HOLY LIBI

THE DEFINITIVE DEPROGRAMMING GUIDE TO THE LIES AND FRAUD OF THE BIBLE

By CONNIE BRYAN

HOLY LIBEL

There is no more ignorant question ever asked in mankind's history than "***What is the harm of religion***?". There is NOTHING MORE HARMFUL than the man-made lies of 'weaponized faith' rampant in the Bible. Like no other work on the topic, I detail those undeniable lies for you here in the pages of this book **using your own King James Bible**…

Deliberately ignoring those lies because Christianity, Judaism or Islam is your 'family tradition' or 'family faith' is no excuse…It only serves to perpetuate and enable the unconscionable degree of harmful divisiveness and bigotry inherent in those lies, **masquerading as 'faith' or 'love'** in the name of God.

By design, you have been lied to by the very institutions you thought you could trust the most. Thank you for having the courage to finally face & awaken to those lies, the primary barrier humanity faces to unity & world peace.

(HOLY LIBEL: The Definitive Deprogramming Guide to the Lies and Fraud of the Bible)

Dedication

This book is dedicated to my Mother. It is the actual **year and a half long text thread** dedicated to the purpose of deprogramming her from the lies of the Bible and church doctrine that have kept her in such a condemning and bigoted mindset toward others 'in the name of God' all of her life.

But as I set out back in 2021 to send her these very detailed and factual texts plainly exposing the many rampant lies of the Bible, **sending her one text every day ending on Mother's Day of 2022**, they were also intended for a worldwide audience that is LONG OVERDUE to awaken to their true shared divine nature - not a tribal, divided one.

As such, this book is also dedicated to all of my readers who find the courage to dedicate themselves to waking others up to our **SHARED ONENESS**, and to the lies of organized religion that have served to hide that powerfully healing truth from humanity for over 2000 years.

To the extent that there is a 'heaven' or a 'hell', WE CREATE IT OURSELVES on this planet! To the extent that there is 'salvation' and future healing peace for humanity, it does not come from an imagined 'savior' coming down on a white horse on a cloud to condemn all 'non-believers'…IT COMES COLLECTIVELY FROM US!

So it is time now for us to stop creating 'hell' and start creating 'heaven' on earth, as we awaken to the realization that in ALL of our diversity, **each and every one of us ARE THE HANDS OF GOD**, and we 'SAVE' ONE ANOTHER with unconditional love and forgiveness, not condemning religious 'beliefs'.

Table of Contents

PREFACE

<u>FREE WILL & THE ORIGINAL SIN FALLACY</u>
(The Great Deception of JudeoChristianity & The Bible Exposed)

Here in the preface, I am going to use a short recent essay of mine as an effective, beginning foundation for the massive amount of lies and fraud I will be detailing for you throughout the upcoming chapters of the rest of the book.

In this essay, '<u>Free Will & The Original Sin Fallacy</u>', I am going to show you the fundamental man-made lie that the rest of the Bible is built upon like a house of cards, and I am going to expose this undeniable, monumental lie from the FIRST story in the Bible about 'Adam & Eve'…

'<u>Free Will & The Original Sin Fallacy</u>'

At some point in the early fabricating of the Christian mythology, the Roman Catholic church realized they had a 'game over' problem, ironically with the very first story that had originally been fabricated by the Jews with their early creation of their culture's religious mythology.

At some point it dawned on the early crafters of Christianity, as it did to me, that 'original sin' upon which ALL the rest of the Bible's guilt trips are predicated, ABSOLUTELY DEPENDS on Adam and Eve ALREADY having the knowledge of good and evil, <u>which we clearly are told 'in the beginning' of the story that they DID NOT!</u>

So the early crafters of the Christian mythology resorted to MORE DECEPTION, crafting & inserting a church doctrine taught and mandated from the pulpit by the Vatican…To be more precise, it was what is referred to as a 'Pauline' doctrine, meaning primarily found in the books attributed to 'Paul' in the New Testament.

This 'decree' by the church (or 'church doctrine') tells you that Adam and Eve committed 'original sin' because they had 'free will'. But the Bible doesn't state that ANYWHERE in the Garden of Eden story…It actually says quite the contrary as I am going to show you.

And so accordingly, church priests, pastors and Sunday school teachers all through the ages tell their members, and ESPECIALLY their innocent children not to what? NOT TO QUESTION ANY OF THEIR TEACHING OR CHURCH DOCTRINE.

But that teaching/doctrine, we can clearly see, IS A BLATANT LIE BASED ON THE STORY IN THE 'SCRIPTURE'! Like I said above, the church saw that too… This is why the church inserted this 'doctrine' because they realized the Creation/Garden story didn't hold water, since on its face it makes it clear Adam and Eve DID NOT already have the knowledge of good and evil, necessary for already having 'free will'.

Adam and Eve are clearly described as completely blameless and innocent, and that is OF COURSE WHY they were easily deceived by 'Satan' in the fable, who God ALLOWED in to what they trusted was their safe garden home, and ALLOWED them to be placed in such dire danger, completely unbeknownst to them due to their childish innocence.

Now remember, God DID have the knowledge of good and evil, and with that knowledge (and WITHOUT Adam and Eve having it to be prepared) God placed them in such danger, and did not deliver them from evil.

So where is the original sin coming from here? Innocent Adam and Eve with ZERO concept of 'right and wrong' or 'good and evil' still? Or this supposedly all knowing God, who knowingly allowed his

7

unequipped, unprepared innocent creation to be placed in such harm's way??

If I as a parent, <u>ALLOW my innocent child to be deceived by a predator,</u> and they engage in some act of fornication under the deceit of that predator, <u>WHO WOULD BE THE SINNER</u> in that scenario? Clearly it would be me the parent, not the innocent child who had no concept yet of 'good and evil'!

Just as in that simple example above, and to put this HUGE CHURCH DECEPTION in very simple terms…

First - You absolutely positively <u>CANNOT already have free will to 'choose to sin' BEFORE you have the KNOWLEDGE OF SIN - synonymous with the KNOWLEDGE OF GOOD AND EVIL</u>!

And second - You absolutely positively CANNOT commit 'original sin' <u>without the 'INTENT' to sin,</u> which entirely DEPENDS on already having the knowledge of 'RIGHT AND WRONG' or 'GOOD AND EVIL'. And we know for a fact, <u>according to the actual story in Genesis chapter 2,</u> that Adam and Eve did not yet have any knowledge of 'good and evil' at the time God allowed Satan the 'master deceiver' to do just that to his completely unsuspecting innocent children.

The shameful, great deception by the crafters of the organized religions of Judeo/Christianity is that you are bad and sinful by nature, when the TRUTH is, you are the OPPOSITE…<u>You are by nature an innocent Holy part of what 'God' is. And so were Adam and Eve in this monstrous Jewish fairy tale.</u>

But when the church or the synagogue tells you over and over from a child that you are bad, you are going to develop a 'LEARNED DELUSION' and begin believing that you are.

And with that learned delusion and deceived mentality will come behavior that is bad, because you have been so conditioned to believe what? That you ARE bad. (Garbage IN, Garbage OUT, as the saying goes)

It's time now, for you to unlearn that deceit and that programmed delusion...You are NOT bad by nature. You are innocent and HOLY by nature!

It's time to WAKE UP to these longstanding institutional religious lies about spirituality and what we truly are...Ironically, those religious lies are the one thing standing in the way of final healing for mankind.

(End of Essay)

In sharing the above essay with my brainwashed, bigoted evangelical fundamentalist mother, I added the following addendum...

I have to be repetitive with you Mother, because I am keenly aware of the brainwashing you have been the victim of as I was, and I know you will try to 'forget' a lot of these truths and facts I am patiently showing you, not to hurt you, but as I said earlier, to once and for all bring you real healing and understanding of spiritual truth and the Divine, NONE of which have ANYTHING to do with an angry, vengeful condemning 'killer God' to teach to innocent children.

Again, the church lie I am exposing is that in order to have 'free will' to CHOOSE whether to do right or wrong...to CHOOSE 'good' or 'evil', you MUST already have the KNOWLEDGE OF GOOD AND EVIL, and so I am exposing that lie using your own Bible...

The story makes it boldly clear that Adam & Eve DID NOT have that knowledge until AFTER 'Satan' was allowed in by who Mother?

By God…ALLOWED to deceive them in their total innocence and perfection, DEVOID OF ANY understanding/knowledge of 'sin'. Therefore, BEFORE having the 'knowledge of good & evil', Adam & Eve could NOT engage in 'original sin' or 'intend' to commit sin, still being completely unaware of sin like a child.

Introduction

You've of course heard the trite expression, 'opening the floodgates of truth'. But nothing could better describe the detailed, eye-opening content of what you are about to read...

And more specifically, this book will be opening not only the floodgates of truth about the lies of the Bible, but it will effectively show you the night and day difference between 'religion' and 'spirituality'…It will effectively replace those lies by two of the world's biggest organized religions, by finally opening the floodgates of real SPIRITUAL TRUTH.

That spiritual truth has, up to now, been denied to you by those Bible lies, accompanied by over two thousand years of the deliberately dishonest, mass 'psy-ops' propaganda of church doctrine regarding the nature of God, that humanity has been so shamefully programmed with for too long now.

I cut my teeth on the Bible as they say, and even as a child I began to recognize quite a number of the lies, contradictions and massive hypocrisies I will be showcasing for you in the following pages. Anytime I ever asked about them, I was always told I was not allowed to question any of them, because it was "HOLY SCRIPTURE" and "God's Word".

But even as a child, something deep down in my heart of hearts always knew that answer did not add up.

This book has been a lifelong project in the making. For many years I have looked for other literary works that specifically detailed the many blatant and obvious, very specific lies and fraud, running rampant and right out in the open in the King James Bible. But to date I haven't found anything like that, which is partly what has driven me to write this book.

Yes, there are plenty of authors who deal with the hypocrisies of organized religion in more generalized ways, and they address some of the hypocritical broad concepts in the Bible.

But I couldn't find anything that was this specific, using common sense and critical thinking, that lets the reader FINALLY SEE for themselves the shocking number of rampant lies in their own Bible, which were

11

deliberately not shown to them by their pastors and church leaders all of their lives until now.

The title 'HOLY LIBEL' specifically means that the content of the 'Holy Bible' is nothing but MAN-MADE LIBEL, with libel of course being generally defined as 'deliberate fraudulent and dishonest written content' in this case falsely attributed to God.

In other words, yes God has a slam dunk, major libel case against the crafters of the Bible, which I am going to be effectively prosecuting in the following pages.

In addition to detailing all of those lies for you, and all of the 'libel' in the Bible about the nature of God, and in addition to a strong, simultaneous focus on replacing those lies with the healing spiritual truth about the TRUE NATURE OF GOD, this book also serves as a very effective deprogramming guide for those who have been traumatized themselves by the lies and mass propaganda of JudeoChristianity, or who also have been looking for such a book to help them deprogram a loved one who has been so falsely conditioned and programmed with those lies about the true nature of God.

Here in 'Holy Libel', I am going to show you the lies and man-made fraud of the Bible undeniably written in plain sight. The primary reasons the vast majority of Jews and Christians have thus far not paid attention to these lies are two-fold…

A.) Because most people don't take the time to actually read the Bible, and simply take the word of their church pastor or synagogue rabbi.

B.) Because they are not reading it using critical thinking, but are blinded by lifelong intense fear & guilt based psychological programming by their family and their church/synagogue, most often from a very early age in childhood. A fundamental part of that programming, especially with respect to Christians, is their being told that if they DON'T believe the Bible, they will be condemned to eternity in Hell.

For one of many examples, I am going to show you Jesus' specifically telling his disciples in not one, but THREE of the so-called 'Gospels', and in answer to their specific question about WHEN his 'second coming' and the 'end times' would be…I am going to show you the many New Testament scripture passages that quote Jesus specifically telling them that his second coming and the end times would in fact happen IN THEIR GENERATION!

Furthermore, he tells them 'The Tribulation' will occur IN THEIR GENERATION, and he tells them the 'forerunner' second coming of Elijah as prophesied by Malachi has already come, and he identifies him as being 'John the Baptist'!

'Church doctrine' deliberately avoids these passages, with preachers misleading followers instead by focusing only on the passage, "No man knows the day or the hour" of Jesus' return, and having that short verse take precedence over what Jesus FALSELY prophesied in THREE different books, Matthew, Mark and Luke, making what I shared above undeniably clear.

Jesus did say at the end of one of those passages that 'no man knows the day or the hour', but the context of that quote was that though he wasn't going to reveal the 'day or the hour', that they COULD KNOW THE GENERATION, and that it was THEIR GENERATION who would witness his second coming!

And then of course he did not return in the clouds on a white horse with an army of genocidal angels to wipe out all non believers, as he claimed was going to happen.

This is just one of many of what I refer to as 'GAME OVER' examples of the fundamental lies of The Bible and church doctrine.

I will be showcasing this fundamental lie and many others throughout this book, but obviously you can't have a so-called 'Holy Savior', and an omnipotent, all knowing 'God in the Flesh' making such a specific false prophecy, and have it repeated not just in ONE, but THREE of the so-called 'Gospels', and then his miraculous return in the clouds doesn't happen!

Obviously, even this one example is exposing as a fraud one of the biggest tenets of Christianity, that lie being that Jesus is yet to come to finally 'fix everything' and 'save' all of his believers, and destroy everyone else.

13

Humanity was not meant to be so divided with such an UPSIDE DOWN, 'weaponized' concept of spirituality and God, and thereby deliberately kept unaware of our ONENESS with each other here on this planet.

Humanity was also not meant to be so selfish, immoral and decadent, using our bodies like they are some sort of amusement park, and thinking that drugs, including alcohol and marijuana, are forms of 'recreation'.

We were meant to be free, but freedom is not 'free', and it requires that we be diligently responsible with it. It requires a degree of risk yes, but not IRRESPONSIBLE, RECKLESS & IMMORAL/DECADENT RISK!

America and humanity in the free world overall, have dropped the ball in this area, and it is time for us to make some BIG overdue changes.

We need to find our moral compass. But again, that has ZERO to do with 'superstitious' organized religion such as JudeoChristianity or Islam, that include beliefs in 'Satan' and 'demons', beliefs that ostensibly are about morals, while they advocate the violent destruction and condemnation of all 'non believers' upon the imagined return someday of their 'savior' coming down riding a horse on a cloud, with countless scriptures throughout the Bible portraying God as ordaining such mass genocide of 'non believers', etc.

ENOUGH with such superstitious condemning concepts of God that have kept humanity divided and at war with one another for too long, shamefully resulting today with THOUSANDS OF THERMO-NUCLEAR WARHEADS pointed at each other, poised to destroy our SHARED HOME!

This fraudulent definition of God that humanity has been programmed with over the last 2 or 3 thousand years has been a deliberate lie, and we are overdue to recognize this ancient original form of 'MASS MEDIA' corruption that was intended to hide from us the power of our awakening to the REAL DIVINE SPIRITUAL NATURE that we all share!

That is where real freedom and real peace and healing are found!

I remember seeing the following powerful message on a sign on the side of a building in Golden, Colorado years ago when I was visiting there for the first time, and it read:

14

"When the LOVE OF POWER is overcome by the POWER OF LOVE, there will be PEACE!"

As we go forward here on this journey together, and as I detail for you the massive lies of the Bible, remember always that 'Love' cannot condemn, it can only forgive…

Love is not ONE CORRECT BELIEF, with all others damned and condemned to eternal torture in some imagined Hell or 'lake of fire', with so-called 'holy scriptures' stating that fate for 'non-believers' repeated all over the Bible.

That is all nothing but man-made superstitious propaganda, again deliberately designed to control the masses with fear of such a bigoted, man-made concept of God.

It is time now for a mass awakening to our true spiritual nature, that we are all ONE, and all a PART of what 'God' is. And as such, we have a responsibility to love and heal one another, not divide off into our religious and political tribes, claiming such tribes are sacrosanct at the condemning EXPENSE of all others, as I will show you that the Bible teaches over and over in both the Old and the New Testaments.

By the way, just on a side note, please notice I haven't made any reference to your spiritual nature having anything to do with 'Luciferians' or 'shape shifting reptilians', etc.

When you hear others trying to get you to buy their books with such equally superstitious nonsense, make sure you don't get fleeced by their con, while they may seem to be benevolent and well meaning.

The very corrupt,esoteric & elite 'powers that be' have always sought to remain in power over the masses by using such false fear based religion and propaganda.

Understand this…Generally over the past few thousand years, any political power seeking to be a world empire has had to have an equally powerful organized religion component as a partner…Christianity (Roman Catholicism) and the Roman Empire were clearly no exception.

It is critical that we FINALLY recognize and separate from the corruption of that system.

We must recognize it in all its corrupt forms…In monopoly corporations, in the current 'mainstream media' and the government those corporate monopolies have bought off, and as is the focus of this book, we must awaken to and finally recognize the man-made shameful lies and fraud of ORGANIZED RELIGION & THE BIBLE.

Once again, let me repeat that JudeoChristianity and Islam were the very FIRST forms of MASS MEDIA and 'psy-ops' (psychological operations) propaganda, fraudulently in the name of God, and they have LIED TO YOU for much, much longer than global corporate monopolies who control the 'mass media' today.

They have done so deliberately, in order to keep you divided and unaware of the unlimited power within you when all of humanity begins to awaken to our SHARED ONENESS with what is 'DIVINE'.

That is when we finally begin to create HEALING, FREEDOM, EQUALITY, PEACE and 'HEAVEN ON EARTH' as we were meant to create together in all of our beautiful diversity like the colors of the rainbow…Free from the division, bigotry, war and condemnation, which I am about to show you is so LIBELOUSLY taught, falsely in the name of God, all throughout the Bible!

Connie Bryan

Chapter One

------ Friday, Jan 29, 2021 ------

Me (1:23 AM)

Mother, **what does RELIGIOUS DOGMA entirely depend on?** It entirely depends on u always considering ANY info other than what u were 'conditioned' with by the church, as being of 'the Devil'. I remember being something like 5 or 6 yrs old, and missing u immensely because u had 'gone away' to Tallahassee for some kind of job. It felt like forever as long as u were gone, but i was very happy at that age as long as Grandmother was near. I never wanted to be away from either of you. I have to say that other than right now and since I awakened spiritually, those early years (before all of the religious extremism you indoctrinated me with) **were the years i remember feeling normal, happy and so content as a child.** You really messed me up soon after that, w the traumatizing lies of your sick, human and animal blood sacrifice images of God, that only an unhealthy person teaches to their little children...**It is a 'learned mental illness' Mother**.

------ Saturday, Jan 30, 2021 ------

Me (2:00 AM)

As i share these very personal examples of the childhood damage u caused with your teachings to me of such a human & animal sacrifice-demanding, blood lusting concept of 'God', in doing so I intend to help u to finally STOP and really THINK about how insane such bloodlust superstitious 'beliefs' are. And just as importantly, i intend to help u recall the SAME trauma that such sick teachings and conditioning by those YOU loved and trusted caused in YOUR LIFE, early as a little innocent child...A child **who had NO business having her innocence polluted and traumatized with such mentally ill superstitious and fear-mongering FALSE images of what is Divine!** I was shaking on my knees in Dr Froehlich's ofc, the pastor of the Presbyterian Christian school you put me in when I was in 6th grade. My teacher decided to take me to his office after I told her in tears that i couldn't be sure these Bible teachings were true, and was afraid I was going to go to Hell...**The reason that horrible childhood memory happened, is entirely because I knew even then as a child how sick, insane and absurd such teachings about God were, but the Mother i loved and trusted with all of my being was force feeding it to me constantly, relentlessly.**

------ Sunday, Jan 31, 2021 ------
Me (1:29 AM)
Because i loved and trusted you so much, the trauma came from trying and trying so hard to believe something so monstrous, <u>against every fiber of my true spirit</u>. The trauma came from how sick it is that adults would EVER think to instill such things in a very young child's mind, **teaching them that they are SO BAD and sinful by nature, so much so that they deserve that God should slaughter them like an animal and send them to burn in Hell for eternity**. That is SHAMEFUL to teach to anyone, let alone a CHILD! What i need u to see is how YOU TOO were similarly traumatized by such early teaching, **by those u thought u could trust, but they led u astray and scarred u psychologically with such insane false images of what is Divine**. This is what resulted in u, as such a Holy innocent child, being programmed to think that u were dirty and evil by nature, when Spiritual Truth is the EXACT OPPOSITE Mother. **What is Divine DOES NOT need an animal or a human blood sacrifice.** **What is Divine NEVER needs to damn or condemn, and teach such damning LACK of forgiveness and love to little developing minds!**

------ Monday, Feb 1, 2021 ------
Me (1:11 AM)
So what was really happening in your personal life that you felt the need to leave me for quite a while and go to Tallahassee? Were u involved at all in a relationship with someone there? You were a very happy person when i remember you in my early childhood, being in a long gay relationship w (name redacted). **What happened that you suddenly refused to be who you are?** I watched you in other similar relationships over the years with (name redacted), physically in your bed together holding each other, or cuddling on the couch together, <u>and it was obviously NORMAL for u. I could see it made u very happy, such close female intimacy. But at some point, you decided to adopt a sick condemning belief system at other gay people's expense??</u>...A sick belief system that conjures up superstitious images of a DAMNING God who must have animal and human blood sacrifices, and you thought u should teach such traumatizing concepts to children as you did to me? **Speaking of which, you would rather stay supportive of such a belief that so wrongly denigrates and condemns your daughter??**

18

------ Tuesday, Feb 2, 2021 ------

Me (12:58 AM)

I am still waiting for an answer to the important questions in my last text...Were u in a relationship w someone when u left me with Grandmother, for what seemed to me like forever at that age? If so was it with another woman? I am trying to figure out what would cause u, being gay yourself...i saw it much of my life...**What would then cause u to become such a HUGE condemning hypocrite toward others who are gay?? And as smart and intelligent as u are, why would u choose to believe such bloody superstitious fairy tales involving animal and human sacrifice?** I am showing u by example with my beautifully healed life, how ugly and in gross error those hypocritical condemning beliefs are toward others. Those around u with likeminded beliefs like your brothers are all buying into a man made bigoted lie. **I am ironically the ONLY one in our family showing you spiritual truth**, that truth being that you are NOT and have NEVER BEEN 'sinful by nature'...That is all a monstrous lie u were traumatized w at a very young age.

------ Wednesday, Feb 3, 2021 ------

Me (3:04 AM)

Since u dont want to answer my question, I will continue now with a lesson on Christianity's bloody human sacrifice symbol, which is of course 'The Cross'. Like so many other examples I will be detailing throughout these deprogramming lessons, **'the cross' was NOT original to Christianity**. The symbol of the cross LONG PREDATES the Christian counterfeiting of it, making it their symbol of human sacrifice to ostensibly satisfy a God who needed such a human sacrifice bloodlust to be satisfied. What the church doesnt teach u is that the 'cross' symbol **was 'co-opted' and changed by the Roman Catholic Church in fabricating that sick human sacrifice fairytale.** The truth is, many ancient cultures LONG predating Christianity, were the original creators of the cross symbol, **THOUSANDS of years before even the Jews!** It would most often have a CIRCLE representing the SUN built into its design. The church doesnt ever want to reveal this, because it totally exposes the truth that they counterfeited a symbol that was an all inclusive, NON HUMAN SACRIFICE, spiritual symbol which was EONS older than them, yet they pretended it was original to Christianity. The 'cross' w the circle behind it is the 'Cross of the Zodiac', which simply represents the FOUR ETERNAL DIRECTIONS of the universe...North, East, South & West, **with the SUN being often referred to by those ancient cultures as 'THE LIGHT OF THE WORLD', also an expression PIONEERED BY THEM, and later**

19

'co-opted' by the crafters of Christianity!

------ Thursday, Feb 4, 2021 ------
Me (2:24 AM)
To continue, when i tell u that the cross symbol comes from the cross at the center of the Zodiac, dont assume i am into astrology. I am not. However, the cross of the four directions of the universe, north, east, south and west, originally known as 'The Cross of the Zodiac' with the circle behind it representing the sun - **THAT is the original SPIRITUAL origin of the cross!** And the truth is that it was COPIED and CHANGED dishonestly by men who sought to redefine it as a fabricated, human blood sacrifice symbol, as a key part of their very sick, new religious propaganda and 'agenda of control'…An agenda to make the masses see themselves as evil by nature, **all being completely fabricated & 'bastardized' lies.** As I said, the original true myth was beautiful and ALL INCLUSIVE of humanity, with no condemnation, and it had no human blood sacrifice element. The Zodiac was not something 'evil'…On the contrary, it was the amazing scientific invention by that ancient Egyptian culture of the YEARLY SOLAR CALENDAR that our current calendar is still based on today! (We will talk more on this in detail later) In 'The Cross of the Zodiac', the SUN is behind the cross because 1.) that invention of the calendar by that earliest civilization in the Nile Valley (later known as Egypt) was entirely based on their early understanding of the 12 months of the SOLAR YEAR, and 2.) **because those MUCH OLDER civilizations NATURALLY recognized that the SUN was the SOURCE of all life and existence on our planet. And THAT is where the concept of 'The SUN of God' comes from, which was later anthropomorphized along with all the constellations those ancient cultures studied.**

------ Friday, Feb 5, 2021 ------
Me (12:57 AM)
I will return to a lot more detail on the proper, genuine 'Sun' of God origin of Christianity in later lessons in this guide. But first i want to share this concise statement from the most recent episode of my cable access television show, "The Connie Bryan Show", which i am just now in what we call 'final edit'. Toward the close of the episode, i remind my viewers of the following fact: The Bible AND the Koran were the **EARLIEST form of 'FRAUDULENT MASS MEDIA'**…Just as massively fraudulent as what masquerades as 'journalism' and the 'news' today. The Bible & the Koran were BOTH counterfeited bastardizations of much older already understood spirituality – The crafters of the Bible

and the Koran took the much older original spiritual myths that supported a healthy, ALL INCLUSIVE understanding of spirituality, and they WEAPONIZED them in seeking to control the masses with fear! The false man made PROPAGANDA of organized religion ALSO, interestingly enough, has had a ONE WORLD CONTROL agenda, has caused MORE WARS AND GENOCIDE than from ANY other source, and continues to be the primary thing standing in the way of world peace, and the CORRECT understanding of SPIRITUALITY. **Once again, The cross was not originally a human blood sacrifice symbol. It was 'The Cross of the Zodiac', referring to ALL THINGS of the universe in ALL DIRECTIONS (North, East, South & West) as being a DIVINE physical expression of what 'God' is!**

------ Saturday, Feb 6, 2021 ------

Me (1:11 AM)

Remember some texts back i asked you, if the story u were told was that instead of being 'crucified' on a cross, that Jesus was HUNG, and you believed that u too are 'HUNG WITH CHRIST' (see how absurd that sounds)...I asked u if u would go around wearing a NOOSE around your neck, instead of a cross? Thats ridiculous, OF COURSE! But how is it more sick & ridiculous as a CROSS around your neck?? How about if Jesus was guillotined, would u b 'GUILLOTINED WITH CHRIST?' **More absurdly, would u go around w a guillotine on a chain around your neck? Would we have guillotines over the altar, and teach our children to sing beautiful hymns like 'THE OLD RUGGED GUILLOTINE'?? No wait, it would be 'The Old RUSTY Guillotine'.** Would u move a church funeral audience to tears singing about the old rusty guillotine Mother? Of course that is absurd, so why is it not absurd w the CROSS? Well, because the ORIGINAL TRUE symbol of wearing a cross WAS **LONG ESTABLISHED thousands of years BEFORE that lie was taught by the church. As the FOUR DIRECTIONS 'Cross of the Zodiac' with the 'SUN of God' shining on all, it had long been a beautiful symbol of ALL INCLUSIVENESS.**

------ Sunday, Feb 7, 2021 ------

Me (2:32 AM)

I'd like to add just a little more history on that symbol. You may have heard of the 'Christian Celtic cross', one of the earliest symbols of the cross adopted by the newly formed Christian religion. **BUT EVEN AS THE CELTIC CHRISTIAN CROSS, some of the earliest versions of it had the circle representing the sun built into it, a result of its much**

older Druid roots! It's important to remember that in that ancient 'Celtic region' at the time of the early origins of the Christian religion, the population was largely DRUID, before the Roman Catholic Church sent St. Patrick to wipe out the so called 'pagan' Druids w genocide, OR convert them to Catholicism/Christianity. St. Patrick launched a horribly violent, successful Christian 'crusade' against the Druids/Celtics. (That is the true origin of the celebration of St Patrick's Day!) Now the reason the Roman Catholic church commissioned such a genocidal crusade by St. Patrick was precisely **because the Druids KNEW the truth, and were at that time VERY EFFECTIVELY engaged in exposing the lies of the Roman Catholic church, and how it was COPYING and CHANGING their much older myths and symbols such as the cross w the sun from Zodiac.**

------ Monday, Feb 8, 2021 ------
Me (12:43 AM)
No amount of pretending otherwise can change hard facts that have been known now for a very long time, that expose Christianity AND Judaism as NOT ORIGINAL…That expose them as only STOLEN and COUNTERFEITED myths and symbols, like the sun and cross, that were falsely literalized and weaponized from their original metaphorical, non-condemning meaning. **As I said, the Druids saw what Rome and the early founders of the Roman Catholic church were doing in fabricating a new religion called Christianity.** They were making BIG progress in exposing that fraud to the masses at that time. They were angering the imperial minded 'powers that be' of Rome, as they were effectively educating people, reminding them how these myths of a 'trinity' and of a 'virgin birth' of a 'savior god/man' were ALL popularly held METAPHORICAL MYTHS, long PREDATING the Christian church founders who were aggressively trying to co-opt them and claim them as 'LITERAL'. **It's important to understand that the whole intended reason for the Church CREATING the Dark Ages is that Rome used that very long period to dumb down the masses after the Druids almost succeeded.**

------ Tuesday, Feb 9, 2021 ------
Me (2:17 AM)
Picking up where i left off, the Druids almost succeeded in exposing the fraud and counterfeiting of age old myths long held by much older cultures who the Greeks and Romans conquered and were trying to rule. The Druids were effectively showing the masses at the time that The Roman Catholic church was copying what they recognized as very

popular longstanding myth motifs engrained in the masses' minds over THOUSANDS of years before Rome existed, and tweaking those myths a little, **making them LITERAL instead of METAPHORICAL as they always had been meant to be.** But such ALL INCLUSIVE, non condemning, NON FEAR BASED beliefs would not work to instill the fear and power Rome sought in their Church and State combination they were crafting, in THEIR agenda for a world dictatorship New World Order THEY sought to force on the world using those counterfeited myths they pretended were original to Christianity. **So as I said, Rome commissioned the genocidal campaign of St. Patrick, who killed or converted all the Druids to shut them up. Shortly afterward, Rome and the Roman Catholic church imposed 'The Dark Ages' for about 1000 yrs from approx 500 AD to 1500 AD.**

------ Wednesday, Feb 10, 2021 ------
Me (12:33 AM)
Like i said, i am sending u these daily texts as my way of trying not to give up on u. You should have noticed by now, a recent sharp increase in people in your 'Conservative evangelical circle' going out of their way to make more and more denigrating and hateful comments about anyone who has or is in the process of changing their gender. **With myself being what you could describe as a Moderate Classical Liberal, and a patriotic American first and foremost**, I've been very concerned about what recently has appeared to be a growing trend of radical Marxist propaganda on the Left, influencing much of the Democratic party. **But simultaneously as a Moderate, I have been deeply saddened by the false, bigoted rhetoric I am hearing more and more from Republican Christian Conservatives**…So deeply saddened to hear what is clearly a growing trend of their wanting to denigrate people simply because they have 'gender disorder'. They do this based largely on their bigoted 'Bible beliefs', **and because they DO NOT WANT TO TRY TO UNDERSTAND that anyone could desperately need such a healing option in their life**. In an upcoming text i will tell u a story of a small local business owner who i was patronizing, who is a religious 'Conservative', who did this in my presence not being aware that I had been through a gender change, and I had to make an effort to educate him despite his resistance.

------ Thursday, Feb 11, 2021 ------
Me (12:48 AM)
This business owner assumed, since i supported his concerns about the Marxist 'radical Left' agenda influencing much of the Democratic Party, that i would certainly agree with his launching into utter disgust with someone who was born a boy wanting to be referred to as a girl, etc... **He was visibly shaken and couldnt believe it when i stopped him and told him he was very wrong and that i had gone through that change**. Why do u suppose he was so shaken Mother? Because BY MY OBVIOUS LOVING, HEALTHY and HAPPY LIFE EXAMPLE, i shattered his false stereotype of those who go through such a challenging change, and in doing so that challenged his ugly condemning religious bigoted conditioning from the Bible, **and his circle of friends from church who reinforce that lie, that false stereotype, that shameful Bible based bigotry, falsely attributed to 'God'**. But even though it shook him deeply, do u think he apologized? No. He was clearly going through all kinds of mental gymnastics in his head to keep from letting go of his relig bigotry.

------ Friday, Feb 12, 2021 -----
Me (1:40 AM)
What was really interesting is he didnt want me to leave. He felt compelled to have me explain it to him, because i had shattered his 'ugly image' of a person like that. And as he struggled w that realization, do u know what he admitted to me? He admitted that **FEAR OF DOUBTING HIS BIBLE BELIEFS was the thing standing in the way of his changing**. See Mother, thats why i am so disgusted w you STILL preferring to embrace such ugly bigoted beliefs, whether it be toward innocent people like me, or innocent gay people like my childhood friend June and her wife, or people with a diverse, but ALL LOVING concept of God. **Deep down u know better! But largely due to fear of doubt, u keep hitting the 'snooze button' on waking up to spiritual truth and standing by your daughter, helping me reach the rest of our LOST family that are also conflicted w fear of doubt.** Its just so horribly wrong how u are being as a Mother toward me with your Bible 'beliefs'.

Me (11:31 PM)
Hopefully u watched the special clip from my show i included in the last text, it is critically important. And when i refer to all of the family as truly the ones who are 'lost', the HUGE difference is the meaning of the word 'lost' has NO 'damnation' component, it simply means lost...**not**

24

the bigoted ugly way you are programmed to view everyone who believes differently than you, or has a natural different sex orientation than you 'approve' of. Understand this Mother, if the issue with you was simply that you held infantile fairytale concepts of God, and if all it was about was you thought everything will be fixed when a 'savior' rides down on a horse from the clouds, i could tolerate that degree of ignorance, IF IT STOPPED THERE **and didnt apply condemnation and damnation toward everyone else who isnt that infantile**...toward everyone else who KNOWS THAT WE ARE ALL HOLY, and as such, being a collective part of God, **it is up to ALL OF US IN ALL OF OUR HOLY DIVERSITY** to wake up and recognize that its up to US to fix everything, not some imagined 'savior' coming down from the clouds someday...And the way we 'fix everything' is with UNIVERSAL LOVE & ACCEPTANCE of each other.

------ Sunday, Feb 14, 2021 ------
Me (2:06 AM)
Thats why i havent given up on you, because it is ME who is your 'savior'. **It is ME who is the unconditional forgiveness, healing and love of 'God' that a condemning, terribly traumatized and horribly misguided person named "(name redacted)" desperately needs**. It is ME Mother, I was sent into your life to help bring u this healing and understanding, not the nightmarish human sacrifice sick fairytales you and i were harmed with mentally at such young ages. The irony that is so hard for your ego to accept, is that it is ME who is ultimately helping to 'save' you and awaken YOU from darkness w such ugly damning beliefs toward your fellow 'parts of God' in all human diversity. **You are NOT 'saved', with all others who do not share YOUR beliefs being damned! That is the DEFINITION of being spiritually LOST!** That word 'lost' has no condemnation to it, it just means u needed your daughter to help 'find' you, the real healthy, loving "(name redacted)" who was traumatized long ago as i was.

------ Monday, Feb 15, 2021 ------
Me (12:59 AM)
When i tell u this critical truth, that WE SAVE EACH OTHER Mother, we enter the heart of powerful healing spiritual truth, **that Christianity has sought to hide and has bastardized by power mongering leaders at its founding.** The truth that brings REAL healing and Light into your life, and just as importantly out to others, is when u finally awaken to the lies of the Bible designed to make u traumatized about your natural self, and to make u FALSELY see yourself as evil, dirty and sinful, so much

so, **u are taught that you deserve to be slaughtered like a cow, HOW SICK AND ABSURD!** Yet u have been SO programmed that u have 'normalized' such sick teachings. Whereas if u heard a similar 'bloody fairytale' from a scared child who was having nightmares, thinking it was true, what would you do? **You would OF COURSE teach them it was A FAIRY TALE!** But you have been SO conditioned w THIS sick bloody fairytale, just as ludicrous as believing in Santa Clause or the Big Bad Wolf, that it has become TRUE, lest u go to Hell.

------ Tuesday, Feb 16, 2021 ------
Me (1:24 AM)
The ancient civilizations in Africa, **before even the Sumerians**... Ten thousand years or more PREDATING the Jews, we now know from indisputable archeological evidence... Those ancient civilizations were who **originated ALL of the myth models** that the Jews, and later the Greeks and Roman conquerors copied, counterfeited and bastardized... mostly the Romans did this fraudulent copying, and the changing of their original metaphorically intended meaning. Let me back up, **just my first stated fact above makes it 'GAME OVER' as they say, for the Bible**, exposing it for the monumental man made fraud that it is, because of that indisputable proof that the Jews, and their claim of being the FIRST of the creation of man in 'the garden', is made a giant mockery of the truth...It is one of the most prominent lies of the Bible, completely exposed now, **because we know civilization existed ten thousand years or more BEFORE the Jews came along, and who were MUCH more advanced**.

------ Wednesday, Feb 17, 2021 ------
Me (2:03 AM)
Lets take a look at Mark chapter 7, vs 1 thru 15, for one of COUNTLESS examples exposing major lies and fraud in the Bible, especially timely w all our heightened germ precautions, which are common sense for the average person...Here in this passage, Jesus SCOFFS at the Pharisees insistence on the need to wash hands before eating to protect from getting sick. He is quoted finding other topic examples to chide them for such ridiculous traditions, **showing his total ignorance of the OBVIOUS health need to wash hands before eating, or coming from market, or to clean utensils**... TRADITION OR NOT, obviously if Jesus was a HEALER and omnipotent as God in flesh, OF COURSE he would not mock such basic important healing knowledge, **to the extent that he is then quoted telling his disciples the blatant lie**

26

that nothing from outside the body can harm them, only what is inside...again with the false teaching that everyone is evil by nature, etc.

------ Thursday, Feb 18, 2021 ------
Me (12:54 AM)
All i can do is trust that as i am taking this dedicated time each night to write these important things to you, that for the most part have been hidden from your knowledge, that u are reading them...Continuing now w Jesus' ignorance of something as basic as germs, and the health importance of washing hands...The REASON the Jews had such a tradition, as with MANY of their traditions, **was they LEARNED them from the much older ancient African Nile Valley civilization, who taught them that 'tradition' for basic PUBLIC HEALTH!** Due to powerful archeological and hieroglyphic evidence in Egypt and the Nile Valley region, anthropologists and religious scholars have known for many decades now that this ancient African people, <u>many thousands of years OLDER than the Old Testament and Jews</u>, **actually invented science, math engineering, agriculture and irrigation, medicine, arts and music...and most importantly, philosophy and SPIRITUALITY! The evidence proved the Jews sojourned under these great African teachers.**

------ Friday, Feb 19, 2021 ------
Me (12:24 AM)
It has been proven for decades now, that the Jews came along many thousands of years AFTER this ancient Nile Valley people who invented civilization and created the popular 'myth motifs' <u>that later the Jews would learn when they sojourned in that Egyptian region for many years</u>...**The Jews would ultimately copy and counterfeit many of those much older myth models as their own, and much later the early Roman crafters of the Christian 'myth' would do the same.** This has been a known fact for a long time Mother, that the precepts of Christianity and Judaism **are ALL neither original nor genuine**, ALL copied and counterfeited and twisted by those who sought to 'DEIFY' their culture and power over those they sought to rule. They would then routinely claim as an EXCUSE that they were 'ordained by God' to commit constant genocide, Crusades, etc. **<u>Neither the Jews nor the Muslims nor the Christians honored the commandment not to kill others IF those others were 'gentiles', 'pagans' 'non believers' as u well know from scripture</u>**

27

------ Saturday, Feb 20, 2021 ------
Me (1:04 AM)
Speaking of the Ten Commandments, **they are a virtual CARBON COPY of 10 of what are known as the "47 Negative Confessions of Ma'at"**, a Holy spiritual confession consisting of 47 bad things that ancient African civilization would testify and routinely give their oath that they had not done to ANYONE, as they recognized w their ancient early spiritual understanding that ALL PEOPLE are EQUALLY A PART OF THE DIVINE. Thats why they are called the "Negative Confessions", because the individual had to honestly be able to testify that they **HAD NOT KILLED ANYONE, they had not committed adultery, or made false witness against others, etc., etc.** The Jews came along THOUSANDS of yrs later, and sojourned under their care for a long time, and took the TEN they called their TEN COMMANDMENTS directly from that MUCH OLDER ancient culture, **claiming them as original from God to Moses, which scholars have exposed for a long time now as a giant fraud. And like i said, the Jews hypocritically often only applied them to other Jews.**

------ Sunday, Feb 21, 2021 ------
Me (1:19 AM)
All throughout the Old Testament, the hypocrisy of the Jews violating those commandments in the name of God, and in the name of being the 'Chosen Race' is mind blowing. If God truly was all about LOVE, and all about those commandments NOT to kill others, or lust after others land and property, or NOT to steal from others, **then God would of course NOT be saying to the Jews all through the Old Testament that those commandments ONLY applied to THEM, and they could go ahead and do all of that and more to those who were not the 'Chosen Race'**. Yet, that is EXACTLY what we see and read OVER AND OVER throughout the Old Testament, genocide after crusade after genocide, God supposedly 'ordaining' the killing of every man, woman and child of so called 'Pagan' nations and races. Pagan meaning simply NOT a Jew, and later for Christians, simply meaning NOT a Christian. **Mother, what i am sick of is your PREFERRING to continue to embrace such racist and murderous, hypocritical, condemning and bigoted teachings of God, when I know DEEP DOWN you know better!** I refuse to accept that my mother could have that ugly of a character.

------ Monday, Feb 22, 2021 ------

Me (12:43 AM)

Let me give u a perfect metaphor of this massive hypocrisy of the Jews, claiming God insisted they strictly follow those 10 commandments, and then they CONSTANTLY violated them over and over toward other races and cultures **ostensibly at God's ordaining & command**. Let's use our nation's founding documents, the U.S. Constitution and the Declaration of Independence. **Do those declare equality for ALL MEN, or just for white Americans only?** OBVIOUSLY, those founding documents declare ALL mankind EQUAL AND FREE, and worthy of individual sovereignty and liberty...Oh, but thats not how we behaved as a nation from that time onward until when? Until the horrendously bloody Civil War was necessary to stop CHRISTIANS FROM ENSLAVING BLACKS MOTHER! Christians!! **The Ku Klux Klan was founded by YOUR DENOMINATION, the Southern Baptists**, who use a large number of so called 'holy scriptures' to this day to justify their sick views. That's because the Bible was written by bigoted men who sought to 'portray' God as having such racist views.

------ Tuesday, Feb 23, 2021 ------

Me (12:54 AM)

To clarify, **obviously i am not saying all** Southern Baptists are racists like the Klan, i am pointing out their being the **ORIGIN** of the Klan, and i am pointing out that MASSIVE hypocrisy, just like the Jew's hypocrisy w the Ten Commandments. **Racism, and preference of a race over others, and accordingly slavery, are each portrayed ALL THROUGHOUT the Bible as being ordained and accepted practice by God**. What i have consistently been trying to show u is that BIGOTED MEN wrote those things, and sought to portray 'God' as being the 'source', so as to 'Deify' their culture over all others, and to 'ordain' their bigotry and hate for other diverse people, as coming from 'God'...As i have told you Mother, IF GOD IS LOVE, there NEVER would have been any such race preference over others, or commanding mass genocide of men women and children, or human enslavement ordained by God, as we see so often in the Bible, **simply due to their being of a different race and culture. It is time to wake up now**.

------ Wednesday, Feb 24, 2021 ------

Me (12:47 AM)

Continuing...Yet another of MANY top doctors has warned of the life threatening dangers of the Pfizer and Moderna so called 'vaccine', this being **Dr J. Glassen, in the peer reviewed, very respected 'Journal of**

Microbiology and Infectious Disease'... He reports the experimental 'vaccine' may cause NEURODEGENERATIVE disease, such as Alzheimer's. As i previously informed u, i have reported for my viewers that the FDA has admitted in their October 2020 report THEY EXPECT MANY deadly 'adverse events', and already we r seeing a growing number of them, but the majority of it will be months and years down the line. So, when i educated u about this, u were for the most part completely unaware of the danger. **And it is the SAME, but much worse regarding the damage that the man made fraud of the Bible has caused in BOTH of our lives from an early age**. I am showing u real healing spiritual truth that you and i were denied most of our lives. But i am patiently bringing it to u now, on a daily basis.

------ Thursday, Feb 25, 2021 ------
Me (12:20 AM)
You were not meant to have **DEVOLVED** as u have into such an ugly, religious condemning woman toward the diversity of others Mother. You are meant to understand the **real spiritual truth**! So it is left to me to forgive your bigoted condemnation, and keep trying to show you. It is not hard to wake up to the truth that what 'God' is would certainly have NOTHING to do with 'blood rituals', animal and human sacrifice to satisfy such bloodlust, along with genocide for non Jewish cultures, etc. It is EASY to see all of that as **man-made, very sick bloody fairy tales**, but you are letting your ego keep u from healing. You dont want to admit that you were so misled and traumatized w such unhealthy teachings, and as a result, you don't want to admit that you so misled and traumatized me. You are NOT a sinful person by nature. You are meant to understand that, and not hold beliefs that denigrate and damn the beautiful vast and diverse HOLY nature of ALL people, **which does not depend on their believing in YOUR same bloody nightmarish superstitious beliefs.**

------ Friday, Feb 26, 2021 ------
Me (12:48 AM)
The Bible has so much fraud and evidence showing huge contradictions, and i am going to show u just one more of many of them here. Lets go bk to the passage in Mark chap 7, that revealed Jesus totally unaware of GERMS and the need for cleanliness w food items. As i said previously, just THAT in itself, since u believe he was here as an omnipotent healer, proves he was NEITHER. But then an even **BIGGER** example occurs at the end of that passage. After Jesus scoffed at the Jews for their practice of washing their hands before eating, he proceeds to double down with his disciples on the totally ridiculous notion. Jesus is quoted telling them

that **NOTHING from OUTSIDE the body can harm or defile you**, that ONLY what is INSIDE you can harm or defile you. Hmmm...Now of course you and I know that 'church doctrine' tries to claim this as part of the Bible's teaching of 'Original Sin'. But we can see on its face how that is a fundamental fraudulent statement, because as you know, the Garden of Eden story decrees that PRIOR to eating from the tree, Adam and Eve were defined as completely innocent...And the story says they were only defiled AFTER what?? **After eating a forbidden fruit** from where?? **OUTSIDE the body!**

------ Saturday, Feb 27, 2021 ------
Me (1:22 AM)
Those are TWO huge 'game over' examples of the man made fraud all over the Bible. Jesus has NO concept of germs, or the basic need for hand and utensil sanitation, <u>and SCOFFS at the Jews for pointing out his disciples' lack of washing hands being a serious health issue,</u> which as i told u we now know they learned from the much, much older ancient African culture among whom they sojourned with, in the Nile Valley region for a time. **Thats already 'GAME OVER' for your claim that he was an all knowing healer,** and then to top that, Jesus contradicts the fundamental basic teaching from the so called 'fall of man' in the Garden, when he erroneously tells them the OPPOSITE of that story, <u>that NOTHING from outside the body can defile you!</u> So, if NOTHING from outside the body can DEFILE you, then the entire 'Garden Story' teaching of Adam and Eve defiling their innocent selves by eating the 'forbidden fruit' from the tree **is a complete SHAM, because Jesus told his disciples that COULD NOT HAPPEN!**

------ Sunday, Feb 28, 2021 ------
Me (1:25 AM)
I am going to talk more about the Garden story from the Bible, that was one of SO many popular ancient myths, **thousands of years older than JudeoChristianity**, but was changed and made a FEAR BASED story of a false image of God who 'SET UP' his innocent children, and then when they were tempted by such a powerful force as 'the Devil' in the FAKE story, God condemns his children and kicks them out of their happy home. This is not an original story...**It is entirely a sick bastardization of the much older worldwide myth of the Garden of Creation.** It is a FEAR-BASED version... a fraudulent counterfeit of a longstanding metaphorical myth shared & taught by MANY older cultures long before and after the 'crafters' of the Bible fraudulently copied and tweaked so many of those much older and universally popular spiritual motifs, <u>that</u>

31

were never meant to be <u>LITERALIZED</u>. I think i said this before, but would u as a parent knowingly allow an evil adult to come in to our home when u werent around, and tempt me to do evil things? **Then why the hell would u believe God would do that?**

Chapter Two

Me (1:10 AM)

This is the ROOT of where the trauma of Christianity has harmed you Mother. This story was counterfeited and then changed from a common much older myth before the Jews learned about it from the ancient African Nile Valley culture, **who taught them what civilization & spirituality were!** Then later when the Jews left their sojourn there and went off to find their own country, their male patriarchal leaders decided to RIP OFF that myth and change it to be damning, and create a fearful image of a MALE God to control their people, and that **'DEIFIED'** their race, claiming their race was preferred and 'CHOSEN' by this 'God' above all others. **It was all a lie by men using fear to have power and control, to define women as inferior and to be subservient to men,** on and on, ALL stemming from that sick counterfeited lie of the Garden myth. Women EQUAL with men?? They werent going to have that! But balanced, absolute equality between both male & female is spiritual truth, and how the original myth is meant to b understood, **That God is BOTH male and female**.

------ Tuesday, Mar 2, 2021 ------
Me (2:19 AM)

You are in such 'fear of doubt', fear of common sense questioning, **that u havent allowed yourself to stop and THINK about what u are 'believing' that is so harmful to your own daughter, and NEEDLESSLY so.** You are believing in something NO PARENT would do to their children, as God is portrayed by the Jewish fiction writers of Genesis. Take your head out of the mud and THINK Mother...**You have been TOLD you HAD to believe in a MONSTER of a 'God',** and had this been a children's fairy tale, causing me nightmares like the giant in 'Jack and the Beanstalk', you would assure me it was just a scary fable! But instead, you treat this sick story like it is totally reasonable and sensible, when it is on its face the OPPOSITE, obviously a man made fear-based FABLE to make people see themselves as innately sinful, bad and evil, so their GUILT and FEAR makes them CONTROLLABLE by those seeking power and control over them. I need my Mother to wake up to this truth, and stop participating in this man-made bigotry in the name of 'God'!

------ Wednesday, Mar 3, 2021 ------

Me (1:06 AM)

Let's continue now, as I showcase for you more of the blatant fraud and contradictions, as we find ALL throughout the Bible, and that you would rather embrace than to stand by me. Mother, why do u think i asked u if u would allow an evil adult into our home while u werent there? <u>Because that is EXACTLY what the Garden story depicts God as doing</u>. God is ALL KNOWING, so how could Satan get access to 'tempt' God's innocent children IN THEIR SAFE, HAPPY HOME, if God did not mastermind and ALLOW such evil to come in to place them in JEOPARDY Mother? Adam and Eve were innocent children, they were not evil by nature before OR AFTER, **anymore than i or a child under your classroom care would be 'evil' for being tempted by a so-called evil MASTER OF DECEPTION!** But they were SET UP while they were innocently TRUSTING that they were safe. And they were betrayed by their own Father they implicitly and innocently trusted for their protection & safety. **Being so innocent, they were EASY PREY for 'The Devil' allowed in by God, yet THEY r not allowed to make a mistake??**

------ Thursday, Mar 4, 2021 ------

Me (1:40 AM)

Let's talk about the reason u so rudely hung up on me when i called to try to talk to u at Christmastime, instead of listening and embracing that effort as most moms would of course 'normally' want to do...Actually let me say that a normal healthy mom would have CALLED ME, would have sent a Christmas wish likely BEFORE her daughter could get one to her. But no, not my devout 'Christian' Mother, who so often has deliberately ignored such things, but yet LOVES TO RECEIVE them from her daughter! **But Mother, how many birthdays and Christmas seasons have you generally not cared to remember a special card until the guilt has OCCASIONALLY gotten to you at the last minute?** And even then you often preferred to just send a one paragraph TEXT, and you showed you are ever ready to reject and hang up on your daughter in a heartbeat, if you don't agree with what I need to talk to you about. Bk to my initial point...You knew why i called and what i wanted to ask u Mother, because i SAID it on the voice mail msg i left before we finally connected. U heard me on that msg ask u <u>**WHAT IS IT that u think u have done that makes u so bad and sinful??**</u> That simple, basic question strikes to the ROOT of the trauma.

------ Friday, Mar 5, 2021 ------
Me (2:54 AM)
You KNOW i am all over the target of the ROOT of what traumatized u Mother, and what created such monumental guilt in your mind that it would allow you to SUSPEND your normal healthy powers of REASON, **and instead choose to embrace such sick superstitious animal and human sacrifice, nightmarish absurd fraudulent fairy tales, more ridiculous than believing in Santa Clause.** But u were made to feel SO GUILTY and bad about yourself at some point, and you were told if u just believe this story of a condemning God who needed a SICK BLOOD SACRIFICE, **if u just believe that, u would not be damned to eternity in Hell for whatever it is u are HIDING from me, that u would hang up on your daughter at Christmastime**...It is time to COME CLEAN with me Mother, and answer the questions i have asked you, that are at the root of this 'learned mental psychosis' u have embraced WRONGLY for too long, at your daughters expense. I am forcing the door open to bring u the **REAL HEALING** that has been kept from u for too long.

------ Saturday, Mar 6, 2021 ------
Me (2:04 AM)
Now in bringing u that true healing, lets revisit the Garden story i covered earlier, and lets look at how that sick perversion of God was revisited in a **very subtle way** by writers of the so called 'Gospels', bk at the time the New Testament was being crafted by the Roman Catholic church. Look at "The Lord's Prayer" in Matt chap 6. Even as a child it NEVER felt right to believe in a God of love for protection, and then to be 'taught' the model of how to pray to him that had to 'PLEAD' with him 'not to LEAD US INTO TEMPTATION', and to plead to him instead of doing so, to reconsider and DELIVER us from evil! Mother, we know for a FACT that **all the gospels were not written by the disciples**. Rome and the early Catholic church commissioned a number of their BISHOPS to write/craft the 'official content' of 'The Gospels', but then placed the disciples' names on them! This is long admitted by the Catholic Church. And their crafting of that ABSURD model of "The Lord's Prayer" was due to their desire to deeply instill and maintain that sick, fear-based image of God that, just like in the Garden story, **was prone to LEAD u into temptation and evil.**

------ Sunday, Mar 7, 2021 ------
Me (1:42 AM)
That sick concept had traumatized SO many and become so engrained in minds of readers of the Jewish Old Test by the time that the Roman Catholic Church decided to officially craft Christianity with the New Test, that the writers of the book of Matthew naturally **portrayed Jesus teaching his disciples how to pray, stressing they should ask God <u>not</u> <u>to lead them into temptation and evil</u>.** Why would anyone ever think they needed to daily beg a loving God to please NOT lead us into temptation and evil? **Because of the lies about the nature of God in that very first story in the Bible, the Garden story.** Innocent Adam and Eve were no match for a 'master deceiver' such as the 'Prince of Darkness' and the story boldly depicts God allowing the Devil in to work his wiles on them. Then when this 'set up' succeeds in getting them to give in to such temptation God led them into, **THEY ARE NOT DELIVERED FROM THAT EVIL! Would u do such a thing to me as a parent Mother, like i asked u earlier? Of course not**. Not knowingly, but u did so unknowingly by traumatizing me with such sick fraudulent monstrous concepts of God that no child should be told they must believe, telling them they are so bad by nature that he will condemn them to Hell if they DON'T believe them.

------ Monday, Mar 8, 2021 ------
Me (2:09 AM)
I am going to go more in depth with this topic in upcoming texts, **and i will prove to u that it was NOT 'free will' at all, if it was God letting in such a 'master deceiver' as 'Satan' to work his masterful evil & deceptive con artistry on Gods innocent children**, who OTHERWISE were obedient, had God NOT 'set them up' to be FOOLED and deceived. But first i want to tell u a story about the black former 'Church of Christ' pastor i tried to share with u sometime bk. His name is Dr Ray Hagins, and he is one of a huge growing number of awakening <u>former</u> 'Christians' **now preaching true spirituality as I am**. In 1996, he went to Nashville to connect with the First Baptist Church there. He noticed a piano, and sat down to play it a little. The white church custodian came up and said, 'What are u doing?' Pastor Ray said, 'Playing the piano', LOL, **and the custodian said, 'You need to go to the OTHER First Baptist Church for the negroes!'** It turns out that church owned & operated BOTH churches, and used their Bibles to justify such racism.

------ Tuesday, Mar 9, 2021 ------

Me (12:50 AM)

That is because, as i touched on in an earlier text, a significant amount of the evidence of the Bible being MAN MADE bigotry and fraud is the unbelievable amount of so called 'holy scripture' that portrays both God and Jesus engaging in racism, racial preference, ordaining slavery as 'punishment', decreeing the Jews as his preferred 'chosen race', Jesus CONSTANTLY being quoted all over the four Gospels saying he did NOT come to bring the Kingdom of God to the 'dogs', but ONLY for the holy tribes of Israel. I could go on and on with the massive evidence in the Bible of God fraudulently being depicted by the writers as **'ordaining' racism and race 'holy superiority'**. I couldnt be more disgusted w you Mother, that u willfully turn a blind eye to that also, on top of the other religious bigotry you hypocritically embrace at my expense and others, when i know deep down in your true heart of hearts, you can see this for the fraud and BS in the name of God that it is. **If i can see it you can TOO!**

------ Wednesday, Mar 10, 2021 ------

Me (1:04 AM)

Again, the psychological trauma that u were subjected to with these monstrous Bible lies about God **has resulted in you thinking you are so bad and evil by nature that you NEED this sick lie to be true**...The lie is OBVIOUS. You see it, you arent so dumb that u dont see it deep down, **but you are trying SO hard to PROTECT THAT LIE,** to hold on to it like a toddler clings to their 'security blankie' or their pacifier, or doesnt want to stop sucking on their thumb, because it is an infantile HABIT that gives them a false sense of security. Mother, you have wasted ENOUGH time, and hurt me ENOUGH with your continuing to hold on to this sick, false image of God that condemns others based on human and animal blood sacrifice fables and superstitions. **As your daughter, my life experience was NOT just to wake me up, but to be YOUR wake up call, and to be the living example of The Light and real spiritual wisdom that was kept from us for so long with such nightmarish, fraudulent teachings of God.**

------ Thursday, Mar 11, 2021 ------

Me (12:46 AM)

Now i am going to expose the Bible's obvious fraud in a big way, returning to that first fraudulent Garden story as i promised. This may take a few texts over a few nights to adequately cover this. **I cant believe i didnt see this truth earlier in my life that i am about to show u, that**

so completely exposes this story as a man made lie. Lets look at where the 'fable' of the so-called 'fall of man' and 'original sin' is told, Genesis chap 3. Now i am using my King James Thompson Chain Reference for this lesson. Right off the bat, before i even read any of the verses, at the top right corner this KJV Bible has the note 'Punishment of Mankind', and right under the type that says 'Chapter 3', it also has the note 'The serpent deceiveth Eve'. The passage begins saying 'The serpent was more subtle than any creature' **making my earlier point clear that God KNEW he was allowing his children to be placed in grave danger, that they as his innocent children were neither aware of nor prepared for**

------ Friday, Mar 12, 2021 ------
Me (12:54 AM)

I am not doing this to hurt you, i am exposing these undeniable lies that YOU TOO have been deliberately DECEIVED with from childhood, **to RESCUE you Mother**...I have been blessed with the wisdom to rescue you from these sick false teachings of the church, and my calling is to preach this truth that exposes these obvious man made lies of a MONSTER of a God who would PLAN and 'SET UP' his own innocent children in the Garden, ALLOW SATAN IN to their home where they were OBEDIENTLY TRUSTING God their father to protect them, and HE is complicit in allowing the Prince of Darkness into their home to con and DECEIVE both Adam and Eve. It is undeniable that they were FOOLED and DECEIVED in their innocence by a master deceiver, and furthermore, **it is undeniable that God enabled and allowed this DANGER to them, this deceiving to happen to them, when otherwise, GET THIS MOTHER... When otherwise they were OBEYING, and not eating of this tree.**

------ Saturday, Mar 13, 2021 ------
Me (1:15 AM)

It's when we wake up to these lies, falsely attrib to 'God' **that we can HEAL and create peace and love**. I will cont to show u in this first Bible story, how GIANT of a lie it is, and that of the church and pastors who 'parrot' the lie that Adam and Eve were 'sinful by nature', and that they showed that sinful nature with their own FREE WILL. **That is a boldface lie, but we were taught that lie as children and we just accepted it**. But even as a child, this story never seemed justified, and i always felt something was wrong with it. Now i have clear wisdom to spell out this fundamental fraud in the name of God. There is NO arguing the point that BOTH of them were completely DECEIVED and fooled.

In vs 13 Eve says she was 'BEGUILED'. The def of beguiled includes being 'enchanted' or 'charmed' in order to MISLEAD and DECEIVE. **If you as my parent ALLOWED an experienced adult to beguile and mislead me, and i act wrongly under that 'enchantment', OBVIOUSLY i wasnt acting of my own FREE WILL!**

------ Sunday, Mar 14, 2021 ------
Me (1:30 AM)
So, i ask u once again, Did Adam and Eve of their **OWN VOLITION** choose to **'SIN'** against God? NO! If u try to say otherwise you now knowingly lying. According to the 'scripture' it is undeniable that they were FOOLED and DECEIVED by a master deceiver. Furthermore, it is undeniable that God enabled and allowed this DANGER to his innocent children. **Thats if we are HONEST about this sick fairytale Mother.** Also, another very sick dishonest angle the church tries to teach is the huge lie that the woman is clearly inferior of a person than the man because she was the 'seductress' and tempted Adam, and he just went ahead and ate of the fruit so she wouldnt be alone in the 'sinful act'. Once agn, according to the scripture, that is a whopper of a lie Mother. Nowhere does it say Eve seduced Adam. **What the passage DOES say in verse 6 is in fact that Adam WAS WITH EVE AT THE SAME TIME, and so they both were beguiled, meaning enchanted and tricked by Satan, not Eve alone.**

------ Monday, Mar 15, 2021 ------
Me (2:36 AM)
By the way Mother, tonight, you might be interested to know that you were featured in my television show episode which i just finished taping earlier this eve. It will take me a few days to do final editing before it is up on my website at conniebryan.com, and later this month released to my national cable access TV network. On this especially powerful episode, in which i spend almost the whole show talking about spiritual truth vs the bigoted man made lies of the Bible and the Koran, i used you as a 'textbook example'. I shared briefly with my cable and internet audience just what it is like and how horribly painful it is to have such an unhealthy, condemning religious bigot for a mother. **By now i have shown u plenty of evidence exposing those manmade lies MASQUERADING as 'holy scripture'** when they are nothing but monstrous fables that dont stand up to any scrutiny, and are manmade excuses to condemn and denigrate much of the diversity of humanity…**the DIVERSITY OF HUMANITY being absolutely what 'GOD' is.**

Me (11:21 PM)

Once again i am spending this dedicated time each night exposing the man made fraud of Christianity and all these Bible lies, **not because i want to cause u pain, but because i am trying to rescue you**. I have shown u the giant lie that Adam and Eve acted of their own 'free will' to 'sin' in their childlike innocence BEFORE they had ANY knowledge of 'good and evil'. I showed that big lie to u right from the actual scripture which states they were NOT acting on their own volition, but were beguiled by Satan, and not only that, i reminded u that God would of course have had to knowingly ALLOW Satan in to take advantage of his innocent children, <u>who as i also reminded u, were obeying Gods directive about the tree in question, and ate of it only after their 'free will' was beguiled and INTERFERED WITH</u>. **They were not acting from ANY 'sinful nature', the story clearly shows they were innocent and obedient until God set them up to have THEIR FREE WILL INTERFERED WITH**. I am spending so much time on this because like a house of cards it exposes the lie the REST of the Bible builds upon.

------ Wednesday, Mar 17, 2021 ------

Me (12:51 AM)

The massive man made lie the entire rest of the Bible builds on like a house of cards is the lie that Adam and Eve demonstrated that we are 'sinful by nature' <u>because they ATE OF THE FORBIDDEN FRUIT of their OWN FREE WILL</u>...And i proved to u Mother, from your own Bible, that is a giant lie. Now u have no choice but to see the truth of that story, that it spells out the FACT that they were unknowingly fooled and beguiled by a master deceiver...**It absolutely was NOT an act of their own volition. On the contrary, up until God ALLOWS Satan to beguile them, they were innocently being OBEDIENT <u>by their TRUE NATURE...by their true 'free will'</u>!** Mother, the story was a man made scary fairytale that thousands of years ago the Jews made up to control their people, making them NEEDLESSLY to be ashamed of, and feel horrible guilt about their true nature. **And of course the Roman Catholic church built upon that horrible lie when they began crafting the New Testament**, and we will look agn at Mark 7 tomorrow.

------ Thursday, Mar 18, 2021 ------

Me (1:23 AM)

Like i showed u in The Lord's Prayer, the Roman Catholic writers who were commissioned to craft the content of 'The Gospels' also **chose to amplify** that sick guilt and fear msg from that Garden story **that they**

40

KNEW had already traumatized so many Jews prior to their crafting 'The New Testament', so as they sought to add more lies to this house of cards, as they crafted their portrayal of Jesus teaching his disciples how to pray, they specifically included **a plea to God our 'father' NOT to lead us into temptation! A plea NOT to lead us into being dangerously deceived and beguiled! THINK Mother!! Why would we need to PLEA to God NOT to lead us in to evil or 'deception'?** That is an insanely sick concept of God drawn from that first insanely fraudulent Garden story. Then, on top of that story that actually showed Adam and Eve always obedient until God allowed them to b so deceived to eat the fruit, u have Jesus as i showed u in Mark 7 **going out of his way to say NOTHING consumed from OUTSIDE the body can defile you!** Hmmm... AGAIN, undermining, contradicting and destroying the entire premise of the Garden story entirely.

------ Friday, Mar 19, 2021 ------
Me (1:18 AM)
And while we are on the subject of 'viruses', 'germs', 'bacteria' and such, lets look at vs 18 of Mark chapter 7 where Jesus...Well, in truth its the ignorant writers of the Book of Mark...But vs 18 is a GIANT 'game over' example of the nonstop lies and fraud of the Bible, as it shows Jesus as he continues with his complete ignorance and unawareness of germs or bacteria, and when he should have known, as the Jews had already learned from the ancient Africans in Egypt who taught them, **he continues to mock the Jews' insistence on the importance of the tradition of hand cleanliness**. He specifically says to his disciples "Are ye so without understanding also? Do ye not perceive that whatsoever thing from without entereth into the man, it cannot defile him?" Then he even MORE specifically shows his total ignorance of germs and need for washing hands to eat when he adds "Because it entereth not into his heart, but into the belly, and goeth out into the draught, PURGING ALL MEATS?" **OK, thats not God, thats an IGNORANT man, and it destroys the Garden story too.**

------ Saturday, Mar 20, 2021 ------
Me (1:26 AM)
Tonight a brief side note...More and more disturbing evidence is mounting of dangerous, sometimes deadly side effects from this EXPERIMENTAL 'MRNA gene therapy'...This past week France, Germany and i think it was Italy suspended the AstraZeneca 'Covid shot' because of a disturbing number of serious & sometimes deadly side effects. **Top doctors are sounding the alarm, and the former chief**

41

science officer for Pfizer, Dr Michael Yeadon, filed a legal injunction calling for Britain to stop all use of all of them for same reason. A man called in to a radio show i listen to and reported that his senior citizen father who he cautioned not to take it, was pressured by his caregivers, and led to believe he could go back to his normal life if he took it, so he did...He was hospitalized w a toxic reaction, and soon after he died. **The nurses told his son that it was the shot, and that they have been seeing this a lot**. Please heed my warnings i have sent to u.

------ Sunday, Mar 21, 2021 ------
Me (1:00 AM)
Continuing w the lessons of spiritual truth...Both u and i were deceived, fooled & beguiled by those we thought we could trust not to lead us wrong, just as that infantile monstrous fairy tale Garden story **portrays a God who would be a part of LEADING his innocent children into such a dangerous potential trap they never saw coming**. This is the perfect example of so many other examples throughout the Bible, that dont hold up to the most simple, basic scrutiny of any kind…that portray a false fear based God who needs animal and ultimately human sacrifice to satisfy 'his' sick blood lust, and gives holy commandments such as 'Thou SHALT NOT KILL!' But then proceeds to tell the Jews to not just fight battles w other cultures, but KILL EVERY MAN, WOMAN AND CHILD in them! Enough Mother! Enough w your bigoted thoughts of, 'Thats because they were sinful cultures', etc **Supposedly, according to that sick Garden story, SO WERE THE JEWS! No, those are more clear evidence of man made lies**.

------ Monday, Mar 22, 2021 ------
Me (12:35 AM)
For important clarity, when i point out the irony that u and I also were both deceived and beguiled by those we innocently trusted not to lead us wrong, i do not mean that you sought to do so intentionally, or those who deceived u did so knowingly. No, it has been a very sick superstitious 'chain' down through generations by the church. But what i am showing u Mother is the sick Garden story undeniably shows God DID intentionally allow his precious innocent creation to be 'lead into temptation' by first creating that tree and that fruit, **and secondly ALLOWING Satan to prey upon his innocent children, WHO BY THE FACT OF THEIR INNOCENCE, DID NOT KNOW GOOD FROM EVIL YET!** So God knowing this, ALLOWS the Master Deceiver access to them in DISGUISE as a snake no less, not looking dangerous or threatening, and they are both OF COURSE easily beguiled, not yet knowing good from

42

evil, until being so fooled, they ate the fruit. **But wait, Jesus says in Mark 7, NOTHING eaten from outside the body can defile you. See, none of it holds up.**

------ Tuesday, Mar 23, 2021 ------
Me (12:39 AM)
Why do u think i am spending so much time on the lies and fraud of the Garden story? It's because i am showing you the fundamental lie YOU have been beguiled and deceived with Mother...That lie being that Adam and Eve were sinful and evil by nature, and by extension u are sinful and evil by nature. I am showing u the actual Bible verses **that u never allowed yourself to THINK about and question before.** You just let the church and others deceive u with this sick lie and this man made, horrendously FALSE image of 'God'. **The story makes it clear Adam and Eve were INNOCENT**. God completed his creation and said it was VERY GOOD. Follow me closely because this is key...God said ONLY if they ate the fruit would they gain the knowledge of WHAT? **GOOD and EVIL**. So in their innocence, without that knowledge, THEY DID NOT KNOW RIGHT FROM WRONG. **As such they were not exercising 'FREE WILL' to 'DO EVIL'**. But God and Satan DID, and used that 'evil knowledge' to fool them!

------ Wednesday, Mar 24, 2021 ------
Me (1:18 AM)
Now that we have honestly and objectively really looked at what those verses are saying, **WHO were the ONLY 'evil' players in the story...IF we r being honest Mother?** As i asked u in a previous text, lets say, as a completely innocent child, u leave me alone at home to go run a lot of errands, and u tell me i can play and do anything i want, but i cant turn on the TV. So i say "Yes Ma'am" Now u know i always did what u told me, you could count on that. But am i suddenly sinful and bad, if YOU, after u leave, knowingly allow an older deceitful, dangerous and untrustworthy adult to have a KEY and unlock our door and enter our home, PRETENDING to be harmless, as God allowed Satan to do to his children...And they tell me **its OK if THEY say i can watch TV**. Then i watch TV and something greatly disturbs me that the stranger was instrumental in having me watch, kinda like a pervert who wants a child to look at dirty pics, u get the idea...**WHO would be the evil, sinful ones in this story??**

43

------ Thursday, Mar 25, 2021 ------

Me (1:51 AM)

Connie Bryan

https://www.conniebryan.com/   Sharing the link to my show website where u can view the latest episode in which u are featured. The title is 'The Truth is Found in the Middle Ground' . The show begins with a funny comedy sketch with some of my comic impersonations including talk radio legend Howard Stern, **and the last hour of the show is the sermon you need to hear, and in which u are prominently discussed at one point**. Now, lets continue with the healing u need Mother...What I have shown you using your own Bible, and will do much more of the same to come, is I have shown u the OBVIOUS LIE that Adam and Eve were evil or sinful by nature, and ON THE CONTRARY, i have SHOWN u Mother, using your own Bible, that the ONLY evil and sinful behavior that is clearly described in that sick fable is God and 'The Devil' setting them up, **deceiving and fooling their totally innocent minds. I bring u the TRUE HEALING u have always needed, in awakening u to the truth that u are INNOCENT by nature**.

------ Friday, Mar 26, 2021 ------

Me (1:51 AM)

To continue, WHERE do u find ANY reference in the Garden story, or anywhere else in the Bible for that matter, where God refers to Adam and Eve being given 'FREE WILL' before they were so craftily deceived? WHERE?? **The answer Mother, is NOWHERE!** And as i detailed earlier, that is because the TRUTH is, one obviously cannot be blamed for KNOWINGLY doing wrong **BEFORE one has the 'knowledge of GOOD and EVIL'!** So, that BS about them being sinful by nature 'BECAUSE GOD GAVE THEM FREE WILL' is **one of MANY such examples where the church inserted that as their 'official doctrine'**, and the masses of unquestioning believers just accepted it without READING the story and saying "Wait a minute, that is not true, it says they DIDNT know good from evil, meaning 'right from wrong', just like an innocent very little child, and they were LED into that 'act of wrong' by a master deceiver, who was allowed to deceive them by God! **Only AFTER could u say they gained free will, AFTER learning good from evil"**

------ Saturday, Mar 27, 2021 ------

Me (2:19 AM)

So again, the church has lied to u and psychologically harmed u with such a sick, distorted fear based image of God...**What father would put**

44

his children, who were totally innocent and completely unaware of what evil was, they only knew good...What father would put those innocent children in such monstrous danger? And then after KNOWING what the outcome would be, that the Devil would trick them easily due to their innocence, **what father would BLAME those innocent children, after he placed them in such a dangerous trap they did not have the knowledge to see coming?** You know the answer Mother, and that is why i remain so disgusted with u, <u>because u know better</u>, yet u still prefer to hold on to your ugly bigotry toward others and align yourself w those who denigrate me, rather than being truly strong spiritually, **and stand with your daughter in finally preaching the TRUTH to our family and others, waking them up to this monstrous man made lie of the Roman Catholic Church**.

------ Sunday, Mar 28, 2021 ------
Me (2:24 AM)
Over the last year, our country has witnessed an extremely unnecessary and abnormal **fear-based germaphobia coming mainly from the 'RADICAL LEFT', that had its own similar 'religious' nature**... I say religious because they are acting just as sick w their fear of a new flu like virus and their hate for those who see through their massive over reaction. They are acting much like YOU are Mother, with your sick fear based superstitions in the name of God, and your damnation toward those who honestly are being true to themselves, <u>and naturally see through your very sick superstitious blood sacrifice beliefs</u>. Both the radical LEFT pushing this absurd germaphobia to control the masses w fear, and the evangelical right pushing their fear based condemnation of all who dont believe like them, **BOTH EXTREMES are the source of inexcusable harm to humanity!**

------ Monday, Mar 29, 2021 ------
Me (2:10 AM)
Its time for u to finally wake up Mother. Mostly you have betrayed YOURSELF first and foremost. You have also so sadly betrayed me as u live in your superstitious guilt ridden lie, falsely believing it is Gods will for u to 'suffer' here in this world, etc. Your calling was NOT to betray who you are and perpetuate such a blood sacrifice guilt and fear concept of God. **Your calling was to BE FREE TO BE WHO YOU ARE! NOT TO CONDEMN YOURSELF FOR WANTING TO BE WHO YOU ARE!** And then in your being traumatized by these religious lies, you went WAY beyond that, as i talked about on my show...You think these bloody fairy tales are your **'salvation'** while u act as a bigot w your

45

beliefs that all others of diverse beliefs who ARE free, and ARE HONESTLY BEING THEMSELVES, like my friend June and countless other beautiful innocent souls, **you choose to want to believe those innocent honest children of God are damned. ENOUGH Mother!** Wake up...You were not meant to be so bigoted and spiritually ignorant.

------ Tuesday, Mar 30, 2021 ------

Me (1:27 AM)

As I continue showing you the REAL spiritual truth you were meant to hear, lets return for a moment to the 'free will' insertion by the church, and the FALSE SPIN they also attributed to it. First, remember that i proved to u with your own King James Bible that **nowhere in the Garden Story does it ever refer to Adam and Eve being given 'free will' to choose between good and evil, or put another way, to 'CHOOSE TO SIN'**, WHY?? Because they DID NOT even have the knowledge of good and evil, until WHEN?? AFTER they were WHAT?? DECEIVED and WHAT?? **BEGUILED and tricked, and Satan was allowed to deceive these perfectly innocent beings by WHO Mother?? GOD!** The church lied and deceived u and countless others over two thousand years with that false doctrine they concocted that u never stopped to really look at or question, like i said in the previous text. Adam and Eve were FREE, HOLY and INNOCENT. The only evil sinful behavior was from God and Satan in the story, **taking advantage of their innocence.**

------ Wednesday, Mar 31, 2021 ------

Me (12:30 AM)

Continuing with this very powerful revelation u were meant to understand Mother...This is SO KEY to waking u up from a life of being deceived by the church. **My special life circumstances of gender dysphoria helped to open my eyes**, and therefore it was meant that I help FINALLY open yours, as i bring this healing truth out to the world to the best of my ability. CLEARLY, if Adam and Eve were to be SO BLAMED for their so called 'sinful act of free will', CLEARLY they would #1, have had to ALREADY HAVE the knowledge of good and evil, in order to have the 'free will' to CHOOSE between the two!! **So the entire 'fall of man' story and assertion u have been taught, that they acted of 'free will' is OBVIOUSLY a complete fraud**...And #2, if they could be so blamed for a 'sinful choice' of FREE WILL, obviously Mother it would necessitate their choosing it ALL ON THEIR OWN, WITHOUT their trusted Father leading them into such danger to be beguiled by Satan! **Left alone, they were always obedient**.

46

CHAPTER THREE

------ Thursday, Apr 1, 2021 ------

Me (1:27 AM)

To continue, In law enforcement in decades past, the police routinely engaged in a corrupt practice, now referred to in legal terms as **'entrapment'**... setting people up, setting a trap, but not only a trap, 'entrapment' is the police going out of their way to LURE and ENTICE someone to commit something illegal, <u>where left to their own 'free will' WITHOUT the undercover police tempting and luring them, they would never have acted of their own volition to seek out and commit that act</u>. The courts have become very strict in holding the police accountable for engaging in 'entrapment' to the extent that we received frequent reminders about it in my law enforcement academy training. **It is basic morality 101, not to actively try to lure otherwise law abiding people into a temporary state of mind to commit an act that without such aggressive tempting and luring by 'the law', <u>that person would never have disobeyed the law</u>. And as i have shown u, there is no denying that is what is described in the fraudulent Garden fable**.

------ Friday, Apr 2, 2021 ------

Me (1:23 AM)

True healing that u were meant to have Mother, and that i am bringing you with these dedicated texts each night, is in realizing that what is 'Divine' is first of all, **not EVER meant to be condemning**, and second of all, we are ALL of us, just like Adam and Eve in your 'garden fable', **INNOCENT and Divine beings, in ALL of our beautiful, innocent 'DIVERSITY'.** What did Jesus say in Mark 7? NOTHING can defile u from outside the body. Like i pointed out, thats Jesus [actually the writer of Mark who no one knows who they were<u>] being totally ignorant of germs and the need to sanitize before eating, and it also **destroys the Garden story premise**</u>. First, they DID NOT have 'free will' because they were innocent w NO concept of wrong or evil, Second they were deceived and LURED not by their will, but God's and Satan's, and lastly Mark 7 makes it clear **NOTHING can defile u that u eat**. If that's true, how can the fruit from the 'tree of the knowledge of good and evil' DEFILE Adam and Eve in their total innocence?? So for multiple reasons, all of that is obviously man made lies about 'God' and about you, and ALL of us. **<u>They are SHAMEFUL lies by the crafters of this false religion, with the intention to hide the truth from humanity that we are ALL Divine.</u>**

------ Saturday, Apr 3, 2021 ------
Me (1:07 AM)
Spiritual truth is not what u and i were taught as children...We as little innocent Divine 'PARTS OF GOD', were lied to and traumatized w such nightmarish images of a condemning God, who would lead his innocent children in the Garden into such danger unbeknownst to them, **instead of ensuring their innocent minds were protected from such an evil master deceiver.** You KNOW BETTER Mother, than to align yourself w such sick ignorant beliefs that are obviously not loving, but are obviously fraudulently **crafted to deliberately paralyze people at a very early age w massive fear, all from an 'agenda of control'. I was sent into your life to ironically be your 'saving wake up call'**...The unique, difficult circumstance i have had to overcome has ironically been MY 'salvation' and wake up call. Mother, u have wasted enough time already aligning yourself with such blatant man made bigotry in the name of God, and at your daughters expense...**Its time to wake up and HELP me in CALLING OUT SUCH LIES**.

------ Sunday, Apr 4, 2021 ------
Me (1:38 AM)
To continue, i am going to show u a well documented quote that Pope Leo X is not just credited with, but famous for saying as a Renaissance era Pope in the year 1514. He was known for admitting and referring to Christianity as **'the Christian fable'**, and at a lavish Good Friday banquet in the Vatican, documented by several witnesses including two Cardinals who included the quote in their letters and diaries, Pope Leo admitted the following in that private lavish Vatican banquet, as leader of the church at that time: **"How well we know what a profitable superstition this FABLE OF CHRIST has been for us and our predecessors."** Pope Leo admitted what the top echelon of the Roman Catholic church has ALWAYS known, but kept from the masses, **because the entire purpose of it by design is to CONTROL the superstitious masses with fear based superstitious FABLES,** by telling them it is the 'The Word of God' with penalty of damnation and excommunication from society if parishioners dared question any of it.

------ Monday, Apr 5, 2021 ------
Me (1:15 AM)
Here we are once agn at Easter time, when u and all those with whom u continue to align yourself love to imagine a bloody human sacrifice,

48

demanded to satisfy the same SICK 'God' who set up his innocent children, allowing them to b placed in such danger by 'Satan'. I put God and Satan in quotes because they are nothing but fraudulent fear based fairy tales designed by the Church to control the barbaric, very ignorant masses long ago. They are obviously man made monstrous images of a God **those men wanted to fabricate in THEIR violent, bigoted, male preference, patriarchal controlling image, not the other way around**. Because when we understand the truth about God, we realize that WE ARE AND HAVE ALWAYS BEEN A HOLY PART OF GOD. Mother, u are NOT sinful by nature. God is WHO YOU ARE BY NATURE! The mistakes u may have made do not define u as 'sinful', they are PART of your HOLY AND PERFECT eternal learning and growth process. **This animal and human blood sacrifice concept is the true 'evil'**

------ Tuesday, Apr 6, 2021 ------
Me (12:52 AM)
To continue, just as i easily showed u using your own Bible that the ONLY 'evil' and 'sinful' behavior in the Garden story was from Satan and God, with Satan deceiving and beguiling those two completely innocent, all trusting children who still had NO concept of good and evil, and God as their trusted Father KNOWINGLY ALLOWING this threat by Satan, and leading his trusting children into such danger...Just as i was easily able to show u that, i have also clearly shown u that to teach innocent people, especially little children that they are so bad and sinful by nature they deserve to die, and that God required a human blood sacrifice or they would be condemned to eternal death...THAT DELIBERATELY TRAUMATIZING, FALSE TEACHING by the Church about God **IS THE REAL SOURCE OF EVIL Mother!** You, Uncle Jimmy, Uncle Billy, NONE of u are living examples of Light and Love...You have been traumatized long ago with man made fraud in the name of God, and u are living a bigoted LIE in the name of God.

------ Wednesday, Apr 7, 2021 ------
Me (12:48 AM)
The Truth Is Found in the MIDDLE Ground – *"The Connie Bryan Show"* – conniebryan.com
https://www.conniebryan.com/2021/04/06/the-truth-is-found-in-the-middle-ground/

Me (1:04 AM)
The link I included above (which you can find on my blog at conniebryan.com) is the full article from which my last TV special

episode on spiritual truth was based, in which you are featured as an example of how hard it is for many to let go of such a sick man made lie, **and the HUGE HARM caused to the world and to children's innocent minds with such a fraudulent, fear based, UPSIDE DOWN concept of what God is.** When u get such 'insane thinking' corrected, u begin to finally be spiritually awakened and FREE AT LAST as Dr Martin Luther King was known for "dreaming" about. When u stop holding on to such bigoted man made lies in the name of God, u **finally begin to create real HOLY healing harmony in your life and others**, as u should by now see, if u are being honest Mother. If you are being honest, you should by now see the healing i have created in my life, in awakening to this Holy truth i have been steadfastly and patiently showing u by example, and that I have been demonstrating with these nightly personal 'text lessons'… a text discipline that isnt super easy to maintain, but i do for you☺. **You and i were lied to about God.**

------ Thursday, Apr 8, 2021 ------
Me (1:39 AM)
Now, i am going to continue to expose to u the MASSIVE lies you have turned a willful blind eye to in the Bible, as we move a few chapters over to the 'Great Flood' monstrous fairy tale**, once agn another condemnation story** written by the early Jewish leaders who sought to elevate themselves over all others as God's preferred 'chosen race'. So, look at Genesis chapter 6 vs 9. My, my, look what it says! Noah was what?? **PERFECT in his generation. Well i could swear the 'script' that you love to call 'scripture' according to church doctrine is in absolute direct OPPOSITION to that. What happened to 'original sin' and there could never be anyone who was perfect or holy?** Well the answer of course is that the Bible is FULL of these MAN MADE LIES as they are fraudulent fables MADE UP by the Jews who were seeking to 'deify their culture', meaning just as Christians and Muslims also do, they were crafting stories to portray themselves as preferred over all others, and use fear of God to control

------ Friday, Apr 9, 2021 ------
Me (1:14 AM)
Next, how many sons of God were there Mother? **Dont say the answer is only ONE,** because as we see clearly in Genesis chapter 6 vs 2, your 'scripture' says "the SONS OF GOD saw the DAUGHTERS OF MEN, and saw that they were fair, and they TOOK THEM WIVES of all which they chose." Then the story describes God as 'REPENTFUL' he made humans, and disgusted with all the bad, corrupt behavior, after it

describes the resulting giants and such, **from the intermixing of the 'SONS OF GOD'**. The church loves to say 'Oh, the sons of God were not sons of God, they were angels'. No Mother, if they were angels it would say ANGELS! **And even if it DID say 'The ANGELS OF GOD', it would still be GOD'S FAULT AND RESPONSIBILITY that he allowed his ANGELS to CORRUPT God's creation! The point would be the same! But your BIBLE plainly says 'THE SONS OF GOD' corrupted mankind!** So here we have yet another GAME OVER example for JudeoChristianity for MULTIPLE reasons. First, your own Bible makes it clear in this early Old Testament passage that there was not ONLY ONE son of God, there were UNTOLD NUMBERS OF THEM! And second, your own Bible is making it clear it was GODS MANY SONS who CAUSED the corruption with their lust and interbreeding, **So GOD and his sons (PLURAL) were the SOURCE of the corruption, not mankind!**

------ Saturday, Apr 10, 2021 ------
Me (2:07 AM)
And as we continue to look at the lies and fraud in the 'scriptures', i cant believe i overlooked this huge example. Look at Gen chapter 4. It explains that Adam and Eve began populating the earth with Cain and Able, but MY GOODNESS, look at what is missing Mother! You guessed it...It appears even the Jewish concoctors of these stories, or some 'editor' of them along the way realized **'Um, hey guys...This isnt going to preach well in Sunday School...I mean, are we really going to paint the detailed picture of INCEST with Cain and Abel's sisters, and all the incest to follow?'** So they lied, and glossed it over, saying in verse 16 oddly that Cain moved away after being cursed for killing his brother Abel, but what do u know, it just skips to saying he 'knew' his wife, who would have HAD to be his sister, as Adam and Eve were the only other humans in this stupid, sick fairy tale. **But as i said, those behind it couldnt teach that obvious incest in synagogue or childrens church very well now could they?**

------ Sunday, Apr 11, 2021 ------
Me (12:53 AM)
Now take a look at Gen 6 vs 12 where it tries to blame all flesh, meaning **ONLY MANKIND** as having corrupted his way. But that is NOT what we just finished reading at the beginning of this flood story in verse two is it? No, it is a blatant lie here in vs 12, because as i showed u in vs 2, it begins by stating that THE SONS OF GOD and their LUST FOR THE DAUGHTERS OF MEN **were the source of the corruption**, oddly very

51

similar to God and Satan being the source of the corruption of Adam and Eve, who as i showed u, the Bible makes it clear had ZERO concept of right vs wrong, good vs evil, and were totally trusting until they were tricked and deceived, **beguiled was the actual word**, by Satan, who could only have been able to beguile and deceive Gods innocent creation HOW MOTHER? HOW?? By leading his unprepared, unaware, innocent children into such dire danger by HOW Mother? **By knowingly setting them up and ALLOWING the 'Devil' in to do that to them. Now the same thing occurs w Sons of God here**

------ Monday, Apr 12, 2021 ------
Me (1:25 AM)
There are so many lies and obvious man made fraud in the Bible, and an extra degree of it in the Creation/Garden story and the Great Flood story, that its hard to cover them all in these nightly text lessons. First, remember what i told u that we now know for a fact that these are two MUCH OLDER popular myths that were pioneered and made a part of their cultures spiritual traditions LONG before the Jews existed, **and we know the Jews SOJOURNED and were taught these and many other such myths by the ancient Kemet (Egyptian) culture**. They werent meant to be counterfeited and bastardized as the Jews did, and to have a fear based image of God superimposed on them that announced to the world the Jews were **'the special chosen race'**...That is why there are so many lies in these beginning fables, because they are the Jews making God in the vengeful, fear-based image **THEY WANTED to control their culture**, not as God truly is, being UNCONDITIONAL LOVE. I will address more of the big lies in the flood story next

------ Tuesday, Apr 13, 2021 ------
Me (1:12 AM)
Ok, believe me i know u Mother, and i know u are mostly burying your head in the sand as they say, trying not to learn what i am exposing to u. But i intend for these lessons to be read by many others, as they will make for an easy read, maybe under a title such as **"The Definitive Guide to The Bible's Lies"**...maybe it should have the subtitle: **"One Daughter's Nightly Texts to SAVE her Bigoted Fundamentalist Mother"**. So i continue not just for you, but to 'save' many others who need help awakening to these sick lies in the name of God, fraudulently traumatizing children especially, like u and i were, teaching such man made condemnation falsely in the name of God. So to continue with the fraud and lies in the FLOOD FABLE, how many of each of every species did God tell Noah to put on the ark? WRONG, if u said 2 of

each, male and female. Oh no, he required 2 of just every CLEAN thing and in ADDITION to that, SEVEN of every UNCLEAN thing! Of course even a second grader can see 2 of all creatures would never fit in the ark.

------ Wednesday, Apr 14, 2021 ------
Me (1:09 AM)
To continue, i need to make a minor correction to my last text...I had it backward. The number was TWO of every UNCLEAN thing, and SEVEN pairs of every CLEAN thing. Now, what does Genesis 6, vs 15 tell us about the size of the boat Mother? "The length of this ark shall be 300 cubits, the breadth of it 50 cubits, and the height of it 30 cubits." So, to hold **not just one pair** of EVERY living creature on the planet, **but a grand total of EIGHT PAIRS**, one pair of unclean, and seven pairs of clean, how big do u imagine this ark must have HAD to be? Do u know how big a cubit is? It is one and one half feet, which makes the ark only 400 feet long, 75 feet wide and only 45 feet tall. Thats a little longer than a football field, which is 300 feet long. Most cruise ships today easily DWARF that size. Theres no holding a fraction of the worlds species of animals on such a boat. As i said earlier, even a second grader without being brainwashed would see this is a huge made up fairy tale.

------ Thursday, Apr 15, 2021 ------
Me (1:32 AM)
Like the important point i made to u in a previous text lesson, IF these superstitious fairy tales you believed in were NOT traumatizing to little innocent children, and were NOT condemning to all who are true to who they are, and who themselves hold unconditionally loving beliefs, and who dont tolerate such sick portrayals of what 'God' is...If **your fables were just harmless fairy tales** that made you feel happy and **did not condemn others**, then i would not be having to call you out for your shameful and disgusting desire to hold on to THEM at your daughters expense, and at all others expense who see it for the man made fraud that it IS in the name of God. I know you, like me, are a huge animal lover. But u arent repulsed by the portrayal of a God who, as i pointed out, **CAUSED any corruption of the human species by, as in the Garden story, ALLOWING his 'SONS OF GOD' to intermarry with mankind, then this 'God' loses his temper and not only blames it all on mankind, but calls ALL THE ANIMALS EVIL TOO??**

------ Friday, Apr 16, 2021 ------
Me (12:14 AM)
And if all the innocent animals on dry land were evil and must be killed as God says in Gen 6 vs7, **WHY WERE THE FISH AND DOLPHINS AND WHALES NOT EVIL TOO Mother?** Actually, the 'scripture' quotes God saying in Gen 6 vs 17 "I will bring a flood of waters upon the earth to destroy ALL flesh wherein is the breath of life from under heaven, and EVERY thing that is in the earth shall die." WOOPS! Bit of a problem, the fish must have been perfect like Noah, huh Mother? All the animals in dry land were evil and corrupt, even though this so called 'holy scripture' makes it clear **the corruption came from 'the Sons of God' lusting after the daughters of men, but this 'God of love' blamed mankind instead, NO MENTION OF ANY punishment for the 'Sons of God' who corrupted it as the story says,** and this loving God not only needed to blame and destroy the innocent men, women and CHILDREN he created, but the innocent animals? But the whales and all the mammals and fish must have been PERFECT like Noah!

------ Saturday, Apr 17, 2021 ------
Me (1:15 AM)
We are only at Gen 6, and it is just piling up, the lies and the man made fraud of these made up hyper fear based images of God, which these Jewish writers - very poor ones i would add -made up in such a fearful image to scare and control the population of their culture. And as i have already educated u, these popular myth models of the 'Garden story' and the 'Great Flood' **WERE NOT EVEN ORIGINAL to the Jews! They counterfeited these myths they learned from the ancient Kemet (Egypt before the Greeks called it Egypt) civilization where the Jews sojourned for many years.** The only thing ORIGINAL in these stories is, after they copied them, how they chose to bastardize them and 'weaponize' them, adding in such a fearful condemning God, and portraying this made up killer God as ordaining THEM as his preferred race, etc. I will address another giant lie in this story tomorrow, but also i am showing u **the crime of those men who SHAMEFULLY used such fear to falsely portray the Divine to children.**

------ Sunday, Apr 18, 2021 ------
Me (1:12 AM)
So just like in the Garden story, here agn these Jewish writers were intent on creating another massive condemnation, and this time a genocidal punishment of mankind, after WHO was the source of the corruption?? Thats right, the SONS OF GOD as i showed u earlier in Gen 6 vs 2. How

54

does a perfect, omnipotent, all knowing, and supposedly 'loving' God allow the SONS OF GOD TO CORRUPT HIS CREATION, **and then blame his creation INSTEAD OF HIMSELF AND HIS SONS?** Actually, we see in vs 6 of chapter 6 that the writers say God REPENTED for making mankind. What does repent mean Mother? **It means, as we all know, to ADMIT you have SINNED, and promise not to keep committing that sin**. So, here we have another GAME OVER example... The Bible describes God in vs 6 as having SINNED. Well yeah! Over and over as i have shown u, **but it isnt really God, its the fake image of God they made up!** Still, that fake God's sin wasnt the 'creating of mankind', it was HIS ALLOWING HIS 'SONS' to corrupt them, and THEN blaming mankind!

------ Monday, Apr 19, 2021 ------
Me (1:04 AM)
It takes **massive delusion** Mother, NOT to see the massive lies and fraudulent portrayal of what is Divine in these first monstrous, man made fables by the Jews. In the manual for mental health, it defines delusion as a 'fixed belief that is either false or derived from deception'. It describes primary delusion, how someone can have a full on chronic delusional psychosis, where they are delusional in a debilitating way about everything, and it also describes **'secondary delusion', which is 'conditioned' over time with false deception, which i have always described as a 'learned psychosis' or 'learned mental illness'**. People like yourself and Uncle Jimmy and Billy, and all the others you continue to align with in the church there in Orlando, **all of them have the same 'learned delusional psychosis' in order to read such stories of a sick killer God, and WANT to believe those lies!** Before i get to the next big lie in flood story, understand that just like Adam and Eve, u too were deceived.

------ Tuesday, Apr 20, 2021 ------
Me (12:20 AM)
Lets talk about that again, because it is the root of your 'learned delusion'. I said 'like Adam and Eve' because remember, **that story doesnt hold up to ANY scrutiny because it says at the beginning that Adam and Eve were perfectly innocent. As i showed u Mother, they had ZERO concept of 'evil', 'sin' or 'wrong'.** The Bible says NOTHING about them having 'free will' before or even AFTER they were DECEIVED and ate the forbidden fruit. As i pointed out to you, that is an **ADDED ON church doctrine** excuse to try to make u believe u and all humanity are evil and sinful by nature, **when the OPPOSITE is the case**. Follow

me here...The ONLY time Adam and Eve could be said to have had an understanding of 'free will' as the church inserted, is ONLY AFTER they were deceived in their divine innocence, and WHAT? And ate from the tree of WHAT?? The KNOWLEDGE OF GOOD AND EVIL. They did not have that knowledge until then, **and that knowledge is PARAMOUNT to have free will to do right or wrong**. More tomorrow.

------ Wednesday, Apr 21, 2021 ------
Me (1:51 AM)
I was inspired to do an article on this, recently posted it on Facebook, and i am going to share it here with u. I couldn't be more thankful for this wisdom that was revealed to me, because it so effectively exposes one of the Bible's BIGGEST lies and massive deceptions, that you and i were both victims of by the church at a very young age. The article is titled **"FREE WILL FALLACY"** and agn i am referring to **BEFORE Adam and Eve were beguiled and deceived by Satan and ate the fruit.** It begins: At some point in the early fabricating of the 'Christian mythology', the Roman Catholic Church realized they had a 'GAME OVER' problem, ironically with the very first story that had been fabricated by the Jews with their early creation of their culture's religious mythology. At some point it dawned on the early crafters of Christianity, **as it did to me**, that 'original sin' upon which ALL the rest of the Bible's 'guilt trips' are predicated, ABSOLUTELY **DEPENDS on Adam and Eve ALREADY having the knowledge of good and evil, which we r clearly told in the beginning of the story they did not!**

------ Thursday, Apr 22, 2021 ------
Me (3:33 AM)
I forgot to tell u, that was just the first two paragraphs, and it's going to take a few nights to transcribe the whole article here... Cont now where i left off: So the early crafters of the Christian mythology resorted to MORE DECEPTION, inserting a 'church doctrine' taught from the pulpit and the Vatican, found NOWHERE in the scripture of the Bible and the Creation/Garden story itself. This 'decree' by the church or 'church doctrine' tells u that Adam and Eve committed 'original sin' why? **BECAUSE they had 'free will'.** And what does 'The Church', through their church priests, pastors and Sunday School teachers all through the ages, routinely tell their members, and especially their innocent children not to do? **NOT TO QUESTION ANY OF THEIR TEACHING OR 'CHURCH DOCTRINE'. But that teaching/doctrine we can clearly see is a BLATANT LIE BASED ON THE STORY IN THE**

'SCRIPTURE'! Like i said above, the church saw that too. More of the article tomorrow showing Adam and Eve could not have 'free will' to choose to sin WITH NO CONCEPT OF WHAT SIN WAS.

------ Friday, Apr 23, 2021 ------
Me (1:33 AM)
I have to be repetitive with you Mother, because i am keenly aware of the brainwashing you have been the victim of, just as i was. And i know you will try to forget a lot of these truths and facts i am patiently showing u. I'm not showing you these lies of the Bible to hurt u, but as i said earlier, to once and for all bring u REAL healing and understanding of spiritual truth and the Divine, **NONE of which have ANYTHING to do with an angry vengeful condemning 'killer God' to teach to innocent children**. Again, I am exposing one of the biggest lies of Christian 'church doctrine', that being that humanity was 'born in sin', because Adam and Eve used 'free will' to 'choose to sin'…That is NOT what that original Garden Story says AT ALL! This is an OBVIOUS LIE by the church, because to have 'free will' to choose whether to do right or wrong, to choose 'good' or 'evil', you MUST FIRST have the KNOWLEDGE OF GOOD AND EVIL, and so i am exposing that lie using your own Bible…**The story makes it boldly clear that Adam & Eve DID NOT have that knowledge until AFTER 'Satan' was ALLOWED in by who Mother? By God! God allows Satan to deceive them in their total innocence and perfection, when they were still DEVOID OF ANY understanding of sin, therefore they could not engage in 'original sin', being unaware of sin like a child!**

------ Saturday, Apr 24, 2021 ------
Me (1:16 AM)
Once agn, what happened to Adam and Eve as spelled out in the garden story... Innocent, unprepared and totally unaware of ANY concept of sin or how they were being fooled into it by Satan, is the exact equivalent of the example i gave in an earlier text lesson, of a parent leaving two innocent children alone in harm's way with a master predator adult who beguiles them with candy or other tantalizing method, **and succeeds in getting them to engage in fornication... WHO IS THE SINNER?** Obvious question, because the innocent children had NO understanding of committing sin. Same with Adam and Eve as the garden fable makes very clear. Cont now w some more of the article where i left off: This is why the Roman Catholic Church inserted this 'doctrine' because they realized the Creation/Garden story didnt hold water, **since on its face it makes it clear Adam and Eve DID NOT already have the knowledge**

57

of good and evil, NECESSARY for already having 'free will'. More from the article tomorrow.

------ Sunday, Apr 25, 2021 ------
Me (1:47 AM)
Continuing from my article where i left off last text: Adam and Eve are clearly described as <u>completely blameless and innocent</u>, and that is of course WHY they were easily deceived by Satan, who God allowed in to what they trusted was their safe garden home, and ALLOWED them to be placed in such dire danger, **completely unbeknownst to them due to their childish innocence**. Now remember, God DID have the knowledge of good and evil, and with that knowledge, and without Adam and Eve having it to be prepared, God placed them in such danger and did not deliver them from evil. <u>So where is the original sin coming from here?</u> Innocent Adam and Eve with ZERO concept of 'right and wrong' or 'good and evil' still? **Or this supposedly all knowing God, who knowingly allowed his unequipped, unprepared innocent creation to be placed in such harm's way??** More to follow tomorrow.

------ Monday, Apr 26, 2021 ------
Me (1:12 AM)
Continuing w the article where i left off yesterday: If i as a parent allow my innocent child to b deceived by a predator, and they engage in some act of fornication under the deceit of that predator, <u>WHO WAS THE SINNER? Clearly it would b me the parent, not the innocent child who had no concept yet of 'good and evil'!</u> Just as in that simple above example, and to put this **HUGE CHURCH DECEPTION** in very simple terms: First, u absolutely positively CANNOT already have free will to 'choose to sin' **BEFORE u have the KNOWLEDGE OF SIN - synonymous with the KNOWLEDGE OF GOOD AND EVIL! And second, u absolutely positively CANNOT commit 'original sin' without the 'INTENT', which entirely DEPENDS on already having the knowledge of 'RIGHT AND WRONG' or 'GOOD AND EVIL'**, which according to the actual story in Genesis chap 2 **Adam and Eve DID NOT**, at the time God allowed the 'master deceiver' to do just that to his completely unsuspecting innocent children. I will finish the last paragraph tomorrow.

------ Tuesday, Apr 27, 2021 ------
Me (12:47 AM)
Concluding the article from where i left off last text: The shameful great deception by the organized religions of Judeo/Christianity is that u are

bad and sinful by nature, when u are the opposite! <u>You are by nature an innocent and Holy part of what 'God' is. And so were Adam and Eve in this monstrous Jewish 'fairy tale'.</u> **But when the church or synagogue tells u over and over from a child that u are bad, u are going to develop a 'learned delusion' and think that u are.** And with that 'deceived' delusion mentality will often come behavior that can be bad, because u have been so conditioned that you ARE bad. (Garbage IN, Garbage OUT as the saying goes.) It's time to wake up to these longstanding institutional religious lies...**<u>the 'GARBAGE' standing in the way of final healing for mankind</u>.** That is the end of the article, and it very succinctly lays out the proof from the actual 'fable' that Adam and Eve were not deciding to 'sin' **because before being deceived, they didnt know what 'sin' was.**

------ Wednesday, Apr 28, 2021 ------
Me (1:18 AM)
Also, i want to address another <u>GREAT DECEPTION</u> in the Garden story by the church, **targeting women as being weak-minded and 'seductresses' because Eve is said to have given the forbidden fruit to Adam.** But the story as written in your Bible does NOT portray her as a temptress AT ALL! As a matter of fact in Gen chapter 3 vs 6, it makes it clear that Adam was NOT ELSEWHERE, with Eve bringing him the fruit after becoming defiled by it, and 'seducing' him or 'tempting' him and he then gives in. **NO, it says the OPPOSITE of that false assertion by church doctrine about Eve!** It says ADAM WAS THERE WITH HER as they were 'seduced' and beguiled by WHO? Satan. See, once agn, <u>the crafters of JudeoChristianity take the blame and 'sinful' behavior AWAY from where it is ORIGINATING from, and dishonestly try to put it on Eve,</u> who to her credit, and NOT ADAM'S, in vs 2 and 3 **EVE SPEAKS STRONGLY in obedience to God, before they are BOTH TRICKED together at the SAME TIME by the <u>ONLY SEDUCTOR</u> in the fable.**

------ Thursday, Apr 29, 2021 ------
Me (1:35 AM)
The 'scripture' which is really a twisted Jewish contrived monstrous fairy tale, twisted even further by Christian founders, plainly states as i said, in chap 3 vs 6 that **Adam was <u>WITH Eve</u>** as they were BOTH brought under the beguiling of Satan. There IS NO DENYING the verse states Adam was with her as they were deceived in their innocence. **Also, there is NOT ONE reference that she seduced Adam, just that she handed him some fruit they were both fooled into eating. There was**

NO 'seductress', only two totally innocent childlike people with ZERO concept of sin, wrongdoing or evil. Yet HOW MANY TIMES Mother, did we hear from the church pulpit, the assertion that this FIRST story about our creation in the Bible shows the 'weaker sex' nature and 'seductress' nature of ALL women, **a false inserted church doctrine used to justify the exalting of men and the inferior, second class defining of women by the church? That is one of the most shameful lies and great deceptions by the church.**

------ Friday, Apr 30, 2021 ------
Me (1:44 AM)
Mothers Day is fast approaching, and i will b getting your special card in the mail, **because you are still loved and so needed by me**, even though u still would much rather embrace such bigotry in the false name of God, at your daughter's expense. I dont think i have ever missed a Mother's Day for u. If i did it was rare and during long periods when you were refusing to acknowledge i even existed, **LONG periods of u ignoring me on my birthdays and the Holidays at Christmas, telling people i had 'died' like u told my childhood best friend Craig**, all because you are so full of massive unnecessary ignorance and religious bigotry regarding things like my gender change, or your sick condemnation of gay people, or anyone who has a different religious belief than you. These nightly spiritual truth lessons are to show u real love, real spiritual understanding that CANNOT and NEVER CONDEMNS, **but always forgives** as i do all your bigotry and misguided condemnation of others. Time for u to wake up.

Chapter Four

------ Saturday, May 1, 2021 ------

Me (1:11 AM)

As i tell u that your harmful bigotry toward me, and toward SO many others is forgiven, **theres a difference between 'being forgiven' and 'being OK' Mother.** That is why i am patiently taking all this time on a daily basis to write these truths to u and show u so many of these Bible lies, and carefully detail for u the evidence of them all being man made bigotry, <u>MASQUERADING as 'Gods word'</u>. **It is NOT OK for u to believe and practice such bigotry and condemnation in the name of God toward others who are different than u!** Why do u think i have spent so much time on the man made lies in the monstrous 'garden fairy tale'? Because as i said to u in a previous text, i am exposing the lies to u in that very first fraudulent portrayal of God, **upon which ALL your 'learned delusion' is falsely based upon**. What is the fundamental lie in that learned delusion that i have exposed to u repeatedly now, using your own Bible? **<u>It is the lie that Adam and Eve were 'sinful by nature'. And neither are YOU!</u>**

------ Sunday, May 2, 2021 ------

Me (1:56 AM)

The story, using your own Bible, **specifically shows how they were by nature innocent**, and the story shows a horrible MAN MADE fear based image of God who would allow for such a devious and dangerous trap for his innocent unprepared children, <u>who COULD NOT have 'free will' to choose to do evil or to 'sin' because, as i have shown u, they did not have an understanding of 'evil' or 'sin', let alone a 'sinful nature' Mother!</u> What i have proven to u, using your own Bible, is that this story is a fraudulent, MAN MADE nightmarish portrayal of God to control their barbaric culture at the time w fear and guilt. They were very poor writers, because as i have shown u repeatedly, **the ones engaging in the true 'evil' in the story, who DID have the knowledge of good and evil, were GOD and SATAN, taking advantage of Adam and Eves blind innocence**. We all are here to make mistakes in order to GROW and LEARN from mistakes. <u>'Mistakes' dont mean u have a 'sinful nature' or deserve condemnation Mother.</u>

------ Monday, May 3, 2021 ------

Me (2:11 AM)

As it turns out, i just discovered the actual date and decree by the Catholic church, inserting 'original sin' and mans being 'born into sin', 'free will' and everything i have been saying. Just as i had already figured out, **it is only 'CHURCH DOCTRINE', not found in the Bible.** It was the Roman Catholic 'decree' in 419 AD at the Council of Carthage that the Garden story showed Adam and Eve were sinful by nature and as such, all others after them are sinful by nature. But YOU are now equipped w the indisputable facts in the story, **and u are now aware that Adam and Eve did not have ANY concept of sin or evil in order to be blamed for choosing to commit 'sin'.** Furthermore, in their unprepared INNOCENT NATURE, they were allowed by God to be PREYED UPON by a master deceiver, so it is absolutely BEYOND ignorant Mother, it is ludicrous and delusional to read those facts in that story, and think that Adam and Eve acted of their own volition, choosing to sin. **Left alone, they were only obedient.**

------ Tuesday, May 4, 2021 ------

Me (2:16 AM)

Now that i have shown u that the 'ORIGINAL SIN' and associated 'FREE WILL' doctrine is NOT mentioned anywhere in the Garden story, but was inserted by the Catholic Bishops as 'official church decree', you can Google 'where is free will mentioned in the Bible' and Christian sources will deceitfully provide u with things like 'Top Bible verses about free will'. **But the verses they use are NOT talking about Adam and Eve when they were completely innocent with no concept of sin at all, and were preyed upon by Satan in their innocence.** Instead, these 'Christian' online sources list verses like 1st Corinthians 10:13 saying 'God will not let u be tempted beyond what you can bear'...OH REALLY?? See, that does NOT add up with the Garden story, **where his innocent children WERE tempted WAY BEYOND their innocent ability to 'bear', having ZERO understanding of 'sin' and therefore not having free will to choose to 'sin', but being 'LED INTO TEMPTATION' and NOT BEING 'DELIVERED FROM EVIL' obviously**

------ Wednesday, May 5, 2021 ------

Me (1:38 AM)

I am once again going to remind u how the predatory act by Satan in the monstrous fairy tale is actually described... Genesis chapter 3 verse 1, describing Satan with the metaphor of a 'serpent', states 'Now the serpent

62

was more subtle than any beast of the field', and my Thompson chain reference King James Bible confirms that i am correctly interpreting Satan's predatory act, **as it shows the synonym for Satan's 'subtleness' as 'CRAFTY'**...So right from the jump in this sick story that seeks to put the blame on two innocent humans w no concept of sin whatsoever, THE STORY ADMITS Satan was more deceitful and crafty than ANY other creature. And remember, God is 'OMNIPOTENT' and 'ALL KNOWING', so he is, as i keep reminding u, ALLOWING his unprepared INNOCENT children to be taken advantage of BEFORE they were equipped with the necessary 'knowledge of good and evil'! **Mother, what traumatized u so badly that u would suspend your powers of common sense and BELIEVE such a sick image of God?**

------ Thursday, May 6, 2021 ------
Me (1:11 AM)
The entire premise that Adam and Eve's act of eating the fruit is what proves that mankind is 'sinful by nature' is DESTROYED when u pay attention to the basic core facts of the story, and then the entire rest of the Bible falls like a house of cards along with it. Look at the admission by God in Genesis chap 3, vs 23. **What does God admit happened to Adam and Eve only AFTER they ate the fruit? That they had 'become as one of US, to KNOW GOOD AND EVIL'.** And then, instead of employing forgiveness, knowing they had been so easily preyed upon and deceived in their complete childlike innocence BEFORE they had any knowledge of good and evil, what does God do, or i should say, what does this sick, monstrous man made image of God do? He not only blames THEM for something they were deceived in their innocence into doing, **but he says they have become just like us, so we must curse them! That makes ZERO SENSE! A parent would WANT their child to be prepared with knowledge of right and wrong, good & evil.**

------ Friday, May 7, 2021 ------
Me (1:02 AM)
So as i make my way back to the other big lie in the flood story i promised to cover, i want to point out the common theme in these sick man made fairy tales, and that theme is **a God who blames his creation, EVEN BLAMES THE EARTH, and curses man, the soil and the innocent ANIMALS**, all the while these 'scriptures', as i have shown u using your own King James Bible, show that it was NOT Gods innocent children who on their own volition sought to disobey him or 'sin', but in BOTH of these fraudulent man made fables, GOD IS THE SOURCE of

setting up and corrupting his innocent creation! I have tried to awaken u to the healing truth that **you are a Divine, holy, sinless and forever a pure PART OF what God is**, not sinful and separate and worthy of damnation without a sick 'blood sacrifice' made for you instead. **That is SICK SUPERSTITION Mother**, and as i have shown u, the garden story actually has God admitting this in Gen chap 3, vs 22 saying Adam and Eve <u>have become just like him.</u>

------ Saturday, May 8, 2021 ------
Me (12:41 AM)
The story FIRST says, right at the start, that they were what?? **INNOCENT, still having ZERO knowledge of good and evil or any concept of sin**...So what does THAT actually tell u about our TRUE NATURE Mother?? **<u>That our true nature is and always was INNOCENT!</u>** And it does not make your innocent nature corrupt just because u mature and learn the knowledge of good and evil. And this is further proven using your own Bible, <u>as i showed u in last nights text, God actually admits Adam and Eves eating the fruit simply matured them to be just like God with that NECESSARY KNOWLEDGE of right and wrong!</u> Listen to me Mother, this is critical. When a little child comes into the world, u can see as they grow and play w other children and the questions they ask u, how totally innocent they are BY NATURE. **Christianity and Judaism and Islam traumatize and ROB them of their innocence, teaching them they are bad by nature, etc. But just teaching them right from wrong DOES NOT corrupt their innocence.**

------ Sunday, May 9, 2021 ------
Me (1:55 AM)
Today being Mother's Day, a friend I had dinner with confided that she gets very depressed on Mother's Day remembering her mother who passed away several years bk, and how she was unable to have a healthy relationship with her. **She shared with me how she gets very sad every Mother's Day, realizing she can never make that happen.** She said it helped her being out with likeminded friends tonight. Her concerns of course, as u should know, are my concerns, and they are the reason why i am sending u these spiritual truth lessons exposing the man made lies in the Bible that are at the root of your inexcusable bigotry toward others, **<u>falsely in the 'name of God'. That is the OPPOSITE of 'love'</u>**.

64

------ Monday, May 10, 2021 ------

Me (12:50 AM)

Bk to the healing lessons u are LONG overdue to wake up to Mother, as i slowly make my way bk to the flood story. But as i have made a point to tell u before, **IF** your bloody human and animal sacrifice, nightmarish fairy tale concepts of God **DID NOT** also involve the condemnation and damnation of others who believe differently than u, then i would just understand that u were 'simple minded' and it wouldnt make me recoil in disgust of my having such a bigoted person for a mother. As i said last text on Mother's Day, it is your inexcusable, dogmatic and willfully blind desire to eagerly express and practice such ugly man made bigotry and condemnation toward others. **And, it is precisely such ugly 'belief' and behavior in that regard that is what is truly in spiritual error.** You were meant to learn this real spiritual truth and wisdom i have learned, from the miracles my life experience has brought and taught me, that i am trying to teach u. **You and i ARE NOT sinful by nature, and 'God' does not condemn.**

------ Tuesday, May 11, 2021 ------

Me (1:27 AM)

Its a step in the right direction that u sent me a short text telling me how this year u managed to get a birthday card out to your daughter, just in time for it not to be an afterthought, as often has been the case in the past. But thats the bare MINIMUM of what a daughter should always b able to count on at important holidays. I have sent you so much unconditional love, and lived SO MANY IMPORTANT HEALING TRUTHS BY EXAMPLE for u for years now, **and yet how many times have i NOT been able to count on just that bare minimum from my mother? All because of your Bible based bigotry that needlessly interferes w you having my back as any daughter should b able to count on, as i have yours!** LONG AGO u have been able to see and learn for yourself how miraculously happy and at peace i am as a result of getting my gender changed, and the joy and prosperity i continue to create because i had the courage to be true to myself and Highest Wisdom, DESPITE you and the family's ugly Bible bigotry. Yet seeing this reality and truth, u continue to let me down by preferring to keep embracing those beliefs at my expense. I need u to wake up Mother.

------ Wednesday, May 12, 2021 ------

Me (1:14 AM)

You have been able to see clearly for a long time now that i created the joy and happiness and healing i desperately needed, with ZERO help from u...**On the contrary, with massive bigotry and resentful rejection by u for a long time, and the rest of the family ongoing, instead of trying to stop and understand it.** The same is the case w gay people who u still shamefully hold condemning beliefs toward, based on man made bigotry masquerading as Gods word. Are u so 'simple minded' Mother, that after <u>your own personal orientation toward being romantically interested in women, that i personally witnessed all my life growing up</u>, are u so 'simple minded' or hypocritical, that knowing that about yourself, and then seeing how healed and happy i am from making the right courageous choice to fix myself, **that u STILL want to cling eagerly to such a condemning bigoted belief at my expense? While u send me heart emoticons??** <u>**Send me the heart emoticons when u tell me that u are beginning to wake up.**</u>

------ Thursday, May 13, 2021 ------
Me (12:13 AM)
You cant be unaware how the conservative evangelical Right has become almost militant with their loud denigrating, now more than ever, of those who have changed gender or are considering the need to do so, and who are living in the role as is required before being approved for the change, which is a long approval process, called the <u>'Benjamin Standards of Care'</u>. **They used to make gay people their favorite ones to aggressively denigrate and condemn w their Bible, but now it has become more the transgender individuals they are targeting, and u are just happy as a clam to remain associated with ALL of that**. And the shameful thing about it Mother, is as i said, that long before now u have been able to see that it is NOT the 'sinful' or 'satanic' or 'demonic' behavior your fellow Bible bigots love to imagine that it is. You know better, but you are so addicted like a drug user to heroin or valium or meth, to those bigoted teachings, **that you prefer to get that 'fix' than to wake up and stand by me**.

------ Friday, May 14, 2021 ------
Me (12:37 AM)
But i am now showing u all the man made bigotry, fraud and lies of the Bible that u have wrongly developed an ugly harmful addiction to, at the expense of your daughter and of so many, just because they are diverse from your beliefs. That has to stop Mother. **You are not in the 'Light'. You and your brothers are all practicing man made hate and bigotry, falsely in the name of God**, and as i have told u before, <u>ironically i am the ONLY member of the family who is preaching and teaching spiritual truth about the nature of God, and showing you all</u>

66

what it truly means to walk in the Light and LOVE ONE ANOTHER. Love has NO ELEMENT OF CONDEMNATION. It is shameful that all of you still associate yourselves with such ignorant condemning bigotry toward others. It is as i said before, **a 'learned delusion', that God would be such a vengeful condemning 'being', who needed his regular fix of animal blood sacrifice in Old Test, and then who needed a HUMAN BLOOD SACRIFICE in the New Test! Thats just sick.**

------ Saturday, May 15, 2021 ------
Me (12:59 AM)
Lets talk about how a healthy minded loving person who is NOT a bigot w their Bible beliefs, would approach BOTH gay people and those like myself who changed gender...They would LEARN from the person's life experience, and thereby have their life experience enriched as they learned, as in the case of someone like me, that it is no different than someone who has a hearing handicap or loss of vision, **but they were able to have that sad life restriction removed and could finally see or hear like they always dreamed of doing like a normal person.** Think about it Mother...You dont say to a handicapped person, whether the handicap is physical OR mental, **you dont say, 'thats how God MADE you'!**...Actually there ARE some 'intellectually challenged' Christian fundamentalists who DO try to teach that such infirmity or physical or mental disorder is due to 'sin' or 'demons' etc. **And those beliefs are also as sick as it gets, all coming agn from MAN MADE bigotry masquerading as Gods word. Spiritual love NEVER condemns.**

Me (11:44 PM)
I have easily and patiently shown u the fraud of the Bible's very FIRST story upon which ALL the rest of it is fraudulently built upon, showing u that Adam and Eve were in total childlike innocence, and were not only preyed upon by a master deceiver as 'Satan', but their own Father ALLOWED them to be preyed upon, **WITHOUT their being aware of what 'sin' was,** which DESTROYS the church doctrine that told u that you are sinful by nature because Adam and Eve chose to sin rather than be obedient. I showed u that it was actually **EVE, not Adam,** who initially spoke up to the 'serpent' and made it clear that they **on their own volition had NO INTENTION of eating from the forbidden tree,** and they both were together, not separate, as they were together fooled in their innocence, not Eve separately, then 'seducing' Adam to 'sin'. The story states Adam was WITH Eve as they were deceived. I have shown u

how without the knowledge of good and evil, they couldnt choose to sin, their nature was innocent.

------ Monday, May 17, 2021 ------
Me (11:18 PM)
Like a child in their innocence making a mistake, as is going to happen, a loving Father, ESPECIALLY one who knew he had ALLOWED them to be so taken advantage of, would of course also in his 'omnipotence' understand they were not equipped or prepared yet with the knowledge of good and evil, and would do what, **IF a loving Father?** CURSE THEM AND KICK THEM OUT OF THEIR HOME?? Of course not! Wake up Mother!! **There would be forgiveness ESPECIALLY because he would know he was complicit in setting up their being preyed upon without the knowledge of sin!** And their newfound knowledge of good and evil AFTER the fact would be what they ultimately needed as they matured. **It was what they needed BEFORE God, in this ignorant fairy tale, allowed his children to be placed in such dire danger, completely unaware and unprepared!** WAKE UP MOTHER! You have been lied to all your life about the nature of what 'God' is, and consequently you have imprisoned yourself as a result of that traumatic lie about God.

------ Wednesday, May 19, 2021 ------
Me (1:53 AM)
There are sooo many examples of the blatant man made lies and fraud in the Bible, many more that i will be showing u in future text lessons, but there is NO EXCUSE for your willfully choosing to hold on to them **when u ARENT a 3 year old who needs to believe in Santa Clause**. At least Santa Clause is an innocent absurd fairy tale...The reason i am holding you and your brothers accountable is because u are old enough and smart enough to SEE these for the sick bloody fairy tales with sick animal and human sacrifice rituals and superstitious bigotry, all at the EXPENSE of others just because they are DIFFERENT in certain ways. I am showing u by my life example u cannot deny, that you are DEAD WRONG in remaining assoc with such SHAMEFUL bigotry in the name of God. **When i remind u often that what is DIVINE (meaning 'spiritual truth') was never meant to be 'weaponized', simply put that means it was never meant to include a select chosen or 'saved' few at the EXPENSE / damnation of others.**

68

------ Thursday, May 20, 2021 ------
Me (12:14 AM)
Everything happens for a reason, and i was brought here as your daughter to help u wake up from these lies that have so traumatized and imprisoned u. **You yourself have a preference for female physical closeness and affection that you showed off and on for ALL of my childhood.** Yet, you shamefully and hypocritically want to embrace condemning bigoted beliefs at the expense of those like my childhood friend June, for finding a wife, **and finding happiness and love**, instead of understanding that as you of ALL people should be able to do, and b happy for her. That is shameful on your part Mother, **and u have to change.** It isnt 'Satanic' or 'demonic' or 'evil' because someone like June is naturally attracted to their same gender, and finds love in their life from another who is the same. **Thats being courageous to be true to yourself, despite even those in your family who u need to accept u, and they reject u falsely in the name of God. Shame on your hypocrisy Mother, you have to change.**

------ Friday, May 21, 2021 ------
Me (1:12 AM)
As i have told u before, i would not lead u astray. **I would not be holding u accountable as i am, if there was one shred of truth to your beliefs that have turned u into such an ugly bigoted person toward those who are different, diverse and believe different ideas than you about 'God'.** Guess what Mother... THATS OK! **PEOPLE ARE A PART OF WHAT GOD IS, AND THEY ARE DIVERSE! It was bigoted MEN who wrote those 'scriptures' condemning the diversity of others they didnt like, period!** Thats the long and short of the truth behind the superstitious lies you are holding on to, needlessly at my expense and many others. Some kind of massive guilt and trauma happened in your life early on that is part of why u bought into this obvious fraudulent, sick superstitious concept of a condemning God, and dogmatically traumatized me with it...But i refused to let such obvious bigoted concepts of God ruin my life. When i asked u what it was at Christmastime, u hung up on me.

------ Saturday, May 22, 2021 ------
Me (1:21 AM)
It was absolutely shameful that u hung up on your daughter at Christmastime, when i was reaching out to try to talk to u and ask u questions that i know are at the root of your believing such sick bigoted superstitious concepts of God, with u shamefully envisioning

69

YOURSELF as 'saved' while proudly envisioning the vast majority of others as 'condemned' simply because they fall into the various categories of your bigotry, i.e. they just believe differently about the nature of God, or they are gay like my childhood friend June as I mentioned earlier. **And as i continue to remind u, the majority of those u cont to eagerly align yourself with also condemn ME just for being myself and fixing my gender, no differently than someone fixing their blindness or deafness or other such fixable handicap**. But you would hang up on your own daughter on at Christmastime, rather than face an honest conversation about what it was that u did that these sick condemning Bible beliefs made u think you deserve to burn in hell. **You are NOT sinful by nature.**

------ Sunday, May 23, 2021 ------
Me (1:26 AM)
True spirituality, not superstitious infantile bloody fairy tales, does not condemn or do harm to others for their being 'diverse'...As i have told u before, spiritual wisdom is the understanding that 'DIVINITY IS DIVERSITY' and ALL of our 'salvation' is guaranteed. We were never NOT SAVED, all of us in our HOLY diverse life experiences are a perfect part of what 'God' is, and we are in an eternal learning process of growth. **As soon as a religious 'faith' teaches that THEY alone have that holiness and deny it to all others, thats when u know that 'faith' is a bigoted, ignorant man made fraud**. And that is what traumatized u many years ago. **I am here showing u Mother, how to heal from that trauma and how to lay that bigotry down**. Adam and Eve were innocent, and if there was going to be a 'test' of their 'free will', they would have needed to have been already given the knowledge of good and evil, **not PREYED upon WITHOUT that knowledge, and then CURSED for a mistake God KNEW they weren't prepared to avoid making!**

------ Monday, May 24, 2021 ------
Me (12:11 AM)
Did u really absorb what i last texted u? "Adam and Eve were innocent, and if there was going to be a 'test' of their 'free will', they would have needed to have been already given the knowledge of good and evil, **not PREYED upon and then CURSED for a mistake God knew they WEREN'T PREPARED TO AVOID MAKING"**. Why were they unprepared to handle a master deceiver like 'Satan' in the story Mother? By now u should know the answer. Because as the story admits, their own trusted Father had up to that point been keeping them in absolute

70

innocence and complete ignorance of what good and evil was, DENYING them the necessary preparation & understanding in order to both recognize and to avoid 'evil'! And how was God doing that Mother? For Adam and Eve to be BLAMED for choosing to do evil, what must they be taught by their Father FIRST?? Thats right, **the KNOWLEDGE of good and evil!** Gen chap 3 vs 22 quotes God admitting he and of course Satan too, had the knowledge of good and evil, and God admits it is UNACCEPTABLE for Adam and Eve to be **LIKE THEM with that 'knowledge'(Of course, TWO MORE giant 'elephant in the room' questions here that the church can never honestly answer are: WHY WOULD IT BE OK FOR GOD AND SATAN TO HAVE THE KNOWLEDGE OF GOOD & EVIL, BUT NOT ADAM & EVE?? IF THEY ARE MADE IN THE IMAGE OF GOD, WHY ARE THEY CONDEMNED FOR ADMITTEDLY BECOMING 'LIKE GOD'??)** But to continue with the passage in vs. 22, God then takes away their eternal life in the Garden of Eden, kicks them out of their home and condemns them to death! So no, you can therefore clearly see they didnt 'surely die' in the fable **from eating the fruit**…The fraudulent writers of the story boldly depict GOD keeping Adam & Eve from the tree of life out of bizarre SPITE**, condemning them for doing something they didn't even have the 'KNOWLEDGE' to 'KNOW' at the time was even 'EVIL'.**

------ Tuesday, May 25, 2021 ------
Me (1:14 AM)
I am spending a lot of time on this topic because as i said before, this very first traumatizing man made lie in the Bible, not just about the nature of God, but a massive lie about mankind's nature, is the fraudulent 'fake foundation' of the rest of the lies of the Bible. Adam and Eve were CLUELESS about good and evil, **so they had ZERO concept of 'sin'**, and they were supposedly made in the image of God. God admits in the story, as i showed u, that HE had the knowledge of good and evil. Of course he did, according to the Bible he's all knowing right? **And being ALL KNOWING, that is precisely why he would have had to KNOW and ALLOW Satan into their Garden home to prey upon their childlike innocence**. And being ALL KNOWING, he'd know they, NOT having the knowledge of good and evil yet, were unprepared for such an evil deceiving predator! **But then he's going to curse and condemn them to death and cast them out for innocently seeking WHAT?? KNOWLEGE!** Turn in Your Bible please to Hosea chap 4 vs 6. What does it say? My people are DESTROYED for LACK OF KNOWLEDGE! **But Adam and Eve are cursed for seeking it??**

71

------ Wednesday, May 26, 2021 ------
Me (1:25 AM)
'My people are DESTROYED for LACK of knowledge'...**MAKE UP YOUR MIND you double-speaking fraudulent writers of these vengeful bloody fables! Because you fools started your fake image of God fables as DESTROYING man, condemning them to death and casting them out of their home FOR INNOCENTLY SEEKING KNOWLEDGE!** Do u see this insanity now Mother? I know you are smart enough to see it. But you are choosing to turn a blind eye to it, **and that is what makes u a bigot, your WANTING to believe these sick man made false depictions of God, to the condemning DETRIMENT of others, just because they imagine the Divine in a different way than u**...Ironically, most of us who see the Divine in a different way <u>are the ones who are bringing real unconditional love and forgiveness and healing to others, not looking at them as LOST and going to Hell</u>. Btw, I almost wrote above, 'Make up your mind God', but the point i am focused on helping u see with all of these examples is that **the Bible is a giant <u>MAN MADE</u> fraudulent book of fear fables.**

------ Thursday, May 27, 2021 ------
Me (1:57 AM)
Do u want to have a healthy, normal mother/daughter relationship? Then you have to get healthy and normal Mother. It is NOT spiritually healthy and normal to believe such condemning bigoted man made lies. You and i were lied to about 'God' growing up, period. Fortunately i awakened to that, <u>and fortunately u are still young enough to wake up to it also, and not remain an ugly bigot, FALSELY in the name of 'God' for the rest of your life</u>. That IS NOT who God is. **My life has been setting the right example for u of real love and forgiveness for ALL, not selectively for a 'chosen' or 'saved' or 'born again' few**. I forgive u for the damage and pain you have created with your bigotry, but its gone on too long, and now it is time for you to change. It is time for u to stop looking at others in such a condemning way, just because they have different styles of approaching the spiritual and the Divine**. Jewish and Roman men seeking to control the masses were who MADE UP that bigotry, making up a God in THEIR im**age.

------ Friday, May 28, 2021 ------
Me (2:13 AM)
Only a bigoted man made image of God would act the absolutely SINFUL way they portrayed God in the very first story in the Bible, and

72

then over and over agn in so many subsequent sick genocidal ways. Thats how u KNOW it is a man made fraudulent portrayal of God. **Like i told u before, the only ones committing evil or 'sin' in the Garden story were the fabled characters of 'God' and 'Satan'. You are a liar Mother, if u continue to try to ignore that truth, and say Adam and Eve CHOSE to sin**, as i have made crystal clear to u the obvious fact as the story tells us, that Adam and Eve did NOT have ANY KNOWLEDGE OF GOOD AND EVIL until AFTER 'God' allowed 'Satan' to deceive them in their total innocence. **A loving father knows he MUST TEACH good and evil to his children to prepare them should they encounter evil. But this man made God CONDEMNED them for falling prey in their unprepared innocence to evil HE set them up for and allowed to prey upon their trusting innocence.**

------ Saturday, May 29, 2021 ------
Me (2:10 AM)
Read agn that last point: "this man made God CONDEMNED them for falling prey in their unprepared innocence to evil **that HE set them up for and allowed to prey upon their trusting innocence**." OPEN YOUR EYES MOTHER! Thats how u can tell this is a made up scary fable. Only sick bigoted men trying to control their culture and justify being allowed to KILL all 'non believers', would 'create' a sick image of God like that. As i have said before, NO LOVING PARENT would EVER allow an evil predator into proximity of their innocent child while they were gone, let alone allow an evil predator INTO THEIR HOME w the innocent unprepared child. Obviously no sane and loving parent would EVER PUNISH their innocent child for falling prey to an evil predator BEFORE they had a mature grasp and understanding of the knowledge of good and evil! But this man made 'God' DOES condemn them for that mistake made in total innocence, **angry BECAUSE they sought naturally and innocently for what Mother? Yeah, KNOWLEDGE.**

------ Sunday, May 30, 2021 ------
Me (1:47 AM)
They were, as u and i are, innocent by nature...They were, as u and i are, HOLY BY NATURE. Sure, according to the fable, **they got the knowledge of good and evil AFTER they were deceived. But before that they had ZERO understanding of evil or sin,** yet this God in this story wants to condemn them for making a natural mistake like that, after God in the story ALSO HAS the knowledge of good and evil, **and he ALLOWS Satan to prey upon their innocence**. I am repeating the obvious insanity of this story to you over and over because thats what it

sometimes takes to help someone wake up from a lifetime of being 'programmed' with such lies about God, and about your true nature. **Remember, in their innocence with no knowledge of sin, they OF COURSE could not be said to have made the so called 'free will' CHOICE to 'sin' against God. They didnt have that KNOWLEDGE yet!** They of course had a natural innocent human interest IN 'knowledge', and God said what again in Hosea chap 4 that i showed u??

------ Monday, May 31, 2021 ------
Me (1:23 AM)
The lies in this very first Bible story are huge. This and many other things in the Bible i remember having a hard time accepting, **<u>God cursing them for being fooled by the Devil, when God was supposed to be their protector as their Father</u>**. You are NOT sinful by nature Mother, and neither is mankind overall. By nature we are honest and good. Some people are traumatized, conditioned by others to be unkind or dishonest, out of hard living or bad upbringing they begin to do wrong to others, but that is NOT the case overall. Do u hear me Mother? Even you probably cant come up w an example of how you are 'sinning' in your life. **You may have made a mistake u are ashamed of, but that doesnt make u SINFUL BY NATURE deserving of damnation but for a human blood sacrifice dying for you, that is beyond sick Mother**. Let me remind u agn of another major example of the lie of the Bible that ALL are sinful by nature, <u>Genesis chap 6 vs 9, where it actually SAYS Noah was 'PERFECT'</u>. Huge contradiction!

Chapter Five

------ Tuesday, Jun 1, 2021 ------

Me (2:14 AM)

How many lies and blatant 180 degree contradictions does it take Mother? I have shown u many more than just that one. But, just that one HUGE contradiction stating that Noah was 'PERFECT' makes it clear that ALL mankind is NOT evil and sinful by nature AFTER the garden 'fable', or there could NOT be 'occasional perfect exceptions' . In crafting that flood fable, the Jewish writers used that 'perfect exception' of Noah in order to justify why HE and his family got to ESCAPE the flood and 'Gods' genocide of the rest of humanity, by building a 400 foot long boat that could hold NINE PAIRS OF EVERY LIVING CREATURE ON THE EARTH, **while God said ALL THE ANIMALS WERE SINFUL TOO**. Oh wait, except those Noah gathered FROM ALL OVER THE WORLD. **Oh but the FISH were perfect!** And its all about 'faith'. No Mother, u might as well be having 'faith' that "Goldilocks and the 3 bears" were real and Goldie was also an 'exception'. **She too was PERFECT and thats why the bears didnt eat her for dinner when they came home to their den to find her asleep on the perfect bed**. More lies to come.

------ Wednesday, Jun 2, 2021 ------

Me (1:09 AM)

The point in my taking this time to detail so many lies and contradictions in the Bible is obviously to show u that these are NOT 'holy scriptures' detailing your origin Mother, they are fraudulent man made fables that dont hold up to the most basic scrutiny. You and i were lied to by others who were lied to by others who were lied to, etc, about the nature of 'God' and all things spiritual. One of the other GIANT lies and 'game over' examples of this that i showed u in a previous lesson, was the Bible story of how the earth began to be populated after Cain killed his brother Able. **How many humans were there? Only 3, after Cain killed his brother (Adam his father and Eve his mother, and himself). There were no sisters yet for Cain to have incest with. Apparently the Jewish writers realized that wasnt going to go well in Sunday School if they wrote that there were brothers and sisters, offspring of Adam and Eve, having sex to populate the earth**. So what does it say in that story? It just says that Cain left to other lands to find a wife. Hmmm, **the church teaches ALL humanity came from Adam and Eve, so a game over lie again**

------ Thursday, Jun 3, 2021 ------

Me (1:48 AM)

Now, speaking of lineage lies, i am going to show u another HUGE 'game over' lie in the Bible regarding the so called lineage of JESUS. When i use the phrase 'game over' w these many examples, i obviously mean they expose ALL of the Bible and Judeo Christianity as the man made intentional fraud that it all is...This next example is a GIANT game over example, like others i have already detailed. What does the Bible say about the requirement of Jesus' lineage? **That his bloodline would come from the house and lineage of David**. Matt chapter 1 vs 1 makes it clear, "The book of the generation of Jesus Christ, the son of David, the son of Abraham"... Well guess what?? The only lineage and genealogy in the Bible for Jesus is of course Matt chap 1 and Luke chap 3, and guess who they BOTH are for? **JOSEPH, not Mary**. NOWHERE in the Bible is virgin Mary's genealogy, and being born of a virgin, WOOPS, the 'writers' of Matt and Luke messed up agn, using only Josephs lineage which does not apply

------ Friday, Jun 4, 2021 ------

Me (1:42 AM)

Simply put, the definition of 'lineage' is one's ancestral **BLOODLINE**. One def when i looked it up incl the specific word **'pedigree'**. This MASSIVE Bible lie has not only had Jewish scholars exposing it as proof of the New Test fraud, but it actually caused many Christian sources, esp online if u do an online search on this, to outright tell a bigger lie even still, **trying to falsely claim that Luke's genealogy for Jesus in Luke chap 3 is Mary's, NOT JOSEPH'S!** And this is a blatant lie of desperation because when u look at the passage, it SPECIFICALLY identifies it as JOSEPH'S lineage in the same way it identifies it as Joseph's in Matthew. But, and this is a HUGE 'but', there is yet ANOTHER LIE, or to be kind, lets call it a **'contradiction'** between those two genealogies for Joseph...**Matt Chap 1 vs 16 says "JACOB begat Joseph husband of Mary". But Luke Chap 3 vs 23 records Jesus as the son of Joseph who was the son of 'HELI.' Hmmm, once agn, not very INERRANT for 'holy scripture' is it?**

------ Saturday, Jun 5, 2021 ------

Me (2:40 AM)

Once agn Mother, the Bible's lies by the writers in the so called Gospels are inescapable and undeniable, on such a fundamental tenet of the

76

'messiah' having to be the 'son of David' that when discovered, it is GAME OVER, clearly exposing the Roman Catholic church fraud and fabrication behind it all. AGAIN, Luke chapter 3 OBVIOUSLY is not Mary's genealogy as lying Christians have tried to assert (if u do a search online on this.) They are making that lie more EASILY SEEN by making such a pitiful claim, **when verse 23 says plain as day that it is JOSEPH'S genealogy QUOTE: "And Jesus himself began to be about 30 years of age, being, as was supposed, the son of Joseph, which was the son of Heli."** SO DID THEY SAY MARY, OR DID THEY SAY JOSEPH? GOOD GRIEF!! Its just mind blowing the length that people will go to with their delusion and such a blatant deceptive claim, thinking people will just accept it and not pay attention, because its the boring 'begats' section of 'The Gospels'... Much more exposing the lies tomorrow.

------ Sunday, Jun 6, 2021 ------
Me (1:59 AM)
Now that i have shown u this fundamental lie where the writers of Matthew and Luke SPECIFICALLY cite **Joseph's lineage**, NOT Mary's lineage, as proof of Jesus' bloodline from David, and as i have reminded u that Jesus was of course NOT related to Joseph whatsoever, **having supposedly been born of a virgin**, lets look at yet ANOTHER example of ANOTHER lie on this same topic where the writers for the book of Romans, present their character 'Paul' ALSO making the same undeniably false claim **that Jesus was 'made of the SEED of David**...Turn if u would to Romans chap 1, vs 3 in your King James Version Bible where Paul plainly decrees that Jesus "was made of the seed of David according to the flesh". So that's not one, **but THREE game over lies from the Bible**, with the writers of Matt, Luke AND Romans all fraudulently using JOSEPH'S bloodline, and applying it to Jesus **as the so called 'evidence' that he is of the 'SEED' of David.** I stress the word seed to show u that IS the meaning of 'lineage'.

------ Monday, Jun 7, 2021 ------
Me (1:10 AM)
Again, that Bible verse attributed to Paul in Romans 1 vs 3 fraudulently states specifically that Jesus was **born of the 'seed' of David,** meaning his BLOODLINE, not any 'legal' reason of Joseph legally being his father. Just like those 'begat' passages in Matthew and Luke were intending to show lineage as actual BLOODLINE, Paul specifically decrees the same in this verse, saying Jesus **was born of the 'seed' and 'flesh' of David.** And whose bloodline is being used as the EVIDENCE

for this Mother? This is IMPORTANT to fully understand. **The reason this is such a GAME OVER lie in the Bible is precisely because the dumb writers actually specified JOSEPH'S bloodline as the 'evidence' for Jesus' being of the bloodline of David**. So you CANT ignore this or make some lame excuse of 'who knows' who Mary's bloodline was, <u>because the Bible deliberately used Joseph's</u>. Take note also of the fact that neither books of Mark or John address the virgin birth AT ALL, as though they had no knowledge of it!

------ Tuesday, Jun 8, 2021 ------
Me (1:05 AM)
Add to that huge lie and contradiction the fact of yet another GAME OVER contradiction on this same topic as i have already mentioned, <u>that being the critical contradiction between the two books of Matthew and Luke, which contradict each other by having TWO DIFFERENT fathers for Joseph</u>, and other differing names in their so called 'messiah bloodline'. **Is that a minor thing of no importance Mother?** You'd be lying to say so. But u have and will try to continue to ignore these things because like a drug, **u are addicted to the sick belief that u need a human sacrifice's blood and death to make u feel 'saved',** instead of understanding that WE HAVE ALWAYS BEEN HOLY AND 'SAVED.' ALL of us are a HOLY PART OF GOD. <u>No one, not you, me or anyone is SEPARATE from what is Holy and Divine, and WE 'SAVE' ONE ANOTHER with our holy love and forgiveness for one another</u>, as we grow in that understanding, WITHOUT CONDITIONS! **Your "conditions" for the "salvation" of others is nothing but man made bigotry**.

------ Wednesday, Jun 9, 2021 ------
Me (1:16 AM)
Its WAY PAST time for u to step away from that ugly bigotry that condemns and denigrates others in the name of God for many varying kinds of diversity or belief! **I am the living example u have needed to help u see those religious lies for the man made hate that they are.** I will be continuing w many more examples of the obvious fraud and lies in the Bible as i have already, but let me state it very simply...**It is not 'sin' or 'evil' to be yourself.** Deep down on some level u know that. You cannot be clueless and unaware of how much people all around u, including your brothers, use their 'Christianity' to denigrate and say such ugly, horrible things behind your back and mine, **at my expense**. And how they condemn others like myself, or the many millions of those who are gay, who are being true to themselves, **and yet u continue to**

78

want to align yourself with such people, at the expense of your daughter, as i have pointed out to u before, and will continue to do so until u WAKE UP Mother.

------ Thursday, Jun 10, 2021 ------
Me (12:25 AM)
Its time to stop burying your head in the sand and LOOK at the things i have shown u. 'SIN' is DOING HARM to others, not just being honest and true to who u are! The vast majority of mankind does NOT do harm to others, and BY NATURE treats others the way they want to be treated. Pull your head out of the sand, as i said, and LOOK at what i showed u in the Garden fable...**WHO is doing ALL THE HARM in that story Mother?** Not the childlike innocent Adam and Eve. They had no idea they were being preyed upon by 'evil'. **The only ones in that sick fable who were doing EVIL were Satan preying upon them, and God who let him in the garden to do so!** And the end of that story has God losing his temper, because Adam and Eve simply became like God, achieving the same knowledge of Good and Evil. But as i pointed out, **they DID NOT UNDERSTAND 'sin' before God allowed Satan to prey upon them in their innocence. LOOK at what i am showing u Mother! This is a sick false portrayal of God. It is a man made lie.**

------ Friday, Jun 11, 2021 ------
Me (1:02 AM)
That first Bible story is so obviously fraudulent. It is not your 'origin' Mother. **You did not come into this world under a curse by God for u to suffer because u are 'sinful by nature'.** And it is shameful that u not only taught that sick man made nightmare crap to me and other children, but that u continue to hold on to such a sick belief still, **and at the EXPENSE of so many others who u hold condemning beliefs toward, because they are being honest and true to themselves**. You are not only living a lie by turning a willful blind eye to the truth i am showing u about those lies, but u are shameful in how u hold such sick beliefs about God at others expense. Spiritual truth has ZERO condemnation, as i have told u. People just have lessons to learn from their unique life paths, **and a lot of those lessons are learned from mistakes, they are not 'sin'. But sexual orientation is NOT a mistake at all, anymore than having blonde hair is a 'sin'. It is who someone is, not damned by God for it.**

------ Saturday, Jun 12, 2021 ------
Me (1:14 AM)
If u will think back, u will recall that i knew when i was still a child at around 12 to 14 that i was likely going to need gender reassignment, and i brought that up to u as we sat in our VW Bug in Grandmother and Granddaddy's front yard that day. You got really really upset that i would tell u i thought i needed to consider the change. I tried for so long after that to hide it and make it go away, **but it was not 'sin' or the result of your sin, or anything bad either of us did, anymore than someone who has any other sort of handicap that can be healed with medical science**. But later when i was older and told u the same thing, u freaked out and thought it must be 'demonic', **until fortunately the Pentecostal 'exorcist' expert u took me to told u flat out that there was nothing wrong with me and i wasnt 'possessed' or controlled by demons.** But Mother, it wasnt anything u did either, and i have never been happier, day after day since i had the courage to heal myself despite family bigotry.

------ Sunday, Jun 13, 2021 ------
Me (2:45 AM)
Sending u these texts each night, sharing these truths and wisdom that u are **way overdue** to grasp, i am trying so hard not to give up on u in the face of your ugly bigotry in the name of God. The degree of hate and victimization and severe discrimination i still have to contend w to this day when some people find out i changed my gender is astounding. Most people dont know because i hardly ever discuss it, but occasionally it comes out, and u should not be surprised at the traumatic experiences i endure from people wanting to retaliate or reject me, the circumstances w the Sheriffs Ofc is but one of countless examples i tried to share w u, **and the ROOT of it is virtually always their bigoted Bible beliefs. That is not love, to call others demonic or living in sin for having the honest courage to be themselves and be happy, as i am, and as my friend June is with her wife, who i use as one of many examples of who u shamefully hold bigoted religious beliefs toward.** You owe it to me to wake up.

------ Monday, Jun 14, 2021 ------

Me (1:05 AM)

I am going to say it again Mother, to begin tonight's lesson. You owe it to me, your daughter, to wake up from the bigoted lies we were taught. Deep down u know better, and i deserve a spiritually healthy minded mother. In the process of showing u so many examples of the man made sick fraud in the Bible masquerading as 'Gods word', i also need to keep reminding u of what your true spiritual nature is, that those lying men didnt want the masses to know. IF the masses were to know that they were a HOLY PART of what God is, how could they be CONTROLLED and kept in subjection? **Especially if WOMEN were to know that they are not only an EQUAL part of God along w men, but the ancient pioneers of true spirituality often identified MORE with the Divine FEMININE energy of the universe, as the life giving half of the balance of male and female.** They pioneered the TRINITY as 'MOTHER FATHER CHILD.' But the sick male dominating patriarchal cultures of the Jews and later the Greco Romans **ERASED those truths.**

------ Tuesday, Jun 15, 2021 ------

Me (1:54 AM)

Take note of what i said about the origin of the 'TRINITY'. As i have told u, the Roman Catholic crafters of the new Christian religion at the time **COUNTERFEITED all of the main tenets u and i were told were original to Christianity. But that claim of originality is a GIGANTIC lie.** The concept of the Trinity is one of many such examples. The ancient African culture of KEMET in the Nile Valley ('Egypt' before the Greeks and Romans conquered it and named it Egypt)… this older culture we now know that pioneered civilization, medicine, agriculture, astronomy, music and the arts, etc...this culture of Kemet, dating back at least several thousands of years BEFORE the Adam and Eve timeline begins in the Bible, they were the creators of the concept of the Triune nature of 'God', and they saw that triune nature represented in the 'FAMILY UNIT': '**THE MOTHER, THE FATHER & THE CHILD'**. As i said in my last text lesson, the PATRIARCHAL Romans and Jews conquered them and kept the concept**, but replaced the Mother w the spirit**.

------ Wednesday, Jun 16, 2021 ------

Me (1:25 AM)

The Jews of course didnt adopt the Trinity myth, but they co-opted other things in crafting their man made religion that they learned from the Kemet culture**, like the ten commandments**, which are IDENTICAL to the SAME TEN much older 'negative confessions of Ma-at', **except the Kemet culture had at least 32 MORE 'commandments' they would swear to all that is Holy that they did not engage in..."I have not killed", "I have not stolen", etc.** The Jews sojourned w them for a long enough period to learn those 42 spiritually practiced 'affirmations', and co-opted the ten they later claimed were original to them, when they were not! And, lets look at the lies and fraud about the ten commandments' BIGGEST one:'Thou shalt not KILL' . The Jews only applied that TO THEMSELVES,,, if even then! They and the Christian church BOTH engaged in murderous genocide after bloody genocide, claiming God ordained it, after supposedly God commanded them NOT to kill. **But its fine if the victims are 'non believers'?**

------ Thursday, Jun 17, 2021 ------
Me (1:47 AM)
This is another evidence of massive fraud i distinctly remember questioning u about many years ago, and u had no answer for it but to say they were evil and non believers so God allows for genocide of them...**How utterly full of SHIT u were…What SHAMEFUL violent bigotry in the name of God!** And the fraud continues to be exposed long after all the Bible documented genocide committed against other cultures by the Jews in violation of that prime commandment. As u know, it went into high gear w the Christian church and the Crusades, **but lets not forget all the needless killing in the name of God by the church, of innocent Native Americans who had their own beautiful way of worshipping their understanding of the 'Divine Spirit' through nature**. And as always, the Christian church used their 'belief' to justify massive genocide of Native Americans. They imposed on THEIR sacred land, tried to make them convert, **and killed them when they refused. But what about 'Thou shalt not kill**?'

------ Friday, Jun 18, 2021 ------
Me (1:34 AM)
It is mindblowing, the amount of killing and genocide the Bible claims was 'ordained' by God, and that the Christian church continued to commit in the same imperialist fashion, over and over, even the genocidal killing in the name of God in the founding of this country and after...The diabolical killing and holocaust in its own rite, of Black slaves, untold numbers of whom were also killed, with the same genocide by 'Christians' happening to the Native Americans, with the Bible used to justify ALL of it...**Mother, it doesnt get ANY more full of SHIT than turning a blind eye to the commandment THOU**

82

SHALT NOT KILL, and saying its ok to kill and commit genocide if we believe those people are NON BELIEVERS who are IN OUR WAY and/or we want their land for ourselves! That is yet another GAME OVER example that the JudeoChristian myth is a gigantic hypocritical, man made bigoted fraud! They falsely created a 'God' that was in THEIR sick vengeful killing image, **and then they set about constantly violating one of this God's prime commandments not to kill??**

------ Saturday, Jun 19, 2021 ------
Me (1:42 AM)
It is critical Mother, that u force yourself to face these lies and this MASSIVE degree of fraud about God and all things spiritual, even though it is a habit u have been conditioned with just as i was. 'God' is NOT what i just finished reviewing for you, that the Bible describes 'him' to be. **First, God is NOT a 'him'**...ONCE AGAIN Mother, this is more of the MAN MADE intention of crafting a male image of God **in order to subjugate the women of the Jews and the Roman Catholic and Christian cultures**, when as i also shared with u, they wanted to use a lot of the myth models they copied from ancient Kemet, but they were sure as hell NOT going to keep women equal w men, because of their cultures' bigoted tradition that men are superior, etc, which is a man made lie. But the ancient African Kemet culture understood that **we are ALL an EQUAL PART of what is 'Divine' and that God is equally BOTH male and female.That is but one manifestation of the balance and harmony of the universe of which we are a part.**

------ Sunday, Jun 20, 2021 ------
Me (1:23 AM)
I cannot stress enough, the monumental, horrendously false extent of the lies you and i were taught by those we trusted, who were also traumatized by such sick man made lies about God. Another quick anecdote to show u the sick conditioning such lies cause with men, **in how they learn to wrongly think of THEIR gender as 'preferred' and 'superior'**...I will never forget the look on Dads face after i had just moved out to California to be close to him. In one of my first heart to heart talks helping him understand gender dysphoria and gender identity, when it is at odds with one's biological sex, i told him how bigoted it is and how COMMON it is to encounter men especially, **who cant believe anyone would want to 'lower' themselves if they were born a male, and then would WANT to be female**, because they are CONDITIONED predominantly by the church to see women as a lesser

83

status, etc. He looked shocked that i would flatly destroy that bigoted belief to him.

----- Monday, Jun 21, 2021 ------
Me (1:19 AM)
Continuing my story from yesterday, Dad seemed shocked i would call out as absurd and bigoted, that common sexist belief most men have, that it is OF COURSE so much more preferable to be male than female. **If u are female, you know how PREFERABLE our gender is** ☺ **and why the overwhelming vast majority of us would NEVER want to be male!** By and large, we are much more in tune with love <u>and nurturing kindness,</u> and in taking in the beauty of the universe we are in...We dont have the violent warmongering tendencies men have as a rule. That isnt to say there arent exceptions w some women, but overall we seek more to be healers, communicators, our gender seeks much more to be compromising and understanding, <u>and isnt as obsessed with competing, or one upping others or dominating them</u>. **We are much more the loving, listening peacemakers, much more sensitive and in close touch w our emotions and very importantly, those of others. We tend to be much more honest than men with being ourselves. But the LIES OF MEN in the Bible teach the opposite**.

------ Tuesday, Jun 22, 2021 ------
Me (2:05 AM)
I cannot stress that last line enough from my last text Mother...The LIES OF MEN in the Bible teach the OPPOSITE. They teach bigotry and misogyny, **demeaning the female sex in the name of God**, nothing but weak bigoted male egos 'making up' a religion <u>to pretend their bigotry was 'holy' and ordained by God.</u> **You have to wake up now Mother, and help me wake others up to these sick lies about God, that are the primary thing standing in the way of finally bringing real healing to mankind!** Lets return agn for a reminder about what is <u>ignored </u>by pastors in that very first garden story in Genesis...The church always wants to misrepresent what that passage ACTUALLY SAYS, that i showed u earlier. **Pastors are LYING when they say Eve was the weak one who sought to sin against God and eat the fruit, and then she 'seduced' Adam**. NO, it says THE OPPOSITE. It says Adam was WITH EVE, as they were BOTH DECEIVED by Satan! She didnt go find him to 'seduce' him, **and EVE, not Adam initially said NO to Satan**.

84

------ Wednesday, Jun 23, 2021 ------

Me (1:29 AM)

I probably should say it differently than i did about Eve initially saying no to Satan in the story. I should say, as i have before, that she was the one, not Adam, (who chap 2 vs 6 states was WITH HER when this was happening) who made it clear that she and Adams **own choice, <u>LEFT ALONE on their own volition,</u> were NOT going to eat of the tree as God told them**. But how have pastors and men in the church always tried to cast Eve? They have added lies to the story, which is no surprise as it is already a made up story by the Jews **who made the woman out to be nothing but an 'afterthought' to serve Adam, etc**. But Christian preachers have always dishonestly portrayed Eve as being the 'seductress' of Adam, going even so far as to try to say Adam would never have eaten the fruit, but only did so because of Eve's seduction, and not wanting her to be the only one punished, which is all man made lies. <u>The story DOES NOT say that anywhere at all, but DOES state they were both together</u>

------ Thursday, Jun 24, 2021 ------

Me (1:20 AM)

The point i have been making is that men have perverted and lied about **not just our true holy SPIRITUAL nature, but lied about men being superior, and women being second class**, all what is known as a patriarchal system, instead of an egalitarian system. Spiritual truth does NOT give preferential status to **either** gender, but as i have told u<u>, they are BOTH EQUAL expressions of the BALANCE of all that is</u>. But men have perverted that truth w their male obsessed superiority, decreeing God to be male, when if we as male and female are 'in the image of God' then God would not be one sex or the other, <u>but would be BOTH</u>! Remember, i believe i told u this before, the ancient Kemet culture that pioneered most of the myth models Christianity and Judaism later copied, wherever they had a representation of God, they always also had a balanced representation of a GODDESS, **because they understood that what God is would most certainly be a balanced combination of BOTH the masculine and feminine energies.**

------ Friday, Jun 25, 2021 ------

Me (1:35 AM)

This is **<u>WHY</u>** things are so violent, bigoted, tribal and selfish in our world, NOT because all mankind is violent, bigoted, tribal and selfish by nature, **but because ORGANIZED RELIGION is violent, bigoted, tribal and selfish by nature, and mankind has been SO dishonestly**

programmed and conditioned by that false religious influence over thousands of years. There is NO MORE denying that truth Mother, like it or not, addicted to it as u are...And it is TIME FOR IT TO STOP! Its time for u to wake up to the massive man made lies of JudeoChristianity's shamefully racist, genocidal, murderous, warmongering and bigoted legacy, **OSTENSIBLY in the name of God**, which is what makes it SO MUCH MORE SHAMEFUL than those in history guilty of bigoted genocide who did it WITHOUT claiming it was Godly 'ordained', and who werent being FLAMING LYING HYPOCRITES in the face of their prime commandment of the ten, THOU SHALT NOT KILL! True spirituality operates by The Golden Rule, unconditionally DOING NO HARM.

------ Saturday, Jun 26, 2021 ------
Me (1:51 AM)
Did u get that important last line?? True spirituality operates under The Golden Rule, unconditionally DOING NO HARM Mother. **Key word, UNCONDITIONALLY**. Those ancient Africans in the Nile River Valley in the area now known as Egypt (many forget Egypt is in AFRICA, so Egyptians originally were Africans) That ancient much older culture we now know from archeology, anthropology and Egyptology **PREDATED the Jewish culture and the Old Test by MANY THOUSANDS of years**. This much older culture of Kemet not only pioneered civilization, agriculture, astronomy, science, medicine and surgery, music and the arts, but it was the world renown pioneer of SPIRITUALITY founded upon EQUALITY and THE GOLDEN RULE, **including most of the world's most popular and widely held MYTHS, such as the virgin birth, baptism, the Trinity (Theirs originally being the FAMILY UNIT of Mother, Father & Child) and the symbolic 'savior God man' myth**, just to name but a few, all orig NOT to Christianity, but to Kemet (later named Egypt by Greeks)

------ Sunday, Jun 27, 2021 ------
Me (2:09 AM)
I want to stress a couple of points from the last text lesson. Remember i shared w u how Kemet, that ancient spiritual and civilization pioneering culture is now proven by anthropology to be MANY THOUSANDS of years OLDER than how far back the Old Testament goes. Well once again, this means what i have been showing u, that the Jews were lying about their being the 'Chosen Race of God' and the 'ORIGIN' of mankind. And not only that, but their lies have been proven for a long time now regarding many of the myths they learned while sojourning in

86

the Kemet (Egyptian) culture, **then falsely claiming them as 'original' when they wrote the Torah**, where as I said, they fraudulently proclaimed themselves as the origin of mankind. Also, the Golden Rule and understanding of the fundamental tenet of DOING NO HARM was practiced UNCONDITIONALLY by Kemet and other cultures LONG before the Jews came on the scene. That ancient Nile Valley culture that pioneered civilization also pioneered what they called **"The spiritual laws of Ma'at", a fundamental part of which was their teaching and understanding of the importance of treating and valuing ALL others as YOU would want to be treated and valued (The Golden Rule)**. By contrast, as i reminded u above, JudeoChristianity has a long legacy of violence and genocide just simply against 'non believers'.

------ Monday, Jun 28, 2021 ------
Me (1:23 AM)
I am going to say it again because u try so hard to 'forget' these facts that immediately expose the fraud and massive hypocrisy of your beliefs. JudeoChristianity has had a LONG well documented legacy of VIOLENT AGGRESSION and GENOCIDE in the name of God, as though the commandment 'Thou shalt not kill' DID NOT EVEN EXIST! And dont say that was BEFORE Jesus' 'teachings of love' in the New Test **because you know all too well of the SAME historical aggressive violence, crusades and murderous genocide in the name of God by the CHRISTIAN CHURCH, same as is documented as the practice of the Jews in the Old Test. NO DIFFERENCE.** The Bible's love is CONDITIONAL, instead of how real love DOES NO HARM UNCONDITIONALLY! **One minute Jesus is talking about 'turning the other cheek' and the next minute, like in Matt chap 10, vs 34, he aggressively decrees that he is NOT come to bring peace, but a SWORD**. You twist yourself into a pretzel to rationalize all of this hypocrisy i am detailing for u here.

------ Tuesday, Jun 29, 2021 ------
Me (12:36 AM)
'Blind faith' in something that is SO FULL of proven lies and constant hypocrisy and bigotry in the name of God **is NOT 'faith', it is 'fraud' in the name of God**. Fraud that has succeeded because it used a fearful monstrous FALSE IMAGE of a condemning violent, vengeful God to teach and traumatize u w a FALSE 'EVIL BY NATURE' image of yourself, telling u your only hope to avoid this monster of a God condemning u to hell is to use 'child like blind faith' and NOT question any of it. But u know QUESTIONING is what is truly 'child like'...The

fact that the Christian Church also has a legacy of focusing a lot on passages they made sure were put in the Bible that tell their 'believers' NOT to question any of it, but to accept it like a child who does what they are told, that **should be a huge tip off to u that u NEED to question it all**, especially when your daughter is showing u so much evidence, much of which u hadnt ever learned before, **precisely BECAUSE u were told to 'believe blindly'**.

------ Wednesday, Jun 30, 2021 ------
Me (1:46 AM)
And as i have been pointing out to u, when 'blind faith' has at its root the fundamental belief that ALL those who question it, and ALL those who simply know better and dont 'blindly believe' it are CONDEMNED to hell by that 'blind faith', <u>then thats a huge red flag</u>. Thats when you can KNOW theres fraud behind it. **Listen closely here Mother...That 'blind belief' that such ETERNAL SUSTAINED HARM is DESERVED by all who DONT share your 'blind beliefs' is the evidence that those beliefs are man made fraud, <u>because they have been 'weaponized'</u>**.

Chapter Six

------ Thursday, Jul 1, 2021 ------
Me (1:55 AM)
That fraudulent aspect of 'weaponizing' JudeoChristianity with such beliefs that 'non believers' DESERVE eternal harm and damnation is all the proof u need all by itself, to have your eyes open to the OPPOSITE of 'unconditional love' that it has hypocritically programmed u to believe. But the fraudulent man made 'weaponizing' of JudeoChristianity, meaning the deeply endemic aspect of HARM that it does, is also, as i have shown u many times already, **harm to YOU and to ME when we were little children, innocent just like the characters of Adam and Eve who were ALSO HARMED in their innocence**... but you and i were horribly harmed by the 'weaponizing' of beliefs, myths that were counterfeited from much older cultures, and that WERE NEVER MEANT to be weaponized and made to be condemning... **But the harm goes much deeper, because as a child, we were LIED to about our TRUE HOLY NATURE.** And that psychological trauma is ironically why u hold on to such bigotry.

------ Friday, Jul 2, 2021 ------
Me (1:52 AM)
What i have been carefully showing u Mother, i realize is difficult for u to face. It was very difficult and shocking for me as i began to learn and honestly face the man made lies, fraud and hypocrisy that are rampant in the Bible. Your ENTIRE frame of reference about not only the nature of God, but YOUR nature **has been nothing but Roman Catholic fabricated LIES Mother**. It doesnt matter that you call yourself a 'Protestant' or a 'Baptist', ALL of Christianity's fundamental tenets were created by Roman Catholic bishops over the course of a few hundred years with various 'councils', like the Council of Nicea under the Roman Emperor Constantine in 325 AD. Like i shared w u in a previous text, **Pope Leo in the 1500s was quoted at a big banquet event, remarking how much profit had come to the church as a result of their 'fable' of Jesus.** It is critical that u begin now to wake up to the REAL nature of 'God' as i have been blessed to awaken to, and have been diligently and patiently sharing with you.

------ Saturday, Jul 3, 2021 ------
Me (2:23 AM)
Think Mother...Look back at all the many violent examples i have been laying out for you. **They do NOT reflect what the true nature of 'God' is. They are obvious bigotry of men.** They are not unconditionally loving, they are highly 'weaponized' as i have reminded u of that genocidal legacy of Judaism, and then continuing with the Roman Catholic fabricating of Christianity, the legacy of killing and aggressive genocidal imperialism in which BOTH the Jews and the Christian church claimed such harm to others was 'ORDAINED' by God...**And u didnt stop to question the MIND BLOWING HYPOCRISY of how that completely contradicts one of the most important of the ten commandments, 'Thou shalt not kill'?** This legacy of genocidal imperialism by JudeoChristianity was also included in the popular rationalizing phrase **'MANIFEST DESTINY'**, meaning their invading and wiping out so many Native Americans was MEANT TO BE and was 'manifest', or 'obvious' destiny ordained by God. **No, the true nature of 'God' is DO NO HARM.**

------ Sunday, Jul 4, 2021 ------
Me (2:03 AM)
Obviously that historical phrase 'manifest destiny' wasnt ONLY about rationalizing the mass genocide of Native Americans and other minorities, but that was a significant part of it. Christianity, in their imperialism of expanding the West to 'the New World' were unapologetic in their claiming this 'destiny' ordained them to do such MASS HARM to those natives whose home land the Christians were invading (they of course called it 'settling') **and who they called 'heathens' because the Native Americans saw the Divine Spirit through nature, not a sick human blood sacrifice**, etc etc. The Native Americans welcomed the 'settling' Christians for the most part and that fact is where we get Thanksgiving from. But over a period of time, as they were being so constantly harmed and betrayed, **of course they fought for their independence, just as we did from Britain.** Many Christians, when u try to share these facts w them, lie to themselves, and try to deny that holocaust on the natives by Christians.

------ Monday, Jul 5, 2021 ------
Me (1:35 AM)
But the truth is that the vast overwhelming majority of the Native Americans were loving and kind, very wise and at peace, **having**

learned to live and see themselves as a **HARMONIOUS PART of what the 'Divine Great Spirit' is**, not separate from some entity that condemns those who believe in 'him' in different ways! Mother, it was not God, but power-mongering lying men who wrote the Bible. They wanted to portray themselves and their cultures as CHOSEN and preferred by God, hence the ORIGIN of most of the bigotry and racism in history TO THE PRESENT. They wanted to portray a God who decreed that nature was for men to DOMINATE, while the Divine truth is what the Native Americans had learned THOUSANDS of years before the arrival of the hypocritical Christian invaders and violent conquerors arrived (oh right, i believe they preferred calling themselves 'missionaries)but my point is the Native Americans knew nature **was NOT for men to 'dominate', but to live in HARMONY with as a PART of them.**

------ Tuesday, Jul 6, 2021 ------
Me (2:44 AM)
So like i told u a few messages back, it is time for u to wake up to the realization that your ENTIRE PARADIGM of belief is a man made bigoted lie in the name of God. As i said, it has traumatized and lied to u and me, **not only about the nature of what 'God' is, but just as importantly, it has traumatized and lied to us about OUR true nature, which is NOT SINFUL or EVIL, but HOLY and LOVING, because WE ARE PART of what 'God' is here in the physical dimension.** That is NOT an egotistical thing to realize, it is a HUMBLING thing to realize! When u realize that ALL man and womankind are EQUALLY a HOLY PART of what God is, you finally begin to understand not just the the need, but your HOLY RESPONSIBILITY to love all diversity UNCONDITIONALLY, without damnation or condemnation beliefs, and u recognize how those sick beliefs contradict the Golden Rule of REAL Spiritual Truth. Yes we make mistakes here, but **making mistakes are HOW WE LEARN AND GROW ETERNALLY! We are unique diverse parts of God**

------ Wednesday, Jul 7, 2021 ------
Me (12:44 AM)
We are touching absolute holiness here in this subject matter, about mistakes being PART of our Holy Spirit's eternal growth process. A huge part of the man made lie u were traumatized with has to do with telling u your mistakes are proof that you are 'bad' or 'sinful' by nature. That is an absolute intentional falsehood to keep the masses in ignorance about their shared holiness, and the power they would have if they learned that

91

spiritual truth about themselves. Remember, even the dumb writers of the lies in the Bible sometimes quoted God saying he made a mistake and 'repented' of his creating mankind, etc, which is all a man made lie. **But the point is they even portray God who is supposedly PERFECT as making mistakes.** You and i and everyone of ALL beliefs, as a part of what God is, are PERFECT, **and mistakes are a PART OF our perfect holiness! We are meant to LEARN and GROW from mistakes, not condemn ourselves as 'sinful by nature' because of them**. Obviously INTENTIONAL HARM of others is evil.

------ Thursday, Jul 8, 2021 ------
Me (12:54 AM)
But 'evil' behavior, meaning behavior that seeks to harm others or treat others the OPPOSITE of The Golden Rule, that behavior is NOT your nature, it is LEARNED and it is conditioned over time. Evil or 'sinful' behavior is intentionally abusing others or treating them in a harmful way. Stop for a minute and think about how the VAST MAJORIY of people of ALL diverse beliefs naturally make every effort NOT to do intentional harm to others. **They NATURALLY PRACTICE THE GOLDEN RULE.** Thats because we are all a HOLY PART of what is Divine, **and it is NOT our nature to do bad things, that is LEARNED BEHAVIOR!** And ironically, as i have shown u MANY shameful examples already, that conditioning, that learning to look at other diverse believing people as deserving eternal harm by God comes from the Bible and the Koran, JudeoChristianity and Islam. All of that bigotry and advocating of genocide and damnation of non believers, **all of that is ANTI LOVING, evil man made conditioning in the name of God**.

------ Friday, Jul 9, 2021 ------
Me (4:21 AM)
Look once more at the very important truth i wrote to u two lessons back: You and i and everyone of ALL beliefs, as a part of what God is, are PERFECT, and mistakes are a PART OF our perfect holiness! We are meant to LEARN and GROW from mistakes, not condemn others for them and call them sinful by nature. Like i have plainly showed u and will cont to remind u, the ones who were doing ALL the evil in the Garden story **were NOT innocent Adam and Eve with ZERO understanding yet of good and evil**. It was God teaming up with and ALLOWING Satan to PREY upon their innocence! It makes me righteously angry that this is just deliberately ignored by u so that u can cont to hold on to such sick man made superstitions about the nature of God, at mankind's expense. Like i have said to u before, **IF u were**

SOOO simple minded that u could only accept nursery rhymes and fairy tales about such a made up God i might could let it go, but i cant when your beliefs make u such a shameful bigot of a person to others.

------ Saturday, Jul 10, 2021 ------
Me (1:09 AM)
Ironically Mother, deliberately ignoring all the MANY obvious hypocrisies and lies in the Bible, and instead holding on to such a bigoted belief that those who DONT believe like u deserve eternal harm and torment... Ironically that <u>DEFINES YOU</u> as a very bad person. That is why i am being so patient and diligent in sending u these lessons on real spiritual truth, because i know u have become such a bigot **because of major psychological trauma**, conditioning u to think you are 'ordained' by such beliefs to look at other diverse people of other faiths and/or sexual orientations as damned by God. <u>But THEY are not looking at u with such condemning beliefs thinking YOU deserve eternal harm and torment.</u> Thats because as i said in my last lesson, **the vast majority of people NATURALLY LOVE others, and naturally want to treat others the way they want to be treated.** Remember i told u that doing harm or ADVOCATING harm to others is evil, and it is NOT NATURAL, it is conditioned by lies and trauma.

------ Sunday, Jul 11, 2021 ------
Me (1:26 AM)
It is time for you to finally grow as i have, and lay down those man made condemning teachings of God, **a superstitious blood sacrifice sick belief system that is completely fraudulent and weaponized, completely OPPOSITE of the UNCONDITIONAL LOVE and UNCONDITIONAL FORGIVENESS of real spiritual truth.** Does that mean those exceptions to the rule, who do harm and evil to others, having been so conditioned, will not have consequences? Of course not Mother. Yes there are SERIOUS consequences for being UNLOVING and intentionally harming others, but those serious consequences are how those very very ignorant misled people will LEARN and GROW. But those serious life consequences, often referred to as 'BAD KARMA' <u>do not include condemnation</u>. They do include **CORRECTION**. See Mother, THAT is how love and forgiveness operate in real spiritual truth...Not in arbitrary damning and God ordained killing, etc as is the sick man made legacy of JudeoChristianity. I am bringing needed correction to u here.

------ Monday, Jul 12, 2021 ------
Me (1:40 AM)
Again, it is time for u to grow and wake up to the **horribly superstitious** man made lies about 'God' that psychologically traumatized u and stunted your spiritual understanding and growth at a very young age. Why do u think i was given to u as your child with the handicap i had and fixed? **I am here for the purpose of teaching you what those sick lies have blocked u from learning.** You should know that i would not lead u astray as i have assured u before in previous lessons in this thread. The Bible was dishonestly and deliberately crafted to hide from u the fact that YOU are a PERFECT and HOLY SPIRIT, and you have <u>NEVER been 'sinful' or 'evil' by nature</u>, **because you have ALWAYS been and always will be a HOLY PART of what 'God' is! You have never been 'separate' from what God is.** Mother, tell me what has you so paralyzed in guilt psychologically, that you would believe such sick, human sacrifice condemning teachings of God. **You hung up on your daughter at Christmastime** and told me 'we have NOTHING to talk about', simply in response to my asking u that question.

------ Tuesday, Jul 13, 2021 ------
Me (1:15 AM)
I remember hearing u stress to me how important to u it was, how much u PRAYED that God would give u a 'son'. But Highest Wisdom and the Universal Divine Spirit, of which YOU and I, and we ALL are a part, found a creative way to teach u, through my life circumstance, **that you were wrong to be making such a 'value judgment', elevating a son over a daughter, and trying to show u from this experience that THEY ARE BOTH EQUAL AND THE SAME.** I personally like to tell u, somewhat jokingly, that as a female i KNOW being a girl is <u>sooo much more preferable</u> ☺ <u>For sooo many good reasons</u>, LOL. The fundamental reason you thought that way is based on the conditioning about male preference as so often taught in the Bible. That, as i have touched on in previous texts, is another GIANT example of the source of JudeoChristianity, and specifically the Roman Catholic church who deviously crafted the New Testament, as being <u>nothing but a sick patriarchal man made agenda</u>.

------ Wednesday, Jul 14, 2021 ------
Me (1:41 AM)
The man made fraud of the Bible is largely rooted in those Jews and Roman Catholics who crafted it being bigoted w their **'male superiority**

complex' that is also at the ROOT of all the weaponizing of it, and all the genocidal violence and killing. The MUCH OLDER ancient culture of Kemet i have been telling u about, who we now know from archeology, anthropology and Egyptology scholars, actually originally pioneered civilization and spirituality... **They knew that women should be EQUALLY in power and that what 'God' is would be BOTH sexes, not MALE CENTRIC!** They did NOT weaponize their understanding of spirituality. Fundamentally they were peace makers, **not genocidal warmongerers as the Bible itself DESCRIBES the patriarchal Jews and Roman Catholics**. ALL cultures at the time of Kemet were enamored by their pioneering of sooo many things...agriculture and irrigation, medicine and surgery, astronomy and SPIRITUALITY. The Greeks and later the Romans conquered them and **counterfeited** their teachings.

------ Thursday, Jul 15, 2021 ------
Me (1:10 AM)
I am going to be showing u much more of the huge lies and fraud in the Bible, and how much of it was co-opted from much older myths that are based in what is known as AstroTheology, **meaning based on the anthropomorphism of the Sun and stars and the 12 constellations, which is why there are so many references to 12...12 months, 12 tribes of Israel, 12 disciples, etc**...But i want to also tell u that i heard from Dad, he has finally decided to end his self imposed alienation toward me. And guess what at least one of his main agendas was to reveal to me...**That he 'sacrificed me on the altar of his career'**. He admitted turning away from me for the most part ALL my life, even as a child, giving all favoritism as i suspected, to the 3 from his second marriage. Then he wanted to say u werent faithful to him...he did not mean infidelity, just devotion-wise, which i countered by telling him u have always kept his last name to this day. More to follow on his Christian hypocritical beliefs....

------ Friday, Jul 16, 2021 ------
Me (1:49 AM)
I put some important info about Dad in my last message last night. It appears u arent giving me the courtesy of even reading the special texts and info i am daily taking special time out to send u. Love doesnt ignore loved ones in such important efforts of discourse Mother. You have a HELL of a lot to learn spiritually, and ethically, in learning that there is also **NO LOVE** in any religious belief that has damning beliefs toward other diverse humans, who have been led on their path to a different way

95

of seeing the Divine Spirit of us all. Back to Dad and his finally wanting to communicate. So the major hypocritical aspect from his admission that he 'sacrificed' me for his career, while he spouts so much Catholic Christian BS in his communication, **is that it was the Catholic church who REQUIRED that he go through their sick process of ANNULING your marriage to him which definitively 'sacrifices' me as it would pretend i wasnt 'legitimate'.** I asked him to explain, still waiting for reply.

------ Saturday, Jul 17, 2021 ------
Me (1:28 AM)
Now look agn at what i said early in my msg to u yesterday, because it bears repeating: "You have a HELL of a lot to learn spiritually, and ethically, in learning that there is also NO LOVE in any religious belief that has damning beliefs toward other diverse humans, who have been led on their path to a different way of seeing the Divine Spirit of us all" The 'damning beliefs' u have been indoctrinated with from the Bible are the man made WEAPONIZING of JudeoChristianity! That is at the core of how u can KNOW it is a fraudulent lie, falsely in the name of God. **Love NEVER condemns Mother. You have to wake up and learn this!** I am not taking all this time and daily effort to share these corrective facts and truths with u because i am some kind of demonic influenced agent of 'the Devil' Mother. Good grief you are so brainwashed with sick superstition, **and the reason this is SO IMPORTANT is because of the way those sick superstitious beliefs harm others and prevent peace in name of God**.

------ Sunday, Jul 18, 2021 ------
Me (1:10 AM)
Again, the reason this is so important is because this man made weaponized, condemning lie u have been fooled with, is the fundamental thing keeping humanity from realizing we are ONE...Such damning superstitious beliefs toward others **PROVE the fraud of such beliefs**. They only prevent us from waking up to our TRUE SPIRITUAL NATURE, **which is that we are ALL THE BODY OF GOD, not just 'Christians', not just 'Muslims', not just 'Mormons', not just 'Jews'.** That 'belief' and 'faith' is NOTHING BUT BIGOTRY, shamefully in the name of God! Understand this: **To the extent there is to be a 'heaven' on earth, WE as the DIVERSE BODY OF GOD will have to create it**, the way each of us created our coming here for this earthly experience as a PART of God in the first place. Look at your hands Mother. Those are the hands of God, not because u are a Christian, **but**

96

because u are a part of God in the physical <u>JUST LIKE THE 7 OR 8 BILLION OTHERS of your fellow PARTS OF GOD</u>. This truth is where REAL HEALING begins Mother.

------ Monday, Jul 19, 2021 ------
Me (1:26 AM)
Once again, That last msg is so special and important for u to hear Mother, because it is in a nutshell the eye opening powerful spiritual truth where REAL HEALING begins, and where the ability to effectively heal others begins...**not in superstitious fearful beliefs of a condemning God who had to CONSTANTLY have a 'blood lust' satisfied w animal blood sacrifices, and ultimately a human blood sacrifice, etc**. That is all sick barbaric superstition from a time when such fear based religion was crafted to control very ignorant barbaric cultures. But this was NOT the case with Kemet, the ancient African culture along the Nile River valley that pioneered this spiritual truth they referred to as 'KRST'. They did not have vowels in their ancient culture that invented civilization, the arts and sciences and astronomy, medicine and early forms of surgery, etc. **<u>They taught their children that 'KRST' was the Divine Spirit that we are ALL a part of, and no one is separate from it</u>**.

------ Tuesday, Jul 20, 2021 ------
Me (1:44 AM)
As the hands of God here in the physical, we are miracle workers and creators...You created your coming here...YOU did that Mother, as a part of what God is. And i did that, as a part of what God is. <u>And what God is is very, very DIVERSE Mother</u>, and we block our ability to be the healers we were meant to be when we adopt unhealthy thinking habits, **ESPECIALLY when those thinking habits become 'beliefs' that are at the EXPENSE of your diverse other 'parts of God' who are just as Holy as you, just on the different path they created, to learn the lessons of UNCONDITIONAL LOVE they were meant to learn**. The biggest lesson we are meant to learn here is our ONENESS Mother! And the man made condemning beliefs of JudeoChristianity and Islam **are superstitious blocks to that lesson and that healing**. Everything is 'THOUGHT' Mother. Creation comes from our eternal unseen consciousness and healing comes naturally where there is healthy thinking. But it is naturally BLOCKED with unhealthy thinking.

------ Wednesday, Jul 21, 2021 ------
Me (1:13 AM)
As i have been so blessed to learn this wisdom, and to begin to achieve this ability to heal others, which i had been steadfastly asking for from a very young age, i have conversely been saddened and amazed at the extent so many people go to in RESISTING healing. Many people LIKE the addictive unhealthy way they think. Many people much like yourself, have been traumatized and lied to from a young age, and **led to falsely believe that God not only will condemn all the rest of humanity just because they have a different spiritual understanding, but that this God expects YOU to SUFFER here in this physical world**. Again Mother, it is critical spiritual truth 101 as i call it, to understand that EVERYTHING IS 'THOUGHT', and unhealthy thought addictions are what block healing. While drug and alcohol addictions are harmful, such addictions to believing that YOU are saved and all others of different spiritual understandings deserve eternal torment, **that is a MUCH more harmful addiction Mother**

------ Thursday, Jul 22, 2021 ------
Me (1:19 AM)
The REASON it is a much more harmful thought addiction is because, as i have been steadfastly showing u for some time now, it is fundamentally advocating HARM for your fellow PARTS OF GOD! Mother, you have in the past shamefully tried to 'rationalize' those beliefs you hold of eternal damnation for others, by trying to tell me that YOU arent saying it, the BIBLE is saying it. **And that is your conscience at a deep level trying to tell u that such a belief is fundamentally in GROSS OPPOSITION to love, forgiveness and everything that real spiritual truth is about.** To dogmatically hold such beliefs that others deserve such eternal harm, and then to back pedal and say, **"Well it isnt ME condemning them, it is God"** is like a member of the Klan who tries to say, "Yeah, i joined the Klan, but it isnt ME who says that Whites should segregate from Blacks, God says it in many places in the Bible, and i just BELIEVE the BIBLE." You have been programmed to believe man made bigotry is 'Gods word'

------ Friday, Jul 23, 2021 ------
Me (1:09 AM)
Not only have u been programmed to believe horrible man made bigotry masquerading as Gods word, but u as my mother, who by now, (actually by long ago) have been able to see firsthand how blessed i have been for having the courage to finally make myself whole with my gender as a

98

female, yet my own mother, witnessing my happiness as a result, and how right that has been for me, **has chosen to continue hold on to the sick bigoted belief system that regularly denigrates and condemns people like your daughter for realizing they need such healing and having the courage to achieve it for themselves thanks to modern medicine**. What did u do Mother, that u feel so paralyzed in thinking u deserve to be condemned if u dont adhere to such beliefs in human and animal sacrifices to satisfy some 'God' who must have a blood lust satisfied? What was it that u did that has your mind so messed up to believe in such bigotry in name of God? Trauma and paralyzing, unnecessary guilt is the only explanation

------ Sunday, Jul 25, 2021 ------
Me (2:19 AM)
I remember being shocked as a teenager when i first read these many verses from three different 'gospels', Matt, Mark and Luke, in which there is no doubt, Jesus is telling his disciples his 2nd Coming, his return bringing the kingdom of God to earth, WOULD HAPPEN IN THEIR GENERATION. I remember being so shocked i pointed it out to u as a serious problem to the teachings of the Christian Church that tells u Jesus is going to come again in the sky and bring the kingdom of Heaven to earth in 'power and glory', **and that these repeated quotes from Jesus make it unequivocally clear that he said that would undoubtedly happen IN THE DISIPLES' GENERATION, and i remember u having no explanation for it, just pretending it didnt say what it clearly says.** I think some dummy tried to twist it and say he was only talking about his appearing to them immediately after his death, but that person was ignoring Jesus' specific quotes that he was prophesying his powerful return with the kingdom of heaven.

------ Tuesday, Jul 27, 2021 ------
Me (1:59 AM)
There is no doubt he is saying clearly that THEY would SEE all those things happen. How do we know there is no doubt? Because Jesus ACTUALLY SAYS THAT verbatim in vs 31. **He says 'Likewise when YE SEE THESE THINGS COME TO PASS', so no one can say he is talking vaguely about some generation thousands of years away in the future.** And if that wasnt clear enough, he adds in vs 32 'THIS GENERATION SHALL NOT PASS AWAY TILL ALL BE FULFILLED'. And then there's even more in this passage. Jesus DOUBLES DOWN on this, to make sure his disciples believed this prediction. In vs 33 he says 'Heaven and earth shall pass away, but my

words shall not pass away', meaning what Mother?? Meaning of course that they could take his words to the bank, in other words. **Oh but no they couldn't, as we know none of that happened! So his words DID pass away, while heaven and earth are STILL here. He was speaking to them, and said specifically THAT generation would not die until his 2nd coming happened. And it was a lie.**

------ Wednesday, Jul 28, 2021 ------
Me (1:59 AM)
You have to face these lies Mother. There is no saying Jesus was talking to YOU or ME or a generation 200 years from now, because not only do those verses i just quoted make it clear he was talking about THEIR generation, **but i am going to show u that Jesus believed it was THEIR generation for the SPECIFIC reason that ELIJAH was prophesied by Malachi to be the forerunner of Jesus' 2nd coming, and in the same context of telling HIS DISIPLES that THEIR generation, NOT YOURS Mother, would see his glorious return, Jesus tells them that John the Baptist WAS Elijah**. And if all that isnt clear enough, in Mark chapter 9, vs one which i will get to later, he wraps it up plainly with a bow, and decrees that there are those standing here TODAY...not today in 2021 Mother...he was talking to those listening to him THEN... who WILL NOT TASTE DEATH until they have seen him return w the kingdom of God in glory. **None of that happened, and u cant be God in the flesh and be caught in such monumental lies**.

------ Thursday, Jul 29, 2021 ------
Me (1:46 AM)
Now i will prove this to u with chapter and verse from your own KJV Bible...Turn pls to Malachi chapter 4 and lets refresh our recollection of Malachi's prophecy. **Vs 5 reads 'Behold i will send u Elijah the prophet, before the coming of the great and dreadful day of the Lord'**. Ok, unless u begin lying now, u have to face the fact Mother, that u have ALWAYS believed Elijah's 2nd coming was to be immediately followed by Jesus. And the disciples CONFIRM that firm belief too, as they respond to Jesus' prophecy that his 2nd Coming will b in THEIR generation, **and they ask him, as i said in a previous lesson, 'So when will we see Elijah as prophesied?'** I am paraphrasing, so better yet, lets look at Matt 17, vs 10 thru 13...'And his disciples asked him, saying why then say the scribes that Elias must first come? **Vs 12 quotes Jesus reply, 'Elias is come already, and they knew him not...Vs 13 says**

'Then the disciples understood that he spake of John the Baptist'.
Much more proof to come.

Chapter Seven

------ Sunday, Aug 1, 2021 ------

Me (2:32 AM)

Now lets continue facing the truth spelled out in actual quotes from Jesus in your own Bible, showing he not only decreed, **but GUARANTEED to his disciples that his so called '2nd coming' would happen IN THEIR GENERATION**. Before we leave Matt chap 10, look at vs 23. Remember in vs 6 and 7 Jesus is quoted telling his disciples **NOT to go to NON JEWS, but to go preach to only the house of Israel, and tell them WHAT? Thats right, 'the kingdom of heaven IS AT HAND' meaning his 2nd coming**. And if that wasn't clear enough, look now at vs 23. Jesus tells his disciples, "for verily i say unto u (which is Jesus saying 'i GUARANTEE what i am about to tell u')...**"Ye shall not have gone over the cities of Israel till the Son of Man be come'** How many times do u need to see it Mother? The context here is not like the sermon on the mount where Jesus is quoted speaking broadly to all. **No, what is so damning about this is obviously he was talking only directly to his disciples!** More examples tomorrow.

------ Monday, Aug 2, 2021 ------

Me (1:58 AM)

The disciples certainly went over the cities of Israel easily MANY, MANY TIMES in the many years to follow after Jesus' prophecy of his return being in their generation, and that never happened. You cant have a God in the flesh making such 'guarantees' about not necessarily the 'day or hour', but DEFINITELY the generation... You cant have that kind of lie coming out of Jesus' mouth, quoted as i will continue to show u in several more chapters, **you cant have such FUNDAMENTALLY fraudulent lies in the Bible and call it 'the word of God'**...ALL of this massive evidence and hypocrisy and bigotry i am consistently showing u is evidence that it is NOT 'HOLY' from spiritual truth, **but it is nothing but man made lies.** Remember back when i showed u how In Mark chapter 7, Jesus is quoted not even being aware of germs or the importance of washing hands to prevent disease? Yes the Jews called it a tradition, **but they learned that tradition from others who taught them about clean sanitary health methods.**

------ Tuesday, Aug 3, 2021 ------

Me (1:38 AM)

To finish my last point about Mark 7 showing Jesus had ZERO knowledge of germs and the importance of teaching his disciples about the REAL HEALTH reason behind that 'tradition'... **You cant have a Holy 'God in the flesh' who is a 'healer of disease', but who doesn't even know of the need for washing your hands for HEALTH REASONS!** Not only did he not tell them this critically important health knowledge, but he tells them **'WHO CARES?'** Yes i paraphrased, but that's the context of what he told his disciples... And even more damning to the entire fundamentals of Christianity, as i showed u before, is that Jesus then OBLITERATES and contradicts the foundation of your whole belief in 'original sin' because of Adam and Eve's eating the 'forbidden fruit', because Jesus proceeds to tell his disciples not only is it ridiculous to think u need to follow some tradition of sanitary washing of hands and utensils before eating, but he IGNORANTLY tells them NOTHING eaten by man can harm or 'defile' him!

------ Wednesday, Aug 4, 2021 ------

Me (12:51 AM)

To continue from my last msg... As Jesus in Mark 7 shows total ignorance of even the most basic understanding of the health risks of unsanitized utensils and hands when consuming food, and as he then tells his disciples NOTHING eaten can harm/defile a person, **he destroys the entire fairy tale, i mean 'story' of Adam and Eve being corrupted and defiled by eating the forbidden fruit!** You cant have God in Genesis losing his temper and cursing Adam and Eve, telling them they are 'sinful' precisely DUE TO their eating a piece of fruit from a tree that would give them an understanding for the VERY FIRST TIME of good and evil, and of right and wrong, which being innocent they had no 'knowledge' of beforehand, as i have covered in great detail...You cant have that FUNDAMENTAL 'story line' and then have Jesus, supposedly 'God' in flesh, IGNORANT of the potential harm of GERMS & DISEASE in consuming food, as well as undermining that basic tenet of the entire Christian fable, i mean 'belief'.

------ Thursday, Aug 5, 2021 ------

Me (12:42 AM)

Now we continue with more chapter and verse examples from your own Bible, **quoting Jesus guaranteeing unequivocally that his '2nd coming' would be in his disciples' generation AT THAT TIME**. Please turn to the last verse of Mark chapter 8, and the first verse of

Mark chap 9. Mark 8:38 reads, "Whosoever shall be ashamed of me and of my words in THIS adulterous and sinful generation, of him also shall the Son of Man be ashamed, when he cometh in the glory of his Father with the holy angels." Now CLEARLY, the context here is that Jesus means his '2nd coming' will occur IN THAT ADULTEROUS & SINFUL GENERATION, and that he will hold that generation accountable. But if u still weren't positive and needed more clarity on that, he gives it to u in the very next vs, **Mark 9:1 which reads, "And he said unto them, VERILY, VERILY i say unto u, that there be some of them that STAND HERE ('them' meaning THEIR GENERATION) which shall NOT TASTE OF DEATH till they have SEEN THE KINGDOM OF GOD COME W POWER."**

------ Saturday, Aug 7, 2021 ------
Me (1:43 AM)
For yet another of so many examples in the 'gospels' of Jesus **guaranteeing his Messianic 2nd coming would be in HIS CURRENT generation's lifespan, and that of his disciples**, lets now look at Mark chap 13, which is entirely devoted to that topic, and his prediction of the destruction of the temple. Vs 3 states that 4 of his disciples asked him when would these things happen, referring to the temple being destroyed, which was NOT any kind of a stretch to predict because of the politics and domination of the Jews by the Romans at that time, it was expected that would likely result. But Jesus begins saying over and over the word "YE" directly to his 4 disciples...As he describes the events and the 'tribulation' by the way in vs 24 that would usher in his 2nd coming, he continuously says, **"When YE see these things", just like he was quoted in all the other examples i have shown u from your own KJV Bible...Again, HE IS NOT TALKING TO YOU MOTHER, he is saying THEIR GENERATION would see it.**

------ Sunday, Aug 8, 2021 ------
Me (1:42 AM)
Cont with commentary on Mark 13, this is one of many specific quotes of Jesus making it clear to his disciples that THEY would SEE the 'end times' happening, NOT a generation thousands of years later. **You are LYING to yourself and to others when u pretend that all of these passages w Jesus making that very assertion dont exist**. I am making u face this truth. He mentions the 'tribulation' in vs 24 and makes it clear THEY, his disciples, would SEE and EXPERIENCE it. Also, verse 3 actually states that Jesus is talking PRIVATELY TO THEM in this 'prophecy' about the so called 'LAST DAYS'. Again, Jesus repeatedly

104

says, "when YE see these things", and among all he describes includes the 'tribulation', and then the 'sun darkened', and the 'stars of heaven shall fall', and then 'the Son of Man coming in the clouds with great power and glory'...**Like so many other passages w Jesus saying the SAME thing to his disciples, that THEIR GENERATION WOULD SEE HIS 2nd coming, did any of that happen?? No.**

------ Monday, Aug 9, 2021 ------
Me (1:59 AM)
It is ALL OVER the Bible in black and white, and i am SHOWING it to u...Even Revelation and Daniel prove this as well. Now that i have shown u all of these passages of Jesus GUARANTEEING to his disciples that THEIR generation would see his return in the clouds w kingdom of heaven, <u>you cant point to some OTHER book like Revelation or a lesser authority than Jesus, supposedly 'GOD in the flesh'</u>. John may be credited w writing Revelation and prophesying about the last days, but remember he was believing everything Jesus told him that i have shown u Mother...**His writings were coming from the assurance in his mind as guaranteed by 'God in the flesh' that those end times he is describing in Revelation were imminent in HIS GENERATION.** Remember in Mark 13 and also in Matt 24, Jesus refers to the 'abomination of desolation' of the temple **that his disciples' generation WOULD SEE, and that when they did, his return would be SO IMMINENT that all should flee to mountains**. More on this tomorrow.

------ Tuesday, Aug 10, 2021 ------
Me (2:23 AM)
Now i am going to show u even more pinpoint detail from your own Bible proving this beyond ANY doubt, with the same kind of detail i have shown u in at least 2 of the 'gospels' **in which Jesus himself was quoted revealing that John the Baptist WAS ALREADY the 2nd coming of Elijah!** <u>Therefore your belief that Elijah's 2nd coming is still to come along w Jesus' 2nd coming is entirely WIPED OUT and proven to be a fraud</u>. Now i am going to show u proof from Revelation, referring to the 'abomination of desolation' that Jesus said would usher in **the 'tribulation' of the end times IN HIS DISCIPLES generation, saying over and over that they would SEE it!** Look at Rev 11, vs 2 and 3, which reads, "But exclude the outer court, do not measure it, **because it has been given to the gentiles. They will trample on the holy city for 42 months. Thats 3 and a half yrs, the 2nd half of the prophesied 7**

year tribulation, and in Mark 13 and Matt 24, Jesus says his disciples' gen would SEE it, and his 2nd coming.

------ Wednesday, Aug 11, 2021 ------
Me (1:31 AM)
So to recap, Jesus not only told his disciples REPEATEDLY and SPECIFICALLY that his 2nd coming was guaranteed to be **IN THEIR CURRENT 'ADULTEROUS' GENERATION**, and he not only told them specifically that **John the Baptist WAS IN FACT ELIJAH'S 2nd coming**, but as i showed u from Johns passage in Rev 11, and as i will show u today in Daniel chap 12, **Jesus even PINPOINTS the 2nd half of the great 'tribulation' as being right before his return!** AND as he does so, we see that he cites that very prophecy of Daniel, and he is quoted saying that last 3 and a half yrs of the tribulation as John also detailed, would occur as Daniel said, IMMEDIATELY AFTER the 'abomination of desolation' which both John in Rev 12 and Daniel chap 9, vs 26 and 27 make clear is simply the gentiles making an abomination of the temple after it is destroyed. The math is just a tad off, John in Rev 12 calling it 1260 days and Daniel 12:12 says that period after the abomination of desolation would be 1290 days, but he wasnt a math whiz.

------ Thursday, Aug 12, 2021 ------
Me (12:56 AM)
So already, in ADDITION to this current example i am showing u in Mark 13, i have shown you many other passages out of your own Bible of Jesus declaring to his disciples **that THEIR GENERATION would witness his 2nd coming 'with the kingdom of heaven in power and glory, etc'**. I am showing you how OBVIOUS this is, not just subject to different readers' interpretation. The MASSIVE lie of the Christian church and of its pastors and priests is how they deliberately ignore this decree shown over and over in the 'gospels', and when they do refer to this topic, what TRITE expression do they love to quote from Jesus in this passage from Mark 13? They ALWAYS ignore ALL of the passages i have detailed for u of Jesus guaranteeing his disciples that THEIR generation would not pass away until his 2nd coming, and INSTEAD, they ONLY quote Jesus entirely out of context in Mark 13, vs 32, where he says not even he knows the specific DAY or HOUR. **That is shamefully out of context and lying from pulpit.**

------ Friday, Aug 13, 2021 ------
Me (1:52 AM)
Just like the other passages i have detailed in Matt, Mark and Luke, here agn in Mark 13, the CONTEXT and **glaring evidence that pastors deliberately ignore is that Jesus is again being quoted telling his disciples that <u>THEY would SEE his 2nd coming</u> at the conclusion of the 'end times' he was describing for them, <u>INCL the 'tribulation'</u> as i have shown u**. Remember, this passage in Mark 13 begins saying 4 of his disciples came to ask him PRIVATELY about the end times. **So it is undeniably clear that Jesus is not talking to YOU or ME, or someone in the year 4021!** He is quoted repeatedly, like in all the other examples i have shown u, saying as he is talking to them PRIVATELY, "When YE see these things" And ONCE AGAIN, before his overused quote by preachers misleading u from the pulpit saying "but of that day and that hour knoweth no man", **what does he tell his disciples only TWO <u>verses above that in vs 31? "Verily i say unto u, that THIS GEN shall not pass till all these things be done"</u>**

------ Monday, Aug 16, 2021 ------
Me (1:23 AM)
I want to begin this next lesson by saying **HAPPY BIRTHDAY Mother**. I know it is on Aug 16th, and technically we r now into the early hours of the 17th, but I wish u a very fun birthday week! Hopefully u can do some extra fun things for yourself. The BEST thing u could consider doing that would change your life in healing ways u cant yet imagine, is to at last finally start to listen to your daughter, who has been carefully and patiently showing u the massive man made lies and fraud of the Bible, **masquerading as 'the gospel'**. As i have assured u before in these lessons, **i would not lead u astray**. <u>If your beliefs were not SO bigoted and SO harmful, not just to yourself, but SO harmful to OTHERS</u>, w a two thousand year legacy of genocidal killing in the name of God, and in direct hypocritical violation of the commandment "Thou shalt not kill"... **If those beliefs weren't SO shamefully condemning of your fellow DIVERSE 'parts of God', i would not be compelled by truth to hold u accountable.**

------ Tuesday, Aug 17, 2021 ------
Me (2:29 AM)
I realized that it was the early hours of the 16th after all, when i sent last nights text and thought it was already the 17th. So i must have been your very first 'happy birthday' msg. I want to deviate just for tonight from continuing w the evidence of the fraud of the Bible and Jesus' so called

107

2nd coming, to once agn warn u about the dangers of this so called 'vaccine' for Covid. Whatever u do, DO NOT take that shot! It is harming and killing growing numbers of people. I have been covering the details of this on my show for the last year and a half. I shared w you the 2 part interview i did w Dr Judy Mikovits, but i have also been detailing the dire warnings about the shot being given by other top doctors and world renown immunologists, including Dr Michael Yeadon, former chief scientist and Vice President of Pfizer, and Dr Peter McCullough. Also chk out Dr David Martin and Dr Sheri Tenpenny. And watch my latest in my 10 part mini-series on 'The Globalists & Their New World Order Exposed' available on demand on my website at conniebryan.com.

------ Wednesday, Aug 18, 2021 ------
Me (2:07 AM)
Tonight lets return to Matt chap 10. I showed u incontrovertible evidence in this chapter already, where Jesus is ONLY talking to his disciples, NOT you or me or anyone 500 yrs from now. He is commissioning them to go spread the 'gospel', that being his imminent 2nd coming w the kingdom of God in power and glory, etc, etc. **He FORBIDS them from taking it to anyone BUT the Jews**. And i showed u the painful truth that pastors and priests do not preach, and seek to ignore, that being vs 23, where just like in many other examples i have shown u of Jesus saying his 2nd coming would b IN THEIR GENERATION, and 'there are some standing here who wont taste death' before his 2nd coming, JUST LIKE THOSE similar passages, here in vs 23 after Jesus tells his disciples to only preach his Messianic return to the tribes of Israel, **what does he AGAIN make absolutely clear?** "For verily i say unto u, (meaning I GUARANTEE this) ye shall not have gone over the cities of Israel till the Son of Man come."

------ Friday, Aug 20, 2021 ------
Me (1:40 AM)
Withdraw and withhold your blessing of peace?? Jesus forbidding his disciples from giving healing and love to anyone BUT the so called 'children of Israel'?? Meaning all others are unworthy by their ethnicity alone?? Mother, HOW LONG ARE U GOING TO REFUSE TO FACE THIS FRAUD IN THE NAME OF GOD? HOW LONG?? Matt 5:46 also completely contradicts Jesus telling them to withdraw their blessing of peace for those they deemed 'unworthy' when it says, "for if ye love them which love u what reward have ye?" **But Jesus quoted in Matt 10, vs 5 and vs 13 didnt give a DAMN about that universal blessing of love for all, commanding his disciples to**

never take his 'gospel' to anyone but JEWS, and even then, to selectively extend a loving blessing of peace to only those they deemed 'worthy'. A normal healthy minded person sees evidence like this in the Bible, and they immediately see the fraud and massive man made hypocrisy masquerading as spiritual truth. **But YOU MOTHER, u see it, but u just keep pretending it isnt there.**

------ Saturday, Aug 21, 2021 ------

Me (1:56 AM)
And u intentionally pretend it isnt there **so u can continue to embrace beliefs at the needless expense of SO many others**, even your own daughter, who u know those with whom u continue to align yourself with, in this sick belief system, ROUTINELY denigrate and say the most horrible things about me and others like me, just because we had a rare diverse gender disorder and had the TRUE FAITH AND COURAGE to what Mother?? **The true faith and courage to BE TRUE TO WHO WE ARE.** By now, though u have just ignored these loving but correcting nightly lessons i have diligently sent u, i know u have read them, even though u have not responded. And if u have at any point refused to even READ these special nightly texts from your daughters heart of hearts, well u are worse of a person than i could have dreamed **in this nightmare i have had to overcome where u and Dad are concerned**. But by now, IF U ARE HONEST, u know what i have shown u exposes the Bible as man made fraud, and it is time to wake up.

Mother (5:19 AM)
Since Dec of last year you have daily voiced your position, your feelings, and your beliefs to me...i have respectfully received, read, skimmed, and looked over what you have sent/my grief regarding you and all you have shared, is great!!!...My response to you is that I pray daily that JESUS will open your eyes and bring you out of your darkness INTO HIS LIGHT!!!

Me (12:51 PM)
I have shown u lie after lie after hypocrisy after shameful hypocrisy, after more lies, **yet u prefer to hold on to such sick bigotry at the expense of your own daughter**, not to mention, as i have told u, at the expense of SO many others your sick bigoted lies in the name of God teach condemnation toward. I am so rightfully ashamed of u for your willful bigotry, despite the evidence of massive man made fraud i have and will continue to show u. You are much like a drug addict Mother, preferring to surround yourself w other sick addicts who support your

109

bigoted lies despite the very unhealthy destructive nature of those lies, **because u dont have the courage to be honest and face those lies you have been SOLD from a young age**. They are not Gods word, as i have shown you already, they are concocted lies from bigoted men MASQUERADING as Gods word, with a long legacy of using those lies in the name of God to commit massive amounts of genocide to other diverse people. Btw, skimming is not reading

------ Sunday, Aug 22, 2021 ------
Me (3:08 AM)
I used the metaphor of a drug addict to describe your addiction to such blatant man made fraudulent teachings about 'God', because it is very fitting. A healthy non addicted person, who isnt traumatized and conditioned from a young age with such a **psychological 'drug' pretending to be 'holy'**, naturally sees such beliefs as delusional, superstitious and bigoted toward others. But you are not allowing yourself to become healthy minded. **You want the drug and how that delusion, that 'fix' makes u feel, even though deep down there IS a part of u that knows better, that u try SO hard to pretend isnt there**...THE SAME WAY you try SO hard to pretend those many examples i quoted to u arent there in the 'gospels', of Jesus specifically telling his disciples his 2nd coming would be IN THEIR GENERATION. **This he was ADAMANT about, as i have shown u, and u pretend it isnt right there in black and white**, because it shows the fraud of the belief. You prefer the addiction to the lies, at my expense.

------ Monday, Aug 23, 2021 ------
Me (1:29 AM)
Once again, let me restate that last point, it is so relevant... Mother, **u prefer your addiction to the lies i am detailing for u, at your own daughter's expense**. And remember, 'skimming' or partly 'glancing' at the disciplined detail i have been steadfastly sending u is NOT 'reading'. That is u trying to turn a blind eye to the evidence i am carefully showing u, just like a drug addict turns a blind eye/ear to ANY info that might mean they couldn't keep getting their daily 'fix'. **I mean, its NOT like i might show u a passage that quotes Moses or Jesus telling u that COFFEE is the 'forbidden bean', Ha Ha!** Seriously Mother, would u STILL be so quick to believe the stupid fairy tale that condemned Adam and Eve for 'sinning' BEFORE they even had ANY concept what 'sinning' or 'good and evil' was...would u still buy into that absurd condemnation of them for falling prey to the master deceiver, who GOD

110

ALLOWED to trick them in their innocence **if the 'forbidden fruit' was COFFEE??**

------ Tuesday, Aug 24, 2021 ------
Me (1:37 AM)
No, coffee addict that we know u are (and me too), if the 'forbidden fruit' was a fresh hot pot of perking **'GARDEN OF EDEN' BRAND COFFEE** that God always kept brewing, and completely childlike and innocent Adam and Eve were tricked by 'the Devil' to go ahead and taste it, after it CONSUMED their sense of smell in the garden, **you would AT LAST FIND YOUR COMMON SENSE** about such an absurd overreaction and condemnation of them by God, who allowed them to be so deceived, **and WHO KNEW they weren't prepared to resist such a master deceiver in their innocence**. Yes, if it was the sweet savor of coffee, you would say NO WAY, that is absolutely entrapping them in their childlike innocence, much like a child who could be easily tricked by an adult to go ahead and eat from a candy jar that their parents had told them not to touch, as i have used as a metaphor to explain the insane absurdity of this fable in previous lessons. You would **NEVER** let such an absurd story stand in the way of u and coffee.

------ Wednesday, Aug 25, 2021 ------
Me (1:28 AM)
Moving on now from the comedy relief of the last 2 texts...Time to return to facing the undeniable evidence again, of the man made fraud of the Bible. Lets begin to recap how i have undeniably shown u MANY of the repeated lies attributed to Jesus, guaranteeing to his disciples that his 2nd coming was not only IMMINENT, **but would happen in THEIR generation**. For example if u recall, IF U HONESTLY READ the passages and proof i sent u, i showed u many chapter and verse examples **from not one but THREE of the so called 'gospels'**, the three that specifically quote Jesus talking about the so called 'end times' to his disciples. Those three are Matt, Mark and Luke. If u recall, in addition to all the specific conversations from those three 'gospels' quoting Jesus saying this verbatim, i showed u Mark chap 1, vs 14 and 15, **where in a 2 verse nutshell, Jesus is quoted, specifically referring to his Messianic 2nd coming, that "THE TIME IS FULFILLED AND THE KINGDOM OF GOD IS AT HAND."**

------ Thursday, Aug 26, 2021 ------

Me (1:31 AM)

Do u know what 'CRITICAL THINKING' is Mother? Among other things, it means **not just blindly 'believing' something when the reality of the facts PROVE the 'belief' is fraudulent**. Another 'critically' important aspect of critical thinking is **'CONTEXT'**. If u have honestly read what i have been carefully detailing for u EVERY NIGHT over the last several months, u will see how diligent i have been about keeping ALL of the evidence IN CONTEXT. When i show u these many different examples, **from THREE different 'gospels'**, with confirmation from both the book of Daniel AND John in the book of Revelation, all of them are in the SAME CONTEXT, that being Jesus' GUARANTEE to his disciples of the ABSOLUTE SPECIFICITY of his 2nd coming 'with the Kingdom of God in power and glory' BEFORE THEIR GENERATION PASSED AWAY. But shamefully, as i have reminded u, ALL Christian pastors take Jesus' quote about not knowing the 'day or hour' OUT OF CONTEXT from those verses i showed u immediately before that one.

------ Friday, Aug 27, 2021 ------

Me (2:26 AM)

Like i carefully showed u in a recent lesson, prior to that verse (Mark 13:32) the ENTIRE CHAPTER of Mark 13 was Jesus being quoted in the PRECISE CONTEXT of a **private conversation ONLY to his disciples**, in which, as i detailed for u, he REPEATEDLY tells them THEY WILL SEE the events of 'the end times'. And i showed u where he even PINPOINTED the GREAT TRIBULATION as occurring during those end times, and in that SAME context, if there was ANY question, he clears it up in verse 30 saying, **"Verily i say unto u, that" WHAT ?? "That THIS generation SHALL NOT PASS till" WHAT ?? "Till ALL THESE THINGS BE DONE".** You cant have any integrity as a preacher or pastor, seeing that context (because it is glaringly obvious) and deliberately **ONLY focus on verse 32, to mislead your congregation into the fraudulent false hope that Jesus' did not know when his 2nd coming would happen!** He made it ABSOLUTELY CLEAR! He falsely guaranteed it would be in THAT generation, just not the exact 'day and hour'.

------ Monday, Aug 30, 2021 ------

Me (1:22 AM)

You KNOW deep down what these facts are showing u, and u have to find the REAL spiritual courage to face it like i have. Lets look at yet

ANOTHER example found in Matt chapter 24...It is the same account, **quoting Jesus talking ONLY TO HIS DISCIPLES, after they came to him privately asking WHEN the 'end times' would be**. This passage gets even MORE specific...Like Mark 13 it quotes Jesus repeatedly telling them THEY WOULD SEE the end times and the GREAT TRIBULATION spoken of by Daniel, but it also quotes Jesus saying not only would they SEE the end times, **but IN THAT SAME CONTEXT he tells them THEY WOULD BE DELIVERED UP to be killed DURING those end times**...You cannot dishonestly take this PRIVATE answer Jesus is directing only to his disciples, and dishonestly claim it was referring to all Christians at an unknown unidentified time far in future. **That is called lying Mother**, and most pastors are doing exactly that! This passage also in vs 34 quotes Jesus guaranteeing THIS GEN shall not pass.

------ Tuesday, Aug 31, 2021 ------
Me (2:14 AM)
I said in the last lesson how this SAME example in Matt 24 gets even more specific, **and it is yet another 'GAME OVER' example for the fundamental beliefs of Christianity**... Because not only does it show that Jesus is fraudulently prophesying that the end times would be SEEN BY HIS DISCIPLES, followed by his Messianic 2nd coming IN THEIR GENERATION (just not specifying the day/hour), but this passage quotes Jesus, not only including the GREAT TRIBULATION in those end times, **but it quotes Jesus including what the Christian church likes to call the 'RAPTURE'!** Jesus makes it very clear, as he tells his disciples THEY WILL WITNESS these end times events, that the concept YOU believe is yet to come, **ALREADY was prophesied to have happened only in THAT generation**, during those end times his disciples were told THEY would witness! Look at Matt 24, vs 40 and 41, **"Then shall two be in the field, the one shall be taken, and the other left. Two women shall be grinding at mill, one taken, the other left."**

113

Chapter Eight

Me (2:07 AM)
The many detailed examples i have shown u from your own Bible prevent u from being able to continue to honestly believe Jesus was talking to ANYONE FAR IN THE FUTURE. Even if u tried to cont to lie to yourself, and cont to take ALL those passages OUT of context, and try to pretend Jesus was NOT talking to his disciples only, you would STILL be shut down in that lie by the undeniable, airtight fact and detail that i showed u, from MULTIPLE examples, that Jesus told his disciples, in answer to their query, 'if we will witness the end times, well then when will we see Elijah's 2nd coming?', **to which i showed u, using your own KJV Bible, that Jesus adamantly told them John the Baptist WAS the 2nd coming of Elijah! So that airtight detail right there PREVENTS u from cont to believe the end times he described were for a generation far in future.** I have to repeat these things because i know u Mother. I know how hard u will keep trying to lie to yourself. You cant anymore. Its time to wake up!

------ Thursday, Sep 2, 2021 ------
Me (2:05 AM)
You cant keep lying to yourself and to others, now that your daughter has carefully shown u that Jesus decreed that John the Baptist WAS the fulfillment of that Old Test prophecy of the end times by Malachi in Malachi chapter 4. Once agn Jesus is quoted making that declaration and identification in both Matt 17, vs10 thru13 AND Matt 11, vs 11 thru 14. Again, as Jesus makes it CRYSTAL CLEAR in all of these passages that not only John the Baptist was the END TIMES FULFILMENT of Malachi's prophecy, but he also decrees to his disciples that THEY WOULD SEE the end times, INCL the great tribulation, **that THEY, not you Mother, not some far in future gen, but he clearly says THEY would be victims of the END TIMES and the 'tribulation'. Not only that but Jesus INCLUDED THE 'RAPTURE' in those same predicted end times as i showed u in yesterday's lesson.** And lest u forget, Jesus told his disciples in Matt 10:23 that they would not complete going over the tribes of Israel till his 2nd coming occurred!

------ Friday, Sep 3, 2021 ------
Me (1:22 AM)
So again, what are these facts from your own Bible SHOWING you??
You know what they are showing you. Why am i taking all this time to
show u all of this RAMPANT FRAUD in the Bible? **It is certainly NOT
to hurt you, but it IS to finally help heal your mind as it was meant
to be healed**, instead of it being imprisoned in such a sick, superstitious
man made horrendous false teaching about not only who and what 'God'
is, **but just as importantly who and what YOU are**! OF COURSE
these examples from your own Bible are showing u that Jesus FALSELY
prophesied his 2nd coming WOULD BE in his disciples' generation.
And you CANNOT be an omnipotent 'Holy Messiah' and be quoted
GUARANTEEING your 'Messianic' return in your disciples' current
generation, telling them John the Baptist fulfilled the end times 2nd
coming of Elijah, etc, **and then it NEVER HAPPENED!** Pastors and
the church keep ignoring and AVOIDING talking about these passages
while they single out the one of Jesus not giving the exact day/hour

------ Saturday, Sep 4, 2021 ------
Me (2:51 AM)
Why do u think i said that exposing all this evidence of Jesus FALSELY
prophesying his 2nd COMING was to help heal u and wake u up to your
TRUE spiritual nature? **What do u think your TRUE spiritual nature
has to do with my taking so much time to show u all these lies in the
Bible**, especially these lies about a so called '2nd coming' of Jesus in the
clouds to 'save all Christians' **and destroy everyone else**, etc, etc? What
could realizing your TRUE spiritual nature have to do with realizing
THAT LIE for the delusional man made fairytale that it is? The answer
is, because your REAL SPIRITUAL NATURE IS THAT YOU AND I
ARE HOLY PARTS OF GOD, **and WE are meant to create heaven on
earth, NOT delusionally believe that only some 'imagined savior'
must come down from the sky on a white horse to finally make
everything ok by KILLING AND CONDEMNING EVERYONE
ELSE!** These delusional fairytales were designed by men to prevent u
from realizing your holiness and that you are NOT sinful, but a PART
OF GOD

------ Sunday, Sep 5, 2021 ------
Me (2:42 AM)
First, any such belief that everything can ONLY be 'fixed' by an
imagined 'SAVIOR' coming down from the sky isnt just delusional, but it
is the **ULTIMATE COP OUT** Mother! I have shared this w u before.

You have been falsely conditioned w such...I am just going to use the word, i know its harsh, but its the appropriate word...You have been deeply conditioned w such 'retarded' concepts that have retarded your proper spiritual growth and understanding of your true ENTIRELY HOLY spiritual nature. **You and i were systematically LIED to about who and what 'God' is.** Fortunately for me, unique circumstances in my life helped me to see those lies in the name of 'God', as i experienced SO MUCH rejection and so much unnecessary bigotry from not only 'Christian' strangers or employers, **but those CLOSEST to me who should have been there for me, and who i needed to help me as i was finding myself and fixing myself. WE SAVE EACH OTHER Mother**, WE CREATE 'salvation', w NO condemnation toward diversity.

------ Monday, Sep 6, 2021 ------
Me (2:01 AM)
You are wasting SO much precious time continuing to embrace a false belief that condemns and denigrates a large diversity of humanity, **most often because 'Christians' would rather denigrate them and believe they r 'condemned' rather than trying to UNDERSTAND THEIR DIVERSE DIFFERENCE from you!** For one prominent example, a recent episode of the 'Tucker Carlson Show' had Tucker's guest, an admitted 'Baptist' i believe he said, **calling all transgender people 'Satanic'.** How do u think Tucker responded? Do u suppose he likely avoided what the guest said about people who have had the misfortune of such a handicap to need a gender change? Do u think he tried to say a POSITIVE, LOVING word for such people, and correct the guest, or even just leave such an ignorantly denigrating and condemning comment hanging, w NO response and move on to the next point? **OH NO! Tucker knew such a denigrating condemning comment 'played to his viewer base' as they say...He said, "Well i am a Methodist and i agree!"**

------ Tuesday, Sep 7, 2021 ------
Me (2:31 AM)
This is so critically important, what i am trying to show u right now. The man made bigoted belief that everything **can ONLY be fixed and healed by an imagined 'messiah' returning in the clouds,** instead of **BY HUMANITY AWAKENING TO OUR SPIRITUAL ONENESS,** And furthermore, such a bigoted belief that fundamental to fixing and 'healing' everything IS NOT ONLY THE DESTROYING, BUT THE ETERNAL CONDEMNATION AND ETERNAL TORTURE of all the

diversity OUTSIDE of your beliefs, of ALL the varied concepts of God by your fellow man…**THAT is the man made lie that is standing in the way of REAL HEALING for humanity!** REAL HEALING COMES FROM US WAKING UP TO OUR SHARED, HOLY COLLECTIVE ONENESS, rather than being deceived into thinking of much of the NATURAL DIVERSE expression and thought of our fellow holy brothers and sisters **as DESERVING OF KILLING AND ETERNAL TORTURE AND DAMNATION.** That is what i mean when i refer to men 'weaponizing' spirituality to further THEIR OWN DESIGNS of power over the masses.

------ Wednesday, Sep 8, 2021 ------
Me (1:57 AM)
Let me give u a good hypothetical example to help u finally grasp the extent of the man made hypocrisy at the core of JudeoChristianity (and to b fair, Islam as well). Even though i know u are generally trying NOT to hear, let alone absorb most of what i am trying to show u Mother, even still at a minimum, u have to have absorbed the fact that i have told u MANY times how **TRUE spirituality loves and forgives ALL, and does so UNCONDITIONALLY!! It doesnt say, 'one is forgiven only under this or that condition'.** Now, imagine that after i spent so much time stressing such a CORE teaching about spiritual truth to u, imagine that LATER i began undercutting and **suddenly 'weaponizing' that message**, and i said that "Actually, that unconditional forgiveness is **ONLY good for BEFORE our 'loving Messiah' comes to destroy u. And if u havent 'converted' to this 'LOVING TRUTH' by then, u are NOT forgiven anymore, love and forgiveness is removed from u!"** Do u see what a massive hypocrite i would be??

------ Thursday, Sep 9, 2021 ------
Me (1:41 AM)
But that is EXACTLY the mind blowing level of hypocrisy that exposes the man made fraud and bigotry in the Bible, **MASQUERADING as 'Gods Word'.** Even as a child i saw this massive hypocrisy, and the few times i asked about it, u and others **NEVER had a rational answer, other than to say something just as hypocritical, like "God doesnt have to be consistent" or "God doesnt have to b understood by u" Wrong Mother!** That was a SHAMEFUL attempt to rationalize such blatant genocidal and condemning teachings 'ordained by God'. Just like i remember saying to u way back then, if God is 'love', and if God is 'forgiving', why wouldnt he understand that many people would be raised by their parents to have many DIFFERENT imagined ideas of him IN

117

HIS ABSENCE, understandably! **And so, when he FINALLY SHOWED HIMSELF at long last, WHY WOULD IT BE TOO LATE THEN, FOR LOVE AND FORGIVENESS for those who either didnt believe before, or believed in him in a different way?** The answer is, its man made bigotry.

------ Friday, Sep 10, 2021 ------
Me (1:39 AM)
Endemic in the fundamental nature of love and forgiveness is that **they DONT SUDDENLY CHANGE to hate and condemnation!** Yet that is the frequent hypocrisy i have shown u from your own Bible here already many times! Fundamental to your delusion of a '2nd coming' of Jesus IS PRECISELY THAT...**That Jesus would NOT let 'unbelievers' see him finally, and be loved and forgiven. OH NO, your belief cant have love and forgiveness anymore at that point**. This as i said yesterday, is something i have tried to show u many times Mother. It perfectly encapsulates and showcases the man made bigoted 'crafting' of such a hypocritical image of God in THEIR condemning image THEY want. As a teenager i could see this massive hypocrisy in the Bible, **but u had me so conditioned to think i HAD to accept it or i TOO would not be loved and forgiven, upon some imagined '2nd coming'**. But REAL love and forgiveness would not change. And as i said, WE are meant to be the love and forgiveness and salvation others need!

------ Saturday, Sep 11, 2021 ------
Me (2:16 AM)
That last line from last night is so powerful and key to what i am trying to help u understand regarding the **man made lies bastardizing spiritual truth in the Bible**. I have said it to u multiple times in previous lessons, and i will probably say it in more as we go along, showing u the fundamental fraudulent **UPSIDE DOWN teaching about what 'God' is in JudeoChristianity and Islam**. ALL THREE of them have caused mass psychosis to humanity, in their WEAPONIZING of their fraudulent teachings of God. This has been the NUMBER ONE cause of not only most of the hate, bigotry and division between mankind, but such UNNECESSARY bigoted and religious division has been the **ROOT cause of more mass killing, genocide and war THAN ANY OTHER REASON in history**…All because of that false teaching EACH of the Big Three religions push, that THEIRS is the only true belief and THEY r the 'chosen' or 'saved' few. But spiritual truth is the OPPOSITE...WE ALL are who 'God' is. **We 'save' each other UNCONDITIONALLY**

------ Sunday, Sep 12, 2021 ------
Me (1:53 AM)
If Christianity was NOT fraudulent Mother, it would be the exception out of the Big Three, meaning it would have NOT weaponized its beliefs with a **legacy of aggressive killing, genocide, imperialism across the globe w endless violent force in the name of Jesus**, while they love to IGNORE the verses in the so called 'gospels' that have Jesus preaching absolute non violence, 'love your enemies', 'turn the other cheek', etc , but they EAGERLY EMBRACE the hypocritical verses like Matt 10:34, quoting this same Jesus saying he did NOT come to bring peace, but he came to bring the SWORD, **meaning violence, killing and war.** So agn, if Christianity were NOT so incredibly fraudulent and full of man made lies about God, it would not have such hypocrisy all throughout the Bible, and it would not WEAPONIZE teachings in the name of Jesus. And u would not see SO MANY verses as i have carefully detailed for u, of Jesus' fraudulent prophecy that his 2nd coming would occur in his disciples' generation.

------ Monday, Sep 13, 2021 ------
Me (1:47 AM)
So keeping in CONTEXT, as i showed u all those verses **in THREE diff 'gospels'** of Jesus answering his disciples question about when would the end times be, and his SPECIFICALLY TELLING THEM his 2nd coming **would occur in THEIR generation**... So when in Matt 10:34 he says he came NOT to bring peace, but the 'sword', what is he referring to?? **He's referring to all the violence and war he FALSELY PROPHESIED was to lead up to his 2nd coming IN THEIR GENERATION, and then all of his violent destroying of all NON JEWS by his army of angels bringing the kingdom of God! HOW BEAUTIFUL, eh?** Remember, i showed u where he pinpointed THE TRIBULATION as something his disciples would suffer and be killed during, along w 'nation rising against nation' in the CONTEXT of violent factions clashing of opposing beliefs. BUT, it is CRITICAL to understand that way bk in that generation there were very few 'nations'. It is understood by Bible scholars that it should read 'tribes' will rise up against 'tribes'.

------ Tuesday, Sep 14, 2021 ------
Me (2:27 AM)
In those multiple passages i detailed for u, Jesus is quoted specifically saying that the 'GOSPEL' in a nutshell was what he was prophesying OVER AND OVER about his 2nd coming, that it would b in **THAT**

GENERATION. I even showed u in one passage where he spoke with targeted anger ABOUT that generation, and i showed u only a fraction of the many places in the 'gospels' where Jesus makes it adamantly clear he WAS NOT COME TO SAVE ANYONE BUT THE JEWS! I showed u specific examples where he told his disciples DO NOT take this 'gospel' to the gentiles, that it was ONLY for the 'children of Israel', **and i showed u where Jesus was then quoted pinpointing his 2nd coming to THEIR generation, agn by specifically telling his disciples that his 2nd coming would not only be in THEIR generation, but that John the Baptist had ALREADY fulfilled Malachi's prophecy about Elijah preceding Jesus 2nd coming, and that they would not even have time to finish going over Israel till his 2nd coming happened!**

------ Wednesday, Sep 15, 2021 ------
Me (2:26 AM)
And it DID NOT HAPPEN. You are engaging not only in massive delusion, but also inexcusable, undeniable dishonesty to ignore these false prophesies by Jesus about his 2nd coming, and continuing to support such a dishonest teaching as to pretend he didnt guarantee it would b in his disciples generation, and dishonestly pretend it is YET to come, **taking that one verse TOTALLY out of context where Jesus says no one knows day or hour**. Agn, that was a tag line after he just finished GUARANTEEING his disciples would WITNESS the end times, the tribulation, **ALL OF IT, and that if not all of them, definitely THEIR gen would be WHEN his 2nd coming happened**! If u arent being dishonest and delusional, u face the fact that Jesus wasnt going to provide the exact DAY or HOUR, but I have shown u the undeniable proof in your own Bible that he guaranteed his 2nd coming to b in THEIR GENERATION. You CANNOT keep lying to yourself in the face of that proof and evidence of massive fraud, when mankind needs truth.

------ Thursday, Sep 16, 2021 ------
Me (2:15 AM)
It doesnt get more critically important than what i am showing u here right now. The REASON humanity is so divided and unloving, so unhealthy and so tribal, and so prone to violent **conflict IS NOT DUE TO SOME 'DEVIL'! That is infantile superstition Mother**. The REASON is because they are simply IGNORANT of their true spiritual nature. And the REASON mankind is so completely ignorant of that key TRUTH is **BY MAN MADE DESIGN over many millennium**... Its because primarily the Big Three man made organized religions,

120

JudeoChristianity and Islam, have thoroughly and fraudulently conditioned mankind <u>NOT TO RECOGNIZE THEIR OWN DIVINE POWER AS AN ASPECT OF WHAT "GOD" IS</u>! It is very important to realize, regardless of whether someone is devoutly religious, agnostic or a complete atheist, one cannot live and breathe here on earth without having been conditioned to a significant degree w the **FALSE teaching that "God" is SEPARATE** from what u are. This false conditioning has been by deliberate design.

------ Friday, Sep 17, 2021 ------
Me (2:31 AM)
It was by design primarily to hold total power and control over the masses, by keeping them ignorant, and from becoming aware of what many of the elite few in what is often referred to as the esoteric elite 'priest classes' KNEW AND STILL KNOW. **But they know also that if they allowed such REAL spiritual truth to come to the knowledge of the masses, they could not continue to hold power and oppression over them.** This is mainly because the fundamental lies of JudeoChristianity i have been carefully detailing for u, <u>entirely depend on a massive dose of conditioning the masses w fear and guilt</u>, THE OPPOSITE of the truth of what u were meant to understand about yourself, **a guiltless all forgiven DIVINE and HOLY ASPECT of what 'God' is here in the physical.** When u adopt such fraudulent 'tribal' and violent-prone 'JESUS BRINGS THE SWORD NOT PEACE' beliefs and think only an external 'savior' who comes down to kill all others is the 'final solution', **<u>C'mon now...Who else does that sound like??</u>**

------ Saturday, Sep 18, 2021 ------
Mother (12:19 PM)
Connie, i am on my knees in my spirit PRAYING GOD THE HOLY FATHER will give you repentance of what you are saying about HIM and HIS HOLY WORD. Your darkness is great!!!...and ONLY HE CAN GIVE YOU LIGHT!!! THAT LIGHT IS HIS SON!!! AND THE TRUTH IS HIS WORD!!!

Me (12:39 PM)
Just like i thought, u are deliberately ignoring all the lies and fraud of the 'word' i have shown u...Simply put, that is shameful Mother, **just as shameful as the massive harm your sick beliefs caused to me growing up**, <u>though i am still patiently showing u the REAL UNCONDITIONAL love and forgiveness of 'God' that never condemns, never denigrates</u>

121

others for their diversity or calls for murderous mass GENOCIDE in the 'name of God' as your SICK beliefs fundamentally do, and as i have carefully detailed for u. Shame on u Mother, for cont to so hypocritically ignore what i have taken so much time to show and will CONTINUE to show u.

------ Monday, Sep 20, 2021 ------
Me (3:20 AM)
Lets look again at your hypocritical outburst, that i need to repent for 'what i have said about Holy God the Father and his word'. What u reacted to WAS NOT what i was saying about 'his word', but what I've been carefully showing u that it SAYS ON ITS OWN Mother! I am showing u the fundamental root of YOUR DARKNESS, **your embracing beliefs in a God who would tell the Jews TO DO EXACTLY IF NOT MORE THAN HITLER DID!!** And i reminded u that u accordingly CRAVE an imagined 'savior' to COME DO THE SAME to all humanity **who believe in 'God' differently**! Lets look at a few more examples of SO MANY in the Bible, of mass genocide ordained by your 'Holy God the Father'. 1st Samuel 15:3, (genocide of all Amalekites): "...but slay both man and woman, infant and suckling." Hosea 13:16 (genocide of Samaritans) "their little ones will be DASHED IN PIECES, and their pregnant women will BE RIPPED OPEN." Numbers 31:18, "but all the WOMEN CHILDREN that have NOT known a man...KEEP ALIVE FOR YOURSELVES."

------ Tuesday, Sep 21, 2021 ------
Me (2:06 AM)
"But all the WOMEN CHILDREN that have not known a man (virgin girls) KEEP ALIVE FOR YOURSELVES"... That isnt a typo Mother, it isnt supposed to be women AND children, your 'Holy Bible' QUOTES your 'Holy God the Father' saying all the virgin female children 'keep alive FOR YOURSELVES'. And i am in 'darkness' for shining the light of truth on such man made fraud masquerading as 'Gods Holy Word'?? Shame on u Mother, for embracing such sick bigotry in the name of God, while your daughter is patiently preaching and showing u the true spiritual Light u were meant to find. You, your brothers, and the younger family members you and they have misled w such lies about the nature of God, ALL OF YOU are not just in darkness, **u r all in PITCH BLACK, and you think your 'imagination' you create in your head is 'sight'. I am the ONLY one in our family preaching the Light, and i am bringing REAL SIGHT to your bigotry and blindness that i was meant to teach u...Thats why i came to u.**

122

------ Wednesday, Sep 22, 2021 ------

Me (1:47 AM)

"And all the women children that have not known a man KEEP ALIVE FOR YOURSELVES" **And thats the 'LIGHT' from your 'Holy God the Father'??** NO! it is the PITCH BLACK DARKNESS you and the rest of the family have been massively deceived with. LOOK AT IT MOTHER!! You have been dishonestly trying NOT to see the undeniable evidence and healing truth i have been steadfastly showing u, with nightly lessons every day over this past year. **LOOK at the PITCH BLACK DARKNESS of evil above, once again on display in your own Bible, with such a sick man made false image of God!** Why do u think i have been so steadfast in showing u these lies and this fraud all over the Bible? As i have told u, its not just to b contrary or rebellious, or to hurt u. It is to finally HEAL you with the healing Light of REAL spiritual wisdom i have been so blessed to have been given. As i said in the last lesson, thats why i was meant to b your daughter. **Not just I, but WE** were meant to awaken, and awaken & heal others.

------ Thursday, Sep 23, 2021 ------

Me (2:22 AM)

Shall we cont to look at your PITCH BLACK DARKNESS **masquerading as 'Holy God the Father's Word'**? Before i add more new examples, lets take another look at Hosea chap 13. As u cannot deny, the Bible says in MANY places, including here in Hosea 13, vs 4, that God is the 'savior' Jesus, and vice versa, that Jesus is God, that they are one and the same. Vs 4 makes clear this passage is the 'word' of your so called 'Holy Father God', and it reads: "Yet i am the Lord thy God from the land of Egypt, and thou shalt know no god but me: for there is NO SAVIOR beside me." I just want it to be CLEAR Mother, u cant dishonestly say Jesus your imagined 'savior' is somehow detached from the following 'word' of the 'Holy Father God'. **Lets now look at vs 16, his calling for the mass genocide of Samaria, with odd specificity toward their INFANTS and PREGNANT WOMEN** "...they shall fall by the sword: **their infants shall be dashed in pieces, and their women with child shall be ripped up." Time to awaken now**

------ Friday, Sep 24, 2021 ------

Me (1:56 AM)

"Their infants shall be DASHED IN PIECES". I thought 'Jesus loves the little children, all the children of the world'. I could swear we used to sing a song like that all the time when i was little. But no,

Jesus, synonymous w your 'Holy Father God' over and over called for their mass genocide IF THEY WERE NOT JEWS! And not just genocide, but CUTTING THEM INTO PIECES! "...and their women with child shall be RIPPED UP**." Wait a minute, i thought Jesus, one and same w God, said 'suffer the children to come unto me, for such is the kingdom of heaven." Matt 19:14**. But u think u can just conveniently ignore the MANY genocidal passages targeting the children, infants and UNBORN BABIES who agn, WERE NOT JEWS!! **And I am the one who needs to repent as i shine a spotlight of truth on this massive BS??** You and the rest of the family are in such PITCH BLACK darkness, and so full of hypocrisy and horse shit, that u all need someone following u around everywhere u go w a wheel barrow and a shovel!

------ Saturday, Sep 25, 2021 ------
Me (1:53 AM)
The fundamental driving desire i have had since as far back as i can remember as a child, was to **GET SPIRITUALITY RIGHT**, for the main purpose of receiving true spiritual wisdom and the ability to heal others. And i ALWAYS had a major check in my spirit with all of the JudeoChristian hypocrisy running rampant in the Bible. Even as a child i was struggling with that check in my spirit that something was not right with it all, but when everyone u trust implicitly is pushing it on u, and u dont want to let them down, u of course just accept it. But **THANK GOD for the unique circumstances in my life, and for the courage and wisdom i had to be true to myself**, that led me to the wisdom of REAL spiritual truth i had always steadfastly been begging God for! As i have told u before, we can easily know when a religious dogma is horse shit and hypocrisy **when it is 'weaponized'**. WHY IS THAT? **Because real spiritual truth and love only bring HEALING to error, and have NO NEED TO HARM AND CONDEMN Mother**.

------ Sunday, Sep 26, 2021 ------
Me (2:01 AM)
That last line from yesterday's msg is so very important to help open your eyes to the man made fraud all throughout the Bible, that i am going to repeat it for emphasis here: "Real spiritual truth and love only bring HEALING to error, **and have NO NEED TO HARM AND CONDEMN Mother**." Real spiritual truth requires that u grow to understand YOU ARE A HOLY PERFECT PART OF WHAT GOD IS here in the physical plane of existence, and real spiritual truth requires that u grow to understand that even as a Holy part of what God is, u are

here to LEARN AND GROW OFTEN FROM MISTAKES that u make. Those mistakes can be terribly painful, **but they do not mean u are 'EVIL' or 'SINFUL' by nature.** Real spiritual truth requires that YOU MUST FORGIVE YOURSELF, take responsibility and learn from those mistakes, not put it on some imagined 'savior' who had to be a human blood sacrifice for your mistakes, to satisfy a sick 'blood lust' of some external God. **What is 'Hell'? It is your inability to FORGIVE.**

------ Tuesday, Sep 28, 2021 ------
Me (2:32 AM)
Again, what i am effectively showing u is this CRITICAL TRUTH humanity is way overdue and in desperate need of learning right now, and that JudeoChristianity and Islam **have DELIBERATELY HIDDEN and BLINDED them from**: Healing begins for ALL OF HUMANITY when we finally wake up to our human and Divine obligation to LAY DOWN the harmful 'weaponized' condemnation, bigotry and the 'sword' of each of the 'Big Three' organized religions, ostensibly in the name of 'God'. Lets return briefly to one of the MANY such sick man made fraudulent images of God that advocates such HARM AND CONDEMNATION. Lets look agn at Numbers 31:18**, "but all the WOMEN CHILDREN that have NOT known a man...KEEP ALIVE FOR YOURSELVES."** This is a prime example i like to use because it includes multiple OBVIOUS man made harm and bigotry pretending to be the 'Light' or 'Gods Word'(as u tried to refer to it)...**This PITCH BLACK DARKNESS is quoting God ordaining child rape and pedophilia, the demeaning of the female sex, and genocide of all that weren't child virgins.**

------ Wednesday, Sep 29, 2021 ------
Me (2:07 AM)
Did u think when i first began this series of daily lessons for u, in order to detail the MASSIVE amount of fraud and man made lies in the Bible, that i was just going to b baselessly attacking Christianity with NO proof or evidence Mother? All of this vast evidence i have detailed for u is **air tight**. It is undeniable that it is the real 'darkness' and the OPPOSITE of the 'Light' that humanity is overdue for and desperately needs right now, and that i am continuing to patiently shine on u here. **I know it is hard on your eyes, having been ironically in such PITCH BLACK DARKNESS masquerading as 'the word of God' for so long now**. I know because i have been where u are, and the Light of real spiritual truth was hard on my eyes, as i awakened from that pitch black darkness. As i have told u before, i would NEVER lead u astray Mother. It is time

for you to face the truth now, of the man made lies of the Bible i have been showing u. **You dont get to refer to the genocide and pedophilia of Numbers 31 as 'OK' because 'God said so'. That is evil.**

Chapter 9

------ Saturday, Oct 2, 2021 ------

Me (1:50 AM)

Also, u tried to characterize all my daily lessons to u as just wanting to expound on my 'unbelief', **which couldn't be more false & opposite from the truth of what I am doing here**. As a matter of fact, that is apparently what set u off after i wrote: "Did u think when i first began this series of daily lessons for u to detail the MASSIVE amount of fraud and man made lies in the Bible**, that i was just going to b baselessly attacking Christianity with NO proof or evidence Mother?"** And i also told u: "You dont get to refer to the genocide and pedophilia of Numbers 31 as 'OK' because 'God said so'. Thats evil." U know i have been carefully showing u strong EVIDENCE from your own Bible that exposes the man made fraud and lies PRETENDING to b 'Gods word'. Again, WHERE is 'the Light' in Numbers 31:17,18? "Now therefore KILL EVERY MALE AMONG THE LITTLE ONES, and every woman that hath known man by lying w him, but all the WOMEN CHILDREN that hath NOT known a man by lying with him KEEP ALIVE FOR YOURSELVES" **The 'Light' says its OK to RAPE VIRGIN CHILDREN?**

------ Saturday, Oct 2, 2021 ------

Me (2:58 AM)

I asked u a simple question. Where is the 'Light' in God ordaining child virgin rape and pedophilia, and the mass genocide of all the male 'little ones'?? **I am not spending all this disciplined time every day putting together these lessons, to just expound to u of my 'disbelief' Mother. OBVIOUSLY i am showing u the UNDENIABLE EVIL in your own Bible, of a sick man made fraudulent image of 'God', that the Christian church has LIED to us about - LIED TO THE WORLD about.** And in so doing, it has lied to us about OUR spiritual nature as well. All any woman considering an abortion need say to u, if u were standing in front of the abortion clinic door w your Bible, is 'Excuse me, but your so called 'Holy' God who u believe was BOTH Jesus and the Father, well THEY were FREQUENT advocates of abortion and mass killing of infants and pregnant women, just look at one example, Hosea 13, vs 16: **"their INFANTS shall b DASHED IN PIECES, and their WOMEN WITH CHILD shall b RIPPED UP."** That is EVIL, not the Light.

Mother (12:19 PM)

Connie, i am so grieved you believe as you do! There is nothing more to say to you than what i have said. My prayers for us both will continue... (Orig msg included a cartoon emoticon of little hearts and a person kneeling praying)

Me (1:36 PM)
Nice try, but all u did was try to avoid the question. A cartoon emoticon of 'hearts' and an emoticon of someone 'praying' doesn't make u a loving person Mother, especially when u r 'praying' with a fraudulent evil and bigoted image of God, at the harmful expense of others. **All it does is make u a FLAMING HYPOCRITE, sending hypocritical heart emoticons as u eagerly EMBRACE SUCH EVIL IN THE NAME OF GOD.** And as your daughter shining the TRUE LIGHT OF GOD'S LOVE on that shameful hypocrisy, i am holding u to that flame. **AGAIN, I asked u a SIMPLE QUESTION... Where is the 'Light' in God ordaining child virgin rape and pedophilia, and the mass genocide of all the male 'little ones'??** Hard to answer that one, huh? Ok, Where is the 'Light' in Hosea 13, vs 16: "their INFANTS shall b DASHED IN PIECES, and their WOMEN WITH CHILD shall b RIPPED UP." ?? That is, as i continue to show u from so many such examples, RAMPANT throughout the Bible, **nothing but man made, bigoted PITCH BLACK DARKNESS masquerading as 'Gods word'.** Answer the question.

Mother (3:15 PM)
It is not for me to "answer" your question, Connie, which is NOT saying there is no answer, IT IS FOR A PERFECT, JUST, AND HOLY GOD to "Help you" with your asking them!!! There are A LOT OF "HARD THINGS IN THE BIBLE" not to be "understood" by mankind...HIS WAYS are not ours!!! [HE DOES TELL US THAT!!!] But I can tell you that "EVERY THING" THAT IS WRITTEN IN HIS HOLY WORD IS FOR HIS HOLY REASONS and HIS HOLY PURPOSES, AND IS PERFECT!!! Unless GOD SHOWS YOU THE WAY, you will not know it...

Me (3:38 PM)
Oh but on the contrary, it ABSOLUTELY is your OBLIGATION to ANSWER for such blatant evil in the name of God Mother! I am on my way to a show where i am performing, but wanted to take a moment to respond to your absurdly bigoted reply...As i told u recently, which

elicited a rather attacking and condemning reply from u, you DONT get to say that the genocide of all others accept the Jews, targeting especially infants, pregnant women, and 'ripping' apart their unborn innocent babies, oh and **telling the Jews they can kill all the male 'little ones' but KEEP the virgin female children FOR THEMSELVES**, on and on repeatedly w such PITCH BLACK EVIL...**You dont get to say thats OK because the God u believe in 'said so'.** That isnt God, that is man-made bigotry masquerading as God, and u are eagerly embracing such bigotry and evil. I am holding u accountable for that, **for the shameful harm u have caused to others by turning such a bigoted blind eye to such evil and hypocrisy**.

------ Sunday, Oct 3, 2021 ------
Me (3:00 AM)
As i have made clear to u in a prior lesson, we can KNOW what is man made fraud pretending to be God's word whenever it is used to deliberately HARM others. Spiritual Light and Love NEVER need to SEEK TO 'HARM' others, **they only HEAL & FORGIVE!** You have become a VERY BAD person to try to claim that those examples are 'HOLY' that i showed u...Clearly evil examples of God ordering the dashing into pieces of infants, ordering the raping of virgin little girls after first killing all male 'little ones', ordering the 'ripping up' of pregnant women, these being only but a few of MANY such acts of genocide the Jews claimed God 'ordained'. NO MOTHER, **We don't find ANYTHING ABOUT 'God' in writings that claim to be 'HOLY' by demonstrating the behavior that HITLER engaged in!** As i said, u have become a very ugly, very bad person as u eagerly seek to EMBRACE such man made bigotry and evil. **I am holding u accountable for that, and for the shameful harm u are a PART OF CAUSING to others, by your choosing to believe such evil and hypocrisy is 'Holy'.**

------ Tuesday, Oct 5, 2021 ------
Me (2:00 AM)
Hold on because stuff is about to 'get real' as they say...Well the expression is usually a different word than 'stuff' but i am keeping this lesson rated G for u Mother. **I know u well, and i know u r already lying to yourself as i show u this perfect parallel of Hitler and his 'Final Solution' with the Jews, and its similar comparison with all the genocide and evil proudly committed by the Jews on 'non Jewish' cultures all throughout the Old Testament, claiming it was ordained by God because they were the 'Chosen Race' of God, etc.**

You r trying to pretend your Bible beliefs in that very same kind of evil mass genocide (especially targeting children and infants) is somehow 'Holy' and has no comparison to Hitler's doing the same. But you know better deep down in your soul. And i am forcing u to face that truth. Your eager belief that Jesus will return in the clouds in a bloody act of genocidal destruction of ALL NON BELIEVERS **is nothing but yet ANOTHER man made bigoted 'Final Solution'.** God doesn't need to behave with such evil like Hitler and like bigoted men do. **What i have patiently been showing u, is that u have been PROGRAMMED with man made lies about God.**

------ Wednesday, Oct 6, 2021 ------
Me (2:15 AM)
Agn, u have been programmed w man made lies about God. Listen to me carefully... Bigoted, tribal minded, hateful MEN committed those genocidal human atrocities described throughout the Bible ALL ON THEIR OWN BIGOTRY, NOT ORDAINED BY GOD! I have explained this to u before, and i will do so agn now... They **fraudulently concocted an image of God in the image THEY wanted, so as to 'justify' their genocide, and to 'DEIFY' their culture as superior and preferred by that 'God', preferred over ALL others**, to the extent that this meant ONLY THEIR JEWISH RACE was 'holy', and the Commandment 'Thou shalt not kill' DID NOT apply to all others who were NOT Jews, and as such were deserving of mass genocide. **Their evil mindset pretending to be acting out 'Gods will' was the SAME EXACT SCRIPT as Hitler followed. In 'Mein Kampf' vol 1, chap 8, Hitler writes that he is fulfilling his mission assigned by God for the necessary security and maintenance of 'our racial stock unmixed'. Mother, it is time to wake up now!**

------ Thursday, Oct 7, 2021 ------
Me (1:44 AM)
My purpose here is to finally wake u up, and bring REAL spiritual truth and healing to everyone who has been programmed with such man made lies FALSELY in the name of God. The KEY TRUTH u have been lied to about, as i have told u before, is that 'God' was NEVER SEPARATE from u, because **YOU ARE AND ALWAYS HAVE BEEN AN ETERNAL PART OF WHAT GOD IS!** And so am i! And so is the ATHEIST who still hasnt understood what 'God' is, and so is the NATIVE AMERICAN who worships and understands the Divine first and foremost through nature, and so is the HINDU and the BUDDHIST, and so is the equally 'programmed' fundamentalist MUSLIM with their

false, bigoted condemning man made beliefs that are synonymous w BOTH Hitler's outlook, and JudeoChristianity's outlook, as i detailed yesterday, to the extent that THEY are the 'CHOSEN ONES', and all others are deserving of destruction, etc. **But THAT is the evil, not 'holiness' Mother,** as u tried to characterize the examples of such man made false teachings in your Bible that I showed u.

------ Friday, Oct 8, 2021 ------

Me (2:02 AM)

Does the atheist, yet to accept his spiritual nature, think YOU deserve to be destroyed because you are NOT an atheist? Does the Hindu or Buddhist think YOU deserve to b a victim of an 'end times' act of mass genocide because YOU are not of THEIR belief? Does the Native American think that God, as she understands God through nature, must bring the same 'FINAL SOLUTION' for YOU, **after Christians invaded her homeland and committed unspeakable acts of genocide to her people, when they OF COURSE refused to be forced to accept such beliefs in a God who would 'ordain' such a violent invasion and betrayal of EVERY TREATY with them??** After all that betrayal, genocide and forcing them onto reservations, often forcibly taking their children away to Christian 're-education' camps against their will, after ALL such unspeakable atrocities by Christians claiming such behavior (reminiscent of Hitler) was 'Gods will', **does she believe YOU deserve the God of the universe to DESTROY YOU and torture u in Hell??**

------ Saturday, Oct 9, 2021 ------

Me (2:45 AM)

No, generally only what are known as the **'Abrahamic religions'** meaning Judaism, Christianity & Islam, or what I usually refer to as 'The Big Three'… ONLY THEY have the trademark WEAPONIZING of 'faith' against all others. Only they think that they are 'saved' and/or preferred over all others by God, and ONLY THEY…most commonly Christianity and Islam… eagerly hold such sick beliefs as u do Mother, **eagerly awaiting a 'Messiah' coming down in the clouds with a VIOLENT GENOCIDAL ARMY OF ANGELS, to wipe out ALL OTHERS in total destruction**. BUT WAIT, THERES MORE! Only fundamentalist Christians and Muslims are so 'programmed' to want to believe that such FINAL SOLUTION end times and **mass "HOLY-CAUST"** for the rest of humanity is NOT ENOUTH. Oh no, it isnt enough to just DESTROY all others. **Your version of 'The Final Solution' is BEYOND anything even Hitler imagined Mother. You (and fundamentalist Muslims too) dogmatically believe the Bible** teaching that all 'non-believers' will be ETERNALLY TORTURED in a 'lake of fire'...**All this evil hypocrisy is awaited in the name of 'Love'. THAT is not God's Love, that is nothing but bigoted man made programming.**

------ Sunday, Oct 10, 2021 ------
Me (2:47 AM)
And in that same fraudulently programmed mindset **u tried to tell me i wouldnt 'find God' until i TOO believed such mass genocide in the name of God was and is 'Holy'**...until i too blindly believed in such evil bigotry masquerading as Gods word. The TRUTH is Mother, with such false programming over many years that 'Love' must condemn and harm others who believe in diverse ways about God, or who are of different sexual orientations, etc... **the TRUTH i am showing you is that u and your brothers and your fellow church members are in nothing but PITCH BLACK DARKNESS.** I am, as i told u before, meant to wake u up finally, to understand 'God' is not found in such damning violent intention toward the diversity of humanity! As i told u in a previous lesson, Love and spiritual truth are ALL POWERFUL **and do not EVER NEED to harm or condemn. They bring HEALING and FORGIVENESS to where there is 'lack' or need for healing, not GENOCIDE and condemnation!** I am finally, once and for all, exposing these sick, harmful & divisive Bible lies about God.

------ Monday, Oct 11, 2021 ------
Me (2:10 AM)
As these lessons are intended to serve as a **'Definitive Guide to the Man Made Lies & Fraud of the Bible'**, let me take a moment to remind other readers of something. Lest other readers make the mistake of thinking that the many 'Final Solution' style genocide examples so often committed by the Jews are somehow 'unrelated' to Jesus, you couldn't be more wrong. In MANY scripture verses, as i have shown several already, **like Matt 10:34, Jesus makes it clear he came NOT to bring peace, but the SWORD.** In a previous lesson i showed u the blatant, man made hypocrisy of that verse, where only 5 chapters prior in Matt 5:44, Jesus is quoted saying 'Love your enemies, BLESS them that hurt u, do good to them that hate u'. **And often Jesus VALIDATES such mass genocide as he BOASTS how that is EXACTLY what is in store for all non believers of THAT GENERATION upon his return in THAT GENERATION. In Matt 10:14-15 he says the mass genocide of Sodom & Gomorrah wont be as bad as what he has planned for them.**

132

------ Tuesday, Oct 12, 2021 ------

Me (12:12 AM)

But as i am consistently showing u in these lessons, **those so called 'holy scriptures' are of course on their face NOT Holy, and DO NOT represent Love and spiritual truth!** Christians like my mom and myself were LIED to and deliberately programmed from a VERY YOUNG age, to believe such PITCH BLACK DARKNESS & EVIL. They were fraudulently and shamefully presented to us when we were but little children, with such nightmarish fear-based examples, **traumatizing us to believe that is what 'God' is.** I am steadfastly showing u many undeniable and specific examples of the rampant hypocritical lies that r present all throughout the Bible, **that ROUTINELY CELEBRATE violence, bigotry, mass genocide, child/virgin rape & pedophilia, demeaning of women as 2nd class humans, and condemnation of all other natural diversity of thought by humanity**, all claimed by Christians, Jews (and lets not forget Muslims too) as being 'ordained' by God/Allah. It is not! **THAT IS THE MAIN LIE...THAT IS THE 'HOLY LIBEL'! It is 'ordained' by bigoted men!!**

------ Wednesday, Oct 13, 2021 ------

Me (1:29 AM)

As i have stressed before, JudeoChristianity and Islam, the Bible & the Koran, were one of the earliest forms of what we call today **'MASS MEDIA'.** As such, the Bible & the Koran were deliberately designed for mass psychological programming...Specifically for the 'DEIFYING' of their respective cultures, mainly by using propaganda, popular superstition and consequently of course, FALSE FEAR. 'Jesus' is defined by these bigoted men who crafted their 'weaponized faith' of Christianity as being **ONE AND THE SAME as the 'God' the Old Testament writers said often called for the child/virgin rape, cutting babies into pieces, 'ripping open' of pregnant women, and the common general 'FINAL SOLUTION' style mass genocide** of other cultures, as i have shown specific scripture examples of. Let me quote one of many such examples where the Bible makes it absolutely clear that Jesus is THE SAME, synonymous with 'God the Father'. **John 1:1 reads, "In the beginning was the Word(Jesus), and the Word was with God, and the Word WAS GOD"**

------ Thursday, Oct 14, 2021 ------

Me (1:45 AM)

As i detailed for u in many lessons a few weeks back, this same 'God' in Mark chapter 13 is described having his disciples come to him privately asking him to REVEAL to them WHEN his 2nd coming would be. IF you will recall, i showed u from your own Bible how he supposedly as 'God', GUARANTEED to them in great detail, that it would happen **IN THEIR GENERATION**. I showed u how he even specified how they would not only SEE the so called 'Tribulation', but would b tortured and killed during it! So CLEARLY it is not 'YET TO COME'. You will also recall i showed u his quotes where **he told them they would experience the specific prophecy by Daniel, that being the 'abomination of desolation', meaning the Romans desecrating the temple mount, etc**. After he GUARANTEES they wiil SEE all of that, in verse 30 he doubles down and says "this generation shall not pass till all these things be done" **This is a giant 'GAME OVER' lie in the Bible! Yet it is actively lied about and avoided by church leaders.**

------ Friday, Oct 15, 2021 ------

Me (3:16 AM)

In addition to these lessons serving as a definitive guide to the rampant man made lies and fraud of the Bible, **i also occasionally spotlight the corresponding lies of 'church doctrine'**… Christian & Jewish denominations, pastors, rabbi's and church/synagogue leaders, who are shamefully complicit in teaching this obviously dishonest and evil hypocrisy in the name of God, **especially to little children.** They OFTEN do so by taking passages from the Bible completely OUT OF CONTEXT. Two such examples are present w the example i gave from Mark chap 13. The writer clarifies undeniably at the beginning of this chapter, that Jesus is speaking PRIVATELY TO HIS DISCIPLES, and actually it says ONLY FOUR of them! But dishonest pastors and Christians in general deliberately overlook that fact, **and falsely teach that Jesus is speaking to ALL Christians in the distant future, a FLAGRANT LIE** used to propagate their other huge lie of Jesus' 2nd Coming to bring their 'Final Solution' genocide to all non believers, when Jesus clearly told his disciples THEIR GENERATION would see it!

------ Saturday, Oct 16, 2021 ------

Me (1:58 AM)

Continuing now on the 2 examples i want to show u in Mark 13 **that Christians deliberately take OUT OF CONTEXT** in order to 'PROGRAM' their followers w lies of a '2nd Coming' and mass violent genocide by Jesus and his 'army of angels' of all others who dont believe like them **(quite a loving and forgiving religion, eh?)** Agn, in the first example they deliberately ignore that Jesus was directing ALL of his discussion about the 'end times' to a specific audience, <u>**ONLY the 4 of his disciples**</u>. And these end times events he guaranteed THEY would experience, and that his 2nd coming would occur IN THEIR GENERATION! <u>Christian pastors lie to their members **'by omission'** in NOT preaching that plain fact in Mark 13, and proceed to play make believe that Jesus was talking to some future UNKNOWN generation.</u> The 2nd example is how they do the SAME w verse 32, where Jesus says the day & hour of his 2nd Coming are unknown. **He didn't give those 4 disciples the exact day & hour OF COURSE, but<u> just 2 verses prior Jesus DID specify and guarantee that it would be IN THEIR GENERATION!</u> That FALSE PROPHECY from Jesus in black and white in your own Bible in THREE DIFFERENT GOSPELS being the case, there is no '2nd Coming' to wipe out the rest of humanity YET TO COME<u>.</u>**

------ Sunday, Oct 17, 2021 ------

Me (2:54 AM)

As i stated before, it is critical, as in basic 'critical thinking', <u>to read things IN CONTEXT</u>. But Christian leaders and pastors know they cant teach these portions of the New Testament 'gospels' in context, because as u can see from the many examples i have detailed for u from your own Bible**, they undeniably show that Jesus fraudulently prophesied to his disciples that his triumphant 2nd coming would definitely occur in their generation.** And remember, i even showed u in Matt chap 11 AND in chap 17 that Jesus' disciples asked for more clarity saying, if it will b in our generation, then when will the prophecy by Malachi of Elijah's 2nd coming happen**? <u>And Jesus told them it ALREADY happened! He told them JOHN THE BAPTIST WAS ELIJAH'S SECOND COMING!</u>** And then OF COURSE, Jesus DID NOT return with the 'kingdom of heaven' and his army of genocidal angels to destroy all non believers as he prophesied in those specific Matt, Mark and Luke examples i showed u. Thats because it is ALL MAN MADE LIES.

------ Monday, Oct 18, 2021 ------

Me (2:14 AM)

The fundamental problem is that as OBVIOUSLY evil, bigoted and advocating of mass genocide all of it is, and as OBVIOUSLY man made and fraudulent all of it is, shamefully in the name of 'God', **the core problem is Mother, that YOU still eagerly WANT to believe such** sick things are true! **You WANT to believe that such mass genocide of ALL 'non believers' will happen by Jesus' army of angels in some still imagined DELUSION of such a 'Final Solution' program that would make Hitler's version look like just a bad summer camp experience!** This is the man made evil & PITCH BLACK DARKNESS i am showing u from your own Bible, that u and your brothers have been utterly programmed and brainwashed with. I am living love, salvation and forgiveness for u by example, **while also holding u accountable for WANTING to associate yourself with a belief that is BUILT on the hypocritical evil, genocide and bigotry i have shown u!** At some point i will venture to guess what it is you did, causing such a level of guilt that u would become so vulnerable to such lies.

------ Tuesday, Oct 19, 2021 ------
Me (1:24 AM)
While we r on this topic, lets also address another HUGE example where Christian pastors and church leaders lie by taking an entire BOOK of the Bible completely out of context, agn in order to eagerly continue to believe Jesus will soon return in the sky on a white horse **and bring their long awaited genocide of ALL other humans who aren't Christians. Of course i am referring to the book of Revelation.** WHO does the Bible claim is the author of the book of Revelation and its bizarre descriptions of end times events? The answer is John, one of the FOUR disciples who came to Jesus privately as we just discussed from Mark chap 13, specifically asking WHEN the end times would happen. And the rest of that entire chapter was Jesus SPECIFICALLY ANSWERING their question, telling them THEY would live to see the end times, and his 2nd coming would b in THEIR generation! **So when John supposedly authors Revelation, describing his dreams of THOSE END TIMES, why would church leaders preach they are STILL TO COME??**

------ Wednesday, Oct 20, 2021 ------
Me (2:47 AM)
It's a FACT that Bible scholars know **that the names on ALL of the books of the Bible ARE NOT the names of those who wrote them.** This is another GIANT LIE of the Bible and its fraudulent writers, who deceitfully put fabricated names on the books they wrote, deliberately misleading the masses into believing, for example, that the 4 so called 'gospels' were actually written by Matt, Mark, Luke & John. In fact, NONE of them were even alive when 'ghost writers' for the newly crafted religion wrote them. But since the church believes John wrote

136

Revelation, it is all the more an even bigger CHURCH DOCTRINE LIE they have perpetuated, trying to claim Revelation is prophesying a YET TO COME 2nd coming of Jesus, **when as i have shown u in great detail, John was under the ABSOLUTE CERTAINTY of belief that Jesus' 2nd coming was, if anything, OVERDUE at that time! As i showed u, he had a PRIVATE TUTORIAL from whom he believed was GOD in the flesh, guaranteeing their 2nd coming would happen in JOHN'S GENERATION.**

------ Thursday, Oct 21, 2021 ------
Me (1:52 AM)
John was there with Jesus to hear not just that private, detailed answer Jesus gave them in Mark 13, but he was there to hear Jesus tell his disciples in Mark 9, vs 1 (speaking of his IMMINENT 2nd coming in THEIR generation as indicated also in the verse prior) "Verily i say unto u, that there be some of them that stand here which shall NOT TASTE OF DEATH, till they have SEEN the Kingdom of God come with power." **John was among the disciples who pressed Jesus, as i have shown u in multiple examples, to tell them when they would see ELIJAH's 2nd coming as the 'forerunner' as prophesied by Malachi, and John knew Jesus was ADAMANT that 'John the Baptist' WAS that prophecy fulfilled!** So there can be no doubt if John authored Revelation, he was ABSOLUTELY NOT writing about end times far in the FUTURE. And to wrap that undeniable fact up with a bow, he BEGINS Revelation in the VERY FIRST VERSE indicating this fact, referring to the book being about "things which **MUST SHORTLY** come to pass."

------ Friday, Oct 22, 2021 ------
Me (3:12 AM)
As I have exposed the lie of the Christian church that ignores the repeated GUARANTEE by Jesus that his 2nd coming would b IN HIS DISCIPLES' GENERATION, and as I have exposed how that lie is not just by deliberately NOT teaching multiple passages where Jesus falsely prophesied that, **but lying by PRETENDING that John's book Revelation was prophesying of end times and Jesus 2nd coming FAR IN THE FUTURE yet to come any day, etc...** In doing so, I have laid out & detailed for you the irrefutable Bible evidence revealing this 'yet to come 2nd^{d} coming' as being nothing but a SHAMEFUL LIE by church leaders! But for them to face and teach those Bible passages i have shown you, would mean there IS NO 2nd coming yet to come, no 'rapture' yet to come, no Jesus and his army of angels coming with

swords to commit their genocidal CHRISTIAN FINAL SOLUTION on all who dont ascribe to such sick beliefs. When u learn these truths i am exposing, its deeply sad to hear John still clinging desperately to Jesus' false prophecy, writing in that VERY FIRST verse telling the reader these things **"MUST SHORTLY COME TO PASS"**

------ Saturday, Oct 23, 2021 ------
Me (1:33 AM)
And OF COURSE, they DID NOT come to pass. But the writer of Revelation not only BEGINS in the first verse with that firm assurance that what they were writing & prophesying MUST shortly come to pass, but they END Revelation with the EXACT SAME statement of firm conviction! The FIRST VERSE proved my point, but the 2nd to the last verse provides even more proof that OF COURSE John was writing his thoughts of the 'end times' to THAT generation at THAT time! Why? Because that is what Jesus had GUARANTEED to him would take place as i have shown u in great detail in previous lessons w scriptures from your own King James Bible, **from not one but THREE of the so called 'gospels'!** Now turn pls to the last chapter of Revelation, chapter 22, the second to the last verse, where he again writes:"He which testifieth these things saith surely i come quickly. Amen. Even so come, Lord Jesus" And btw, WHY does the King James Bible refer to him as **'John the DIVINE'??** (See attached pic) So many lies!

THE REVELATION
OF SAINT JOHN THE DIVINE

The Apostle

of the book.

Personality | Lamb | as. | acle of God. | vants.

aspired, | [ch.14.13.

(3).

tnesses.

mised for | Obedience

es.

ng.

it.

Time.

CHAPTER 1

The preface. 7 The coming of Christ.

THE Revelation of Jĕ´ṣus Christ, which God gave unto him, to shew unto his servants things which must shortly come to pass; and he sent and signified it by his angel unto his servant Jŏhn:

2 Who bare record of the word of God, and of the testimony of Jĕ´ṣus Christ, and of all things that he saw.

3 Blessed is he that readeth, and they that hear the words of this prophecy, and keep those things which are written therein: for the time is at

and, What thou seest, write in a book, and send it unto the seven churches which are in A´ṣiā; unto Ĕph´e-sŭs, and unto Smŷr´nā, and unto Pĕr´ga-mŏs, and unto Thŷ-a-tī´rā, and unto Sär´dis, and unto Phĭl-a-dĕl´phĭ-ā, and unto Lā-ŏd-ĭ-çē´ā.

12 And I turned to see the voice that spake with me. And being turned, I saw seven golden candlesticks;

13 And in the midst of the seven candlesticks one like unto the Son of man, clothed with a garment down to the foot, and girt about the paps

3961 Writin | 417 "Wor | **The Sev** | 272 Asia. | 1142, 4365 I | 2736, 4403 I | 3147, 4410 8 | 2050 Laodi | 2495 Vision | 3241 Seven, | 637 Candl | **Vision of** | C | p.p.Da | 722 Son of | 682 Glorifi | 52 Robe

138

------ Sunday, Oct 24, 2021 ------

Me (1:14 AM)

A FUNDAMENTAL CORNERSTONE of Christianity is the undeniable fact that **Christians do not believe ANY human was ever 'DIVINE' accept Jesus**. Right there u can see yet another huge lie of the King James Bible, just in the TITLE of Revelation! Now for others in the future who may read this, who call themselves Christians because you were told by your parents that is your religion...**By this i mean u arent a bigot 'fundamentalist' like my mom, who believes all other people of different faiths are condemned to Hell**...You havent read much of the Bible, maybe Psalm 23 'The Lord is my shepherd', Maybe 'The Lord's Prayer', and 'Love thy neighbor', but u CANT IMAGINE that there could b such a genocidal, Hitler type "Final Solution" planned by God/Jesus...Well turn pls to Revelation chap 19, vs13-15 for one of MANY such examples: **"And he was clothed w a vesture dipped in blood and his name is called the Word of God. And the armies which were in heaven (angels) followed him upon white horses...Out of his mouth goeth a sharp sword that with it he should smite the nations"**

------ Monday, Oct 25, 2021 ------

Me (2:28 AM)

There are a few more points i want to cover before moving on from Revelation. Again John makes it obvious that this book and his prophecy he is writing are ENTIRELY SYNONYMOUS with Jesus' prophecy to return in the clouds on a white horse **IN JOHN'S GENERATION**, as i have detailed w multiple examples from 3 of the 'gospels' QUOTING Jesus guaranteeing that to his disciples. **It is VERY important to note that in those passages, Jesus commonly uses the phrase 'the time is at hand', or 'the time is fulfilled' IN THE CONTEXT of his guarantee to his disciples that his 2nd coming is IMMINENT, and that it WILL OCCUR in their generation!** With that, see Rev 1, vs 3: "Blessed is he that readeth and they that hear the words of this prophecy... FOR THE TIME IS AT HAND." Agn, The church has LIED in a shameful way to portray this as written for a different generation in the future. And worse yet is WHY they do so...Largely because of their bigoted 'programming' to WANT Jesus' "Final Solution" genocide against all others.

------ Tuesday, Oct 26, 2021 ------

Me (1:38 AM)

Listen to me closely Mother. Unless one is 'programmed' to believe in such mass genocide in the name of God/Jesus, **one NATURALLY KNOWS it is the epitome of evil and the OPPOSITE of the**

'Light'...The OPPOSITE of spiritual truth, love & forgiveness...The OPPOSITE of the Golden Rule. Unless one is programmed w such TRAUMATIZING LIES about the violent, genocidal condemning nature of God, one NATURALLY KNOWS it is NOT the nature of Divine Truth & Holiness, but conversely it is nothing but the nature of ignorant bigoted men. **As i have told u, 'The Light' has NO NEED TO COMMIT GENOCIDE as it shines on others who are in PITCH BLACK DARKNES! 'The Light' has NO NEED to bring mass murderous harm targeting little babies as 'God/Jesus' routinely have demanded, as i have shown u here w MANY examples from your own Bible!** As i shine that 'Light' by example here, understand that it CANNOT HARM OR CONDEMN...The true love of God only HEALS & FORGIVES, as it brings healing and forgiving correction, NOT GENOCIDE!

------ Wednesday, Oct 27, 2021 ------
Me (2:09 AM)
As i have explained in a previous lesson Mother, what you have been programmed with for all of your life has been a man made, fear based 'weaponized' image of God. It is a very harmful, false image of God that has kept u and your brothers in **PITCH BLACK DARKNESS** all these years. I am finally shining the **TRUE LIGHT of God** on the upside down, bigoted man made image u have been lied to about for so long. I am about to detail here yet another of the BIGGEST examples of infanticide of little innocent babies and children ordered by God/Jesus (remember God & Jesus, as John 1:1 makes clear, are ONE AND THE SAME.) Mother, it is overdue for u to wake up and realize that LOVE, and THE LIGHT of spiritual truth DOES NOT AND CANNOT BEHAVE IN THIS DIABOLICAL WAY! **To do so is only to TEACH humanity to behave so evil!! Spiritual Truth & The Light teach LOVE and FORGIVENESS always, not mass genocide of innocent children, as we see being BOASTED about in Exodus and the sick 'Passover' story, as a way for God to proudly demonstrate his power!**

------ Thursday, Oct 28, 2021 ------
Me (2:55 AM)
As virtually all Jewish faith resources and websites such as **Chabad.org** will confirm, 'Passover' is THE MOST CELEBRATED of all Jewish holidays. For a 7 or 8 day period they carry on this extended 'celebration', having big gatherings, drinking wine and eating very festive meals. **And many often proudly admit they are celebrating being God's "Chosen**

People" who he delivered from "slavery" under the Egyptians by SHOWING HIS AWESOME POWER with a series of increasingly deadly plagues, the last being God TARGETING THE FIRSTBORN CHILDREN AND INFANTS of the Egyptians with MASS GENOCIDE/INFANTICIDE. Any Jewish resource will also confirm they are SPECIFICALLY 'celebrating' God's ANGEL OF DEATH 'passing over' THEIR homes and THEIR children, and killing only the Egyptians' first born BABIES & CHILDREN, hence the name of the festive holiday 'Passover'. **Does that sound like a story that people should 'CELEBRATE', let alone have a WEEK LONG FESTIVAL ABOUT?? Only when u r PROGRAMMED w such PITCH BLACK DARKNESS & 'HOLY LIBEL'!**

------ Friday, Oct 29, 2021 ------
Me (3:22 AM)
I am going to b exposing more powerful, undeniable man made lies in the next few lessons on this topic from your Bible. **First, how do u think it would strike most people if the truth was that Pharaoh DID NOT REFUSE to let the Jews go?** Because that is the general story the masses have been told, right? That is the general lie that the masses have been programmed with by JudeoChristianity. In the coming lessons, I will show u that your Bible makes this adamantly clear, not only MULTIPLE times, but right from the START of the story!! Turn pls to Exodus 7, vs 3, where God is quoted, **"And i will HARDEN PHARAOH'S HEART, and multiply my signs and wonders in the land of Egypt."** Christian pastors do their usual lying by taking verses out of obvious context, such as the very next vs: "But Pharaoh shall not harken unto u, that i may lay my hand upon Egypt." But Pharaoh DID harken to Moses, many times as I am about to show you from your own Bible…And listen closely now because this is very important…**The story describes God REPEATEDLY TAKING AWAY PHARAOH'S FREE WILL! What happened to the all important 'free will' required for sin??**

------ Saturday, Oct 30, 2021 ------
Me (2:35 AM)
Agn, I ask you: What happened to the all important 'FREE WILL' required for sin Mother? All through this story, Pharaoh's own FREE WILL TO LET THE JEWS GO is SUPERSEDED BY GOD! Why?? Because as i showed u, the writers of this sick, evil FABLE quoted God in verse 3 telling Moses he will 'harden Pharaoh's heart' in order to **'multiply my signs and my wonders'**. But as we know, it wasnt

141

just to impress and 'awe' the Egyptians to win them over, as the TRUE LIGHT & MIRACLE OF LOVE can & will do...Oh no, this was a pure selfish genocidal evil plan that, as i have told u before, along w the MANY other genocide examples, a few of which i have previously detailed, of God calling for the killing of ALL the little boys and the RAPING of ALL the little virgin female children, or the 'ripping up' of pregnant women, etc... **All of it has only served as a 'HOW TO' INSTRUCTION MANUAL for humanity's acts of genocide and tribal warmongering ever since! And 'GOD' REPEATEDLY PREVENTS Pharaoh from his own FREE WILL DESIRE to let them go in order to do it!**

------ Sunday, Oct 31, 2021 ------
Me (2:29 AM)
This evidence, this evil in the name of God i am showing u from your own Bible, is for u to finally realize **it is NOT GODS WORD!** You have been programmed w a very, very sick and bigoted MAN MADE IMAGE of God. But let me continue detailing the evidence of the HUGE JudeoChristian lie that Pharaoh would not let the Jews go...**All one has to do is take the time to actually READ the whole story, and u find the EXACT OPPOSITE is the case!** Pharaoh repeatedly was going to let them go, but as i showed u in chap 7 vs 3, the writers of the fable quote God saying he will harden Pharaoh's heart so he can show his power, **ultimately to commit MASS INFANTICIDE.** For the first example of many, see chap 7 vs 12 after the rods 'turned to serpents'. It says "he hardened Pharaoh's heart that he harkened not unto them". When God SUPERSEDES and 'hardens Pharaoh's heart', **this by definition means Pharaoh was WILLING to let them go, but his own free will was deliberately 'interfered with' by God. When you actually read the entire story, you are shocked to see that Pharaoh WAS willing to let them go!**

142

Chapter Ten

------ Monday, Nov 1, 2021 ------

Me (1:51 AM)

This is yet another MASSIVE lie by both the Christian and the Jewish 'faiths'. They both DELIBERATELY lie by 'omitting' these verses i am showing u, **while intentionally & falsely presenting the fundamental reason for 'God's wrath' being that Pharaoh & the Egyptians REFUSED every opportunity God gave them after each curse, to let the Jews go.** But I am revealing here, using your own KJV Bible, this yet another 'GAME OVER' lie of JudeoChristianity! Not just once, but TEN TIMES we find this fact right there in the so called 'scripture' of the story. I showed u the FIRST 2 already. Turn now to Exodus 10, vs 1: **"...Go in unto Pharaoh, <u>for I HAVE HARDENED HIS HEART, AND THE HEART OF HIS SERVANTS</u>, that i might show these my signs before him".** And now turn pls to chap 11, vs 9-10: **"And the Lord said unto Moses, Pharaoh SHALL NOT HARKEN UNTO U, that my wonders may b multiplied in the land of Egypt...<u>and the Lord HARDENED Pharaoh's heart SO THAT HE WOULD NOT LET THE CHILDREN OF ISRAEL GO...</u>"**

------ Tuesday, Nov 2, 2021 ------

Me (2:06 AM)

And what do the Jewish writers of this story quote God decreeing in chapter 11, vs 5? "AND ALL THE FIRSTBORN IN THE LAND OF EGYPT SHALL DIE, from the firstborn of Pharaoh that sitteth upon his throne to the firstborn of the MAIDSERVANT THAT IS BEHIND THE MILL." (??) **First of all, does infanticide of little babies and children fit the definition of 'showing my SIGNS and WONDERS'??** Only to people who have been PROGRAMMED with such bigotry would not only think that is an acceptable act by God to show his 'wonders', and in so doing to portray THEM as his 'PREFERRED, CHOSEN RACE', **protecting THEIR children, while committing mass genocide of the NON JEWS - not just the Egyptians, but their SERVANTS AS WELL!** What did the innocent children and babies have to do w the Jews being held in Egypt?? What did the innocent SERVANTS have to do w it?? NOTHING! **<u>But this merits a WEEK LONG CELEBRATION every year by Jews who teach this HORSE SH#T to their children! ALL based on the LIE that Pharaoh wouldn't let them go.</u>**

------ Wednesday, Nov 3, 2021 ------
Me (3:09 AM)

Why have YOU as a teacher Mother, always taught that HUGE LIE to me and children in your charge? Its right there TEN TIMES throughout the story! It even BEGINS as i showed u in Exodus chap 7, vs 3 with God BOLDLY STATING that Pharaoh's heart would be hardened by him, meaning God would use his 'omnipotent power' to FORCIBLY CHANGE Pharaoh's WILLINGNESS to let the Jews go, all so he could 'show his wonders'! **I ask u agn Mother, does the mass infanticide of all the firstborn children of the Egyptians sound like a 'wonder' of God to be CELEBRATED WITH A WEEK LONG FESTIVE PARTY? I ask u agn, WHY did u teach such a lie that Pharaoh REFUSED to let the Jews go, and therefore DESERVED what God did??** By now, you should know the true answer. It is because you were dishonestly PROGRAMMED w that lie as a child by those u trusted and thought u had to believe. And i havent even revealed the MOST shocking evidence yet! **Surely a loving God would NOT do all this if Pharaoh actually ASKED HIM FOR FORGIVESS??**

------ Thursday, Nov 4, 2021 ------
Me (2:16 AM)

SURELY we wouldn't discover not one, but TWO "faiths", the leaders of which routinely preach such a MASSIVE LIE from the Bible, that Pharaoh and the Egyptians DESERVED such curses and genocide from God BECAUSE THEY REFUSED to let the Jews go, **if the OPPOSITE EVIDENCE is right in the story, that Pharaoh not only was repeatedly WILLING to let the Jews go, but that he ACTUALLY ASKED GOD'S FORGIVENESS!!** But shamefully, we DO have two of the world's biggest religions, FAMOUS for not only teaching this lie to children about God committing infanticide on 'NON BELIEVING' cultures, but CELEBRATING it every year, in the Jew's case with a week long festival! Yet we see clearly w this evidence i am showing u from your own Bible, that u r celebrating a man made LIE. Turn pls to Exodus chap 10, vs 16-17: **"Then Pharaoh called for Moses and Aaron in haste, and he said i have sinned against the Lord your God and against u. Now therefore FORGIVE, i pray thee, my sin..." MY MY, THATS NOT THE STORY WE'VE HEARD!!**

144

------ Friday, Nov 5, 2021 ------
Me (2:36 AM)
Pharaoh ASKED FOR FORGIVENESS!! Quote: **"now therefore forgive, i pray thee, my sin..."** This is one of MANY times he WANTED TO COMPLY and let the Jews go, and here in your own Bible, we see Pharaoh not only wanted to comply, but of HIS OWN FREE WILL, WANTED TO SHOW HIS CONTRITION! And lo and behold, what do we find happens yet again just 3 verses later in the story? God INTERFERES w Pharaoh's free will contrition and decision to comply! Chap 10, vs 20: **"But the Lord hardened Pharaoh's heart, so he would not let the Children of Israel go." Is any of this what we always hear from Rabbis and pastors in their pulpits? No. All we hear is the massive lie that Pharaoh and the Egyptians DESERVED the curses and infanticide by God because Pharaoh REFUSED to let 'Gods chosen people' go.** It doesnt get any bigger of a lie than that by a religious 'faith', accept to ignore Jesus telling his disciples repeatedly that his 2nd coming will happen in THEIR generation, and pretend he never said that lie.

------ Saturday, Nov 6, 2021 ------
Me (1:32 AM)
To give u one WRITTEN example of this **very deliberate lie** perpetuated by the Christian and Jewish faiths, it is actually even in the concordance reference notes section in my Thompson Chain Reference King James Bible. Directly next to chapter 10 vs 20 that we just discussed, where God INTERFERES w Pharaoh's own free will to not only let the Jews go, **but to ask for FORGIVENESS**, what do u suppose the Christian 'researchers' wrote in the reference note section of my Bible, about that verse of God hardening Pharaoh's heart?? **"STUBBORNESS"!!** So there is that HUGE LIE agn! I have shown you in your OWN BIBLE the actual passages showing the OPPOSITE over and over**...Pharaoh was NOT being 'stubborn', but in addition to repeatedly AGREEING to let the Jews go, Pharaoh is quoted even ASKING FOR FORGIVENESS FROM GOD, and complying w Moses requests, only to have God INTERFERE w his free will and HARDEN HIS HEART!** I shouldnt have to keep explaining it, it is so plainly obvious on its face. But those who, like u Mother, have been 'sold' SO MANY of these sick lies about God, need it to be repetitively shown to them, because u tend to have 'selective memory' when u have been so deeply conditioned w such lies.

------ Sunday, Nov 7, 2021 ------

Me (1:52 AM)

Lets get even more REAL in exposing these giant lies by looking agn at that last verse, Exodus 10, vs 20. What did it say was the REASON God forcibly CHANGED Pharaohs mind? It says, "But the Lord HARDENED Pharaoh's heart SO THAT HE WOULD NOT LET THE CHILDREN OF ISRAEL GO." But what does that really expose as the REAL reason God kept interfering w Pharaoh's WILLINGNESS TO COMPLY? **Because that would RUIN HIS PLANS FOR THE INFANTICIDE!** For other readers seeing this for the first time, u will naturally recoil in horror at yet another shameful dishonest 'HOLY LIBEL' depiction of God in the Bible, **that reveals how the church has lied to u that the curses and genocide of the Egyptians were ALL because Pharaoh REFUSED to let the Jews go. Now, u cant deny that the Bible repeatedly states the OPPOSITE! God kept interfering w Pharaoh's free will, as Pharaoh was repeatedly trying to COMPLY, so that God could finally get to his act of killing all the first born children! And THAT is nothing but 'HOLY LIBEL'…a shameful man made lie and FRAUDULENT image of God!**

------ Monday, Nov 8, 2021 ------

Me (2:33 AM)

This is yet another of so much evidence i have documented in these lessons over the last 11 months now**, exposing the ROOT** of the massive man made fraud, hypocrisy and lies RAMPANT in both the Bible AND the church 'doctrines' taught from the pulpits of both Christianity and Judaism 'faiths'. Many who call themselves Christians or Jews, but rarely read a Bible or Torah, and rarely attend church or synagogue other than Easter or the Passover 'FESTIVAL WEEK', **may read this evidence and be stunned to realize for the FIRST TIME, just how genocidal and evil God and Jesus behave in the Bible (remember 'God' and 'Jesus' are one and the same as stated in John 1:1).** Now, for other readers, i will reveal a truth about my Mother that is even more shocking. She and MANY other heavily 'programmed' Christians & Jews like her who regularly read the Bible, **THEY KNOW that Pharaoh was WILLING to let the Jews go, and THEY DONT CARE about the fact he asked for forgiveness only to have God forcibly 'harden his heart' in order to get to the infanticide**!

------ Tuesday, Nov 9, 2021 ------

Me (12:22 AM)

I said in yesterday's lesson that this Bible story is yet more evidence upon which i am shining the light of REAL spiritual truth, and that exposes the ROOT of the man made lies and fraud all throughout the Bible, that the vast majority who call themselves Christians & Jews hardly ever bother to take the time to READ for themselves. **WHAT IS THE ROOT i have been consistently showing u? What is the ROOT OF THE LIES in this 'Passover' story?** Its not the lie that Pharaoh refused to let the Jews go...That is a HUGE shameful lie perpetrated by the leaders of the Jewish and Christian faiths, but its NOT THE ROOT of the overall fraud of the Bible and JudeoChristianity. **The ROOT here in this story and in so many other examples i have detailed, is the fraudulent man made WEAPONIZING of the two 'faiths' to the bigoted detriment and FINAL SOLUTION style genocide and eternal condemnation of ALL others, simply because of their diverse, different ways of expressing their understanding of spirituality!**

------ Wednesday, Nov 10, 2021 ------

Me (2:22 AM)

Listen to me carefully Mother, because the following words are where real healing begins. **There is NOTHING about true spirituality for anyone to be afraid of! NOT ANYONE!!** There is NOTHING about spiritual truth and 'The Light' that needs a 'BLOOD SACRIFICE' of animals for thousands of years, ultimately leading to a HUMAN BLOOD SACRIFICE in order to satisfy such a sick blood lust craving by some 'male entity' who is vowing to CONDEMN you if u dont satisfy, embrace and worship such a diabolically sick blood lust belief system!! As i have pointed out in prior lessons, you automatically refer to such sick blood lust animal and human sacrifices as 'DEVIL WORSHIP' when u hear about them being done by OTHERS, but in the PINNACLE OF HYPOCRISY, u pretend such a mentally ill, sick evil practice is not the CORNERSTONE of JudeoChristianity!! **Again Mother, it is 'HOLY LIBEL'...It is PITCH BLACK DARKNESS that teaches such a sick concept of "God" to little children. Man made bigotry & lies need such fear, NOT THE LIGHT!**

------ Thursday, Nov 11, 2021 ------

Me (1:55 AM)

But you WANT TO BELIEVE THE LIES. **They are like DRUGS that you are addicted to.** You are like a child who is turning 12 or 13 and

147

becoming a teenager, too old to keep believing in Santa Clause, and she STILL REFUSES to believe Santa Clause was a lie taught to her by her parents. **But at least a belief in Santa does not involve CONDEMNATION OF ALL OTHER CHILDREN WHO DONT!!** Yet, it is an interesting 'preparatory fable'. Its an oddly similar myth to JudeoChristianity we teach our kids. Its often the FIRST METHOD parents use to begin teaching their child about 'good vs bad' or 'right & wrong', with the whole 'naughty or nice' angle, and therefore naturally, a little child begins to see Santa as the all seeing omnipotent miracle working 'God' figure. **And their parents tell them only if they are 'good' all year will they get presents, otherwise they will b on Santa's 'naughty list'. Then when the child is older, this 'white lie' myth is replaced w the much more fear based man made lies i have detailed here**.

------ Friday, Nov 12, 2021 ------
Me (2:53 AM)
Speaking of the lies i have detailed here, i meant to briefly clarify something relating to the lie that Pharaoh 'refused' to let the Jews go. Remember i told u there are about 10 such references throughout the fable, stating that God interfered w Pharaoh's free will, as he stated to Moses he would repeatedly do in Exodus 7, vs 3 & 4. You will find a few of them have the FULL wording **'God hardened Pharaoh's heart'** etc. But u will find a few that leave out the full reference to God doing it, and the wording just says 'Pharaoh hardened his heart'. But as i reminded u above, u have to remember from the beginning in vs 3 & 4 of chap 7, **God is QUOTED decreeing that HE will harden Pharaoh's heart in order to bring all his curses (which as I showed you, include the genocidal killing of all the innocent firstborn Egyptian children.)** Its amazing how many people 'selectively' read the Bible to avoid having to FACE so many of the blatant lies in it! I have to take the time to remind u of this lest u see a few of those examples and 'forget' chap 7, vs 3 & 4.

------ Saturday, Nov 13, 2021 ------
Me (2:55 AM)
Continuing w how these man made lies act like 'drugs' you are addicted to Mother. One of the BIGGEST and most appealing LIES of Christianity that attracts a very large number of people, ESPECIALLY Catholic priests, is Paul's undeniable 'CON ARTISTRY' in Romans chap 7, vs 15-25. **This passage is one of the MOST hypocritical lies of the New Testament, right up there w the lies i showed u of Jesus GUARANTEEING his 2nd coming to occur DURING his and his**

148

disciples' generation. **And pastors/priests pretend not to see that and pretend it is yet to come**. Keep in mind, Paul is making these statements about his utter INABILITY TO DO GOOD, or to do the right thing as he KNOWS he should, **long AFTER he has had his supposed Damascus Road 'BORN AGAIN' experience!** Lets look at this 'i cant help but do bad things even though i want to stop' utter horse shit for a religious teaching! Vs 15 says "For what i would, that do i NOT, but what i HATE that do i". That is NOT 'living in the Light' Mother.

------ Sunday, Nov 14, 2021 ------
Me (2:21 AM)
Continuing w these wildly popular lies crafted by the Catholic founders of Christianity, and attributed to Paul, **as he says here in this passage that it is <u>NOT HIS FAULT that he CANNOT DO GOOD, even though he knows he should</u>**. We began w vs 15 yesterday. Today lets look at the 17th verse: "Now then it is NO MORE I that do it, BUT SIN that dwelleth in me. (We r going to need a shovel and a large wheel barrow momentarily.) In vs 18-20 he continues: "...for to WILL is present w me, but HOW TO PERFORM THAT WHICH IS GOOD I FIND NOT. For the good that i would i do not: but the evil which i would not, that i do. Now if i do that i would not, IT IS NO MORE I THAT DO IT, BUT SIN THAT DWELLETH IN ME." **We r going to need something much bigger than a wheel barrow!** WAKE UP MOTHER!! This is undeniably, as i said yesterday, utter horse shit!! **<u>You dont get to say you 'cant help but do bad instead of good' and continue to do EVIL by claiming its NOT YOU, but 'SIN' in u, and that the literal BLOOD from a HUMAN SACRIFICE makes it OK</u>**.

------ Monday, Nov 15, 2021 ------
Me (3:23 AM)
And what SPOTLIGHTS & UNDERLINES this for the obvious 'GAME OVER' lie that it is would b what Paul is quoted saying only ONE CHAPTER EARLIER! Turn pls to Romans chap 6, verse 11-14. Here he DEMANDS THE EXACT OPPOSITE from the reader: **"<u>Let NOT sin therefore reign in your mortal body, that ye should obey it in the LUSTS thereof.</u>"** But as i showed u yesterday in chap 7, Paul decrees that **SIN REIGNS HIS BODY & HE CANNOT DO GOOD!! But that its 'OK' <u>because its NOT HIM, its 'SIN' which he is NO LONGER RESPONSIBLE FOR</u>, allegedly due to a human blood sacrifice. It doesnt get more sick or hypocritical than this!** But lets not stop there, lets continue underlining his undeniable hypocrisy w more from chap 6 prior. Vs 13 reads: **"Neither yield ye your members as**

instruments of unrighteousness unto sin..." And vs 14: **"For sin shall not have dominion over u..."** And vs 15: **"...shall we sin because we r not under the law, but under grace? God forbid"** **Hmmm. But in chap 7 he says he STILL REGULARLY DOES EVIL, AND CANT DO GOOD??**

------ Tuesday, Nov 16, 2021 ------
Me (3:12 AM)
So once agn, lets hear from 'Saint Paul the Apostle' in Romans chap 7 vs 19: **"For the GOOD that i would i DO NOT: but the EVIL i would not, that i do."** As i stated in the last lesson, there r plenty of other OPPOSITE verses where Paul demands that the reader LIVE HOLY, DO GOOD AND NOT EVIL. But as i said, that only PROVES my point by underlining the lies and horse shit hypocrisy in this passage and others **where he gives himself and ALL 'BELIEVERS' a free pass claiming such daily sinful behavior is 'not his fault' and by extension 'not your fault'**, because u cant help it, u r after all just an evil doer by nature, which is the height of dishonest shameful, horse shit and hypocrisy!! Agn, for example, IT DOESNT MATTER that he writes the OPPOSITE in Romans 12, vs 1-2: "...present your bodies a living sacrifice, holy, acceptable unto God...and be NOT conformed to this world, but be ye transformed by the RENEWING OF YOUR MIND." **This while saying he CANT STOP SINNING, but it isnt him!!**

------ Wednesday, Nov 17, 2021 ------
Me (2:48 AM)
In other words, Paul's shameful lie i am exposing here, using Romans 12 vs 2, is MAGNIFIED by that verse where he says "but be ye transformed by the renewing of your mind, that ye may prove what is that GOOD, ACCEPTABLE & PERFECT will of God." But obviously the ENTIRE CONTEXT of his passage in chapter 7, where he claims his regular engaging in what he **KNOWS to be wrong,** and his ongoing INABILITY TO DO GOOD doesn't just suggest, **but PROVES he is a con artist liar in chapter 12, vs 2.** He is showing that the TRUTH is **he himself has NOT been 'transformed' by the 'renewing of his mind',** and he is telling the reader that (wink wink) 'Its ok if u keep being like me, doing evil, generally unable to do good. Its ok because u just can't help it. But now it ISNT REALLY YOU. Now, If u just believe this human blood sacrifice story, **even though (wink wink) I may say in other passages that u must be transformed to do good, the truth is, just like me, u cant renew your mind, and its 'sins fault', not yours.'** **What a giant, very popular received con indeed!**

------ Thursday, Nov 18, 2021 ------

Me (2:34 AM)

Lets shine some more true spiritual LIGHT on the **PITCH BLACK DARKNESS** of Paul's whopper of a con act in chap 7, vs 20 & 21, and then i want u to let me know if u would ever have accepted THIS excuse from me as a child if i misbehaved or was bad after being told to b good: Vs 20 & 21: "Now if i do that i would not, IT IS NO MORE I THAT DO IT, BUT SIN that dwelleth in me. I find then a LAW, that WHEN I WOULD DO GOOD, EVIL IS PRESENT W ME." **Does it sound like Paul was "transformed by the renewing of his mind" as he spouts this lie masquerading as the 'word of God', saying he CANT HELP HIMSELF in continuing to do evil??** I cant believe HOW MANY TIMES i remember pastors wanting to preach this passage from the pulpit. OF COURSE, because what better recruiting message could there be to preach than this in order to lock in more **TITHING MEMBERS**?? In case u didn't know, 'Saint Paul' and the books attributed to him are a fabricated construct of the early crafting of Christianity by Rome & the Roman Catholic church. No surprise there

------ Friday, Nov 19, 2021 ------

Me (2:56 AM)

"Now if i do that i would not, it is NO MORE I that do it but sin that dwelleth in me" **This is one of the biggest lies in the New Testament, crafted by the Roman Catholic Church. I asked u in the last lesson Mother, whether u would have accepted that line from me if i delib acted badly after being told to b good.** The answer obviously is NO. And why is that? Precisely because you intrinsically KNOW this is a massive lie by Paul. You naturally know that its NOT true, that we as humans CANT HELP but do evil and sin when we know better! ESPECIALLY CHILDREN! In vs 18 where Paul tries to decree that inside himself (and by extension ALL humans) 'dwelleth no good thing', thats the COMPLETE OPPOSITE of spiritual truth, and of humanity's TRUE SHARED DIVINE NATURE! Children are innocent and good BY NATURE, not evil and sinful. **As i told u before, the mistakes we make DO NOT equate to us being 'evil'. We are meant to make mistakes so we can learn from them…that doesn't make us 'sinful by nature'. People are CONDITIONED to be bad, including by these lies of organized religion.**

------ Saturday, Nov 20, 2021 ------

Me (2:21 AM)

Look at this shameful con act in the name of God once agn, and notice what i put in all caps: "Now if i do that i would not, it is NO MORE I that do it but sin that dwelleth in me" Just to make sure u and other future readers dont miss it, **Paul is describing his regular CONTINUED sinful, evil behavior, and his admitted utter inability to do good as <u>NO MORE</u> him doing it!** Its important not to miss the reason he says NO MORE in this con he is running. And that is because he means no more AFTER he has adopted this belief in God needing a human blood sacrifice to satisfy his blood lust. Thats sick enough in itself, and just becomes more bewilderingly shameful when he tells everyone who reads his horse shit that they OF COURSE cant help but continue a life of sin and evil just like him, <u>but AFTER THEY JOIN HIM in such a belief, they dont have to b responsible for the evil or bad they do or did,</u> **because <u>IF THEY ADOPT THIS 'BELIEF', well then, suddenly it NO MORE is or was them doing evil!</u>**

------ Sunday, Nov 21, 2021 ------

Me (3:07 AM)

This is, in a general sense, the SAME lie perpetrated by the writers of the fraudulent story of Adam and Eve's so called 'sinful nature' that i spent a great deal of time showing u when i began these lessons. I showed u that the Bible itself identified them as EXACTLY THE OPPOSITE! **<u>Your own Bible describes them as being COMPLETELY INNOCENT.</u>** They were, just as u and i and ALL of humanity, ABSOLUTELY NOT 'sinful by nature'. They made an error or mistake THAT ANY INNOCENT CHILD WOULD MAKE, if their Father they trusted to protect them in their innocent home, SECRETLY planned w the master deceiver (Satan), allowing him into the garden to have his way w these innocent, blameless & unprepared children. SHAME on Jews & Christians who deliberately ignore this OBVIOUS TRUTH, and lie to their own children, **programming them from kindergarten age or <u>EARLIER, to believe they are 'all bad by nature'! SHAMEFUL is an understatement for that LIE to children!! Remember, what did Adam & Eve NOT HAVE THE KNOWLEDGE OF?</u>**

------ Monday, Nov 22, 2021 ------

Me (2:44 AM)

Once agn, what did Adam & Eve NOT HAVE THE KNOWLEDGE OF? As i showed u in our beginning lessons, your own Bible makes it a CENTRAL POINT to the story that until they were deceived and

152

PREYED UPON in their childlike innocence by Satan, **they were innocent PRECISELY BECAUSE they did not have the KNOWLEDGE OF GOOD & EVIL!** Your own Bible is telling u that BY NATURE, they were NOT SINFUL, BUT INNOCENT. And as i pointed out to u before, **who were the only two characters in the story who WERE SINNING and being 'EVIL' in setting up these innocent childlike new beings who were (as i and so many others also are doing to this day) completely TRUSTING God to protect them and 'DELIVER THEM FROM EVIL'??** Your own Bible shows that the ONLY ones engaging in EVIL in this sick lie of a nightmarish fairytale were 'God' and his secret partnership w 'the Devil', **KNOWING in his omnipotence that Adam & Eve didnt even know who Satan was, what 'sin' or 'evil' was, let alone have 'free will' at that point to DECIDE to 'sin'!**

------ Tuesday, Nov 23, 2021 ------
Me (1:43 AM)
I need to clarify my wording from yesterday...Since they had no concept of evil or sin, where i said that in their total innocence, Adam & Eve were completely trusting God to 'deliver them from evil', i should have just said 'trusting God like an innocent child in all things', because as i have shown, without the foreknowledge and understanding of 'good and evil', **they had no concept of 'evil' or 'sin' or even of being harmed or deceived, that's how innocent and trusting like little children they were**. And then that very first story in the Bible is regularly taught to little children in Sunday School, making them think that's what God could do to them! Making them in their total sweetness and innocence, believe they r bad and evil by nature! This, as i have made clear to u before, is the fundamental, sick & shameful man made lie upon which the entire rest of the Bible's 'HOUSE OF FRAUDULENT CARDS' rests upon! And shouldn't u b asking a very common sense question? **Why after they DID learn of good & evil, was it not made a NECESSARY LIFE LESSON instead of a CURSE?**

------ Wednesday, Nov 24, 2021 ------
Me (3:22 AM)
It came to me in my meditations, that another HUGE tell tale sign of this man made lie is that IF we r to believe the God of the Bible is loving and forgiving (as i have already shown in much detail, the Bible repeatedly describes his character as most often THE OPPOSITE, acting more evil than we ever see the so called 'Devil' being described) But IF we r to believe this God to b fundamentally all about LOVE & FORGIVENESS,

then obviously, if EVER there was a time for a 'Father' to demonstrate that **(AFTER SETTING UP HIS INNOCENT CHILDREN TO BE PREYED UPON IN THEIR INNOCENCE BY SATAN)** it would have been THEN, in that first story w Adam & Eve! Every loving human parent knows their most important responsibility to their innocent children is first, to keep them SAFE from such a predator, and secondly to TEACH THEM THE KNOWLEDGE OF RIGHT AND WRONG... GOOD AND EVIL! <u>Yet here, we have Adam and Eve's 'Father' not only SECRETLY SETTING THEM UP to b in dire danger, but CURSING them for then being tricked into gaining that KNOWLEDGE!</u>

------ Thursday, Nov 25, 2021 ------
Me (2:06 AM)
Happy Thanksgiving! There is SO much to b thankful for this year! I'm especially thankful for the answers to my prayers over many years, diligently asking for the wisdom and full understanding of spiritual truth. I am thankful to b able to not only teach that to u, **but also in the process, to show u the rampant man made lies of the Bible that serve to BLIND u to your true oneness with ALL humanity as an eternal PART OF WHAT GOD IS**, irrespective of varying diverse beliefs, cultures or sexual orientations, etc. Let's cont where i left off yesterday, and soon i will return to Paul's con act using this SAME LIE of 'original sin'. I am now going to show u something pastors usually avoid when covering this first Bible story. Turn pls to Genesis 3, vs 22: "And the Lord God said, behold the man is become as ONE OF US, to know good and evil". **Hmmm...So they were childlike and innocent, tricked in their innocence to gain 'knowledge', and lo and behold, your own Bible says this resulted in their being ONE WITH GOD! <u>Think about that...How could they be EVIL BY NATURE if they were ONE WITH GOD, after finally GAINING the knowledge of what 'sin' was, which we've seen that they DID NOT have prior to being deceived??</u>**

------ Friday, Nov 26, 2021 ------
Me (2:28 AM)
This is so important in helping to awaken u from many years of **false programming that u are 'sinful by nature'.** This example is generally avoided by most Bible teachers because it absolutely shows, just like the earlier passage describing them as innocent, not having any knowledge of good or evil...this verse in chap 3 further puts a GIANT exclamation point on the fact that they could NOT be 'sinful by nature' if the Bible

154

quotes God saying they simply **finally gained the knowledge of good and evil, and are become as ONE OF US**. Unless u believe God is sinful and evil by nature... Unless we are to say God is NOT Holy and Divine, then it is clear this is a major revealing verse that Adam and Eve's nature became ONE WITH GOD, therefore Holy & Divine. **I cant stress the fact enough that BEFORE they were deceived as childlike beings by a master predator at Gods allowing, they had NO concept of 'sin', therefore they could not INTEND or 'WILL' to sin.**

------ Saturday, Nov 27, 2021 ------
Me (1:41 AM)
A few lessons back i said shouldn't u b asking a basic common sense question about what is conspicuous in its ABSENCE in this fable. After they DID learn of good & evil, WHY at that moment was it not made a NECESSARY LIFE LESSON instead of a CURSE?? **If EVER there was the PROPER time for anything like The Ten Commandments to be taught, or general parental style teaching and instruction regarding the Golden Rule and ethics, etc, OF COURSE IT WOULD BE THEN AND THERE!** Instead, we see these innocent childlike beings who had NO instruction on such things, HAD NO CONCEPT OF 'SIN' OR 'EVIL', we see them get taken advantage of in that unprepared innocence, and after they innocently get deceived that its really OK to eat the fruit and gain KNOWLEDGE (remember they didnt have a clue the 'talking snake' from that early version of Sesame Street was 'evil'. He may as well have been ELMO**!) instead of empowering them to UNDERSTAND such necessary KNOWLEDGE in life just as God had, HE commits the only evil in the story**

Mother (7:08 AM)
"You" are calling GOD "evil!" and HIS HOLY PLAN for mankind! /my heart is terrified for you! You have crossed a terrible line!!! I cannot bear to read any more of your words against GOD and HIS HOLY WORD! Please, respect my request, and stop sending them to me...
I cannot bear to read anymore!!!

------ Sunday, Nov 28, 2021 ------
Me (2:37 AM)
Mother, u are not being honest, because if i am to believe u TRULY have read 'my words', instead of apparently only a SENTENCE OR TWO here and there, u would LONG before now understand that **i have been calling YOU out on YOUR 'evil pitch black darkness' beliefs. I have diligently shown u the evidence from your own Bible, that**

UNDENIABLY describes God as vengefully engaging in MORE EVIL than anything the Bible ever says about 'the Devil'! Reread what i wrote u on Nov 24th, about God and Satan setting up his innocent childlike new creation, knowing they had NO CONCEPT of evil! And instead of using it as a parent would, as a TEACHING opportunity, God CURSES his innocent children, who COULD NOT have 'free will' or 'CHOOSE' to sin because they had NO KNOWLEDGE OF 'GOOD & EVIL'! Thats nothing but a SICK and EVIL portrayal of God. This and MANY other such examples i have shown u in order NOT to proclaim God as 'evil', but obviously to WAKE U UP to these being EVIL MAN MADE LIES ABOUT GOD!!

------ Monday, Nov 29, 2021 ------
Me (2:27 AM)
What i have been carefully and patiently showing u is that the organized religion of JudeoChristianity (and Islam as well) is EVIL, primarily due to their **LIBELOUS, false and evil portrayal of who & what 'God' is**. I have made that CRYSTAL CLEAR over and over Mother! Yet u act as though u either have IGNORED my daily messages and the specificity of their content, or u have somehow now become incapable of such basic 'word comprehension'. **Your last outburst is very revealing in how it shows your deeply rooted belief that such a sick, evil God WOULD & SHOULD harm your own daughter for merely pointing out that EVIL so OFTEN engaged in as the writers of the Bible describe him! Instead of u realizing that i am describing THEIR portrayal of God as evil**, though i have made that point very clear even in the very title of this book, it is shameful on your part to WANT to believe that i am the evil one, 'deserving' of eternal harm and damnation for having the honest courage to expose those lies.

------ Tuesday, Nov 30, 2021 ------
Me (1:53 AM)
This is going to b a special 2 texts lesson, as i need a little more space for this one today. In the last couple of days, i have had something very SPECIAL from my childhood involving your Dad (my Granddad), brought to my awareness, prompting me to give to u as an example, in shining the Light of real spiritual truth on the **PITCH BLACK DARKNESS** of all the man made lies about God in the Bible. As u know, i have used the Bible's very FIRST story frequently in these lessons to carefully show u **that the only truly 'sinful' or 'evil' actions in that first story of Adam & Eve are UNDENIABLY committed by the 'characters' of God and Satan**, and that IN FACT, we now know it

156

was a 'bastardized' fable, stolen and tweaked from those who science and archeology have now proven to b a much older civilization who ORIGINALLY AUTHORED that spiritual creation myth, **NEVER meant to b either weaponized, or 'cursing' of the first man and woman for 'sinning', as Jewish writers did, let alone taken literally...(Cont Tomorrow)**

Me (2:33 AM)
Now for the special story: I was about 5 or 6 yrs old, in the care of Grandmother and Granddaddy in Orlando, Florida. I think it was when u had left me w them, going away for some job in Tallahassee, Florida. Grandmother almost had lunch ready one day, and Granddaddy was going to b home soon on his lunch break from work. She said i could play in the front yard, **but not to leave the yard.** I absolutely intended to do what she said, but some other children playing 2 or 3 houses down caught my ear, and i went to the edge of our yard to see them. They saw me and we waved at each other. I wanted to make friends, and i think they actually were calling me over. In my innocence, i didn't think i was doing wrong by trying to get a little closer to talk to them, and before i knew it, i was in the yard next to us, trying to meet them. **The next moment i heard Granddaddy very angry, and pulling off his BELT, as he came toward me saying "Your Grandmother told u to stay in the yard, didnt she?" I ran toward him apologizing...**
(Cont Tomorrow)

Chapter Eleven

------ Wednesday, Dec 1, 2021 ------

Me (2:08 AM)

(This will take TWO texts also) Before i cont, what do u expect happened? Many evangelical fundamentalists who r programmed with fear and guilt to believe the rampant, sick lies of the Bible would b quick to say, **"Thats right, u deserve a belt whipping for your SIN and deliberate disobeying of your Grandmother! SPARE THE ROD, SPOIL THE CHILD!!"** (Or they could quote any number of other evil and sick passages in the Bible attrib to God ordaining the abusive striking and beating of children to teach them a lesson for their 'evil sinful nature', otherwise how will they learn, right??) So i ask u, is that where your head is on this so far? **Bring on the BELT WHIPPING??** Well thankfully, Granddaddy thought better as he saw me run to him saying i was sorry, and he UNDERSTOOD that it was natural that i was pulled toward those other kids. He also saw i was not going all the way to them, but i had only gone halfway, and i thought i could still hear Grandmother from that close to our yard...

Me (2:29 AM)

Keeping in mind the Adam & Eve story, lets apply God and Satan's behavior to my example w Granddaddy. How evil would it have been if he PLANNED for those kids to attract my attention and wave at me, and call me toward them? What if he did what God did to Adam & Eve, and SET THE WHOLE THING UP, knowing my natural innocent reaction would surely b to come closer to them if they waved and invited me? **OBVIOUSLY that would b evil 'sinful' and abusive behavior on HIS part.** As i have carefully shown u using your own Bible, the story BEGINS making it clear they were innocent childlike beings WITHOUT ANY concept or understanding of 'good & evil' or 'right & wrong'. So in that kind of total innocence, they were INCAPABLE of this complete HORSE SH#T, made up assertion by Christianity that they chose to 'sin' w FREE WILL! **Why did Granddaddy have the moral wisdom to see my innocent mistake and forgive me, but God wanted to CURSE Adam & Eve in their innocence?? Answer: Because that is an evil lie.**

------ Thursday, Dec 2, 2021 ------

Me (2:43 AM)

What am i trying to do here w these lessons, and all of this EVIDENCE i am carefully showing u of the rampant lies in the Bible, and its shameful 'LIBEL' about the nature of God? **I am trying to get u to THINK!** As i have said before, w this series of lessons ultimately serving as what i hope to be a DEFINITIVE GUIDE to the man made fraud and lies of the Bible, designed for the DEPROGRAMMING of those so harmed & psychologically traumatized w such lies, often from a very early age...With that as my main goal here, **by necessity there must be a fair amount of REPETITION**. We can already see why, with your last outburst, where u apparently fixated on one place where i pointed out how the Bible clearly depicts God and Satan as the ONLY ones who were 'sinful' or 'evil' in the Garden story, as they together preyed upon Adam & Eves TOTAL INNOCENCE, and God then CURSES them for becoming ONE w him. **We see how instead of u THINKING & PROCESSING that along w SO MANY OTHER similar such man made lies i have shown u, u attacked me for calling 'Gods plan' EVIL.**

------ Friday, Dec 3, 2021 ------

Me (2:44 AM)

So shall we cont w some repetition of THE EVIL OF GOD i have already shown u from your own Bible? I showed u Genesis 7, where just before God decides to commit his BIGGEST act of WORLDWIDE GENOCIDE on mankind for becoming 'adulterers and fornicators', the Bible makes the ONSET & ORIGIN of such behavior clear, being when THE **'SONS OF GOD'** came and had their way w the 'DAUGHTERS OF MEN'. So just like God's evil partnership w Satan in allowing Adam & Eve to b preyed upon in their total innocence, but then CURSED them for being deceived, **ONCE AGAIN we see your own Bible admitting the evil of the 'SONS OF GOD' corrupting the daughters of men and humanity**, so that just like the story i showed u of God INTERFERING w PHARAOH'S FREE WILL to let the Jews leave Egypt just so he could get to his FINAL CURSE OF INFANTICIDE of all the first born Egyptian children, just like BOTH those stories **we see God ALLOWING HIS 'SONS' (Wait, what happened to there's only ONE 'SON OF GOD'?) to set mankind up to b CURSED AGAIN!**

------ Saturday, Dec 4, 2021 ------

Me (1:27 AM)

One correction is needed from the message yesterday...Where I cited Genesis chap 7, **I meant chap 6**. So let's quote vs 1 and 2 to get a nice, concise picture of 'GODS PLAN', just like his similar behavior in the Garden story. Now keep in mind that this passage in your Bible is detailing & describing <u>WHO CORRUPTED MANKIND</u> at the dawn of their beginning to multiply: **"And it came to pass, when men began to multiply on the face of the earth, and daughters were born unto them, that the SONS OF GOD saw the daughters of men that they were fair; and they TOOK THEM WIVES OF ALL WHICH THEY CHOSE."** Meaning what Mother?? <u>**Meaning GOD'S SONS forcibly took human girls to have their way sexually w them AT WILL!**</u> Oh, but it says they 'took them WIVES'. That doesn't matter! Its a euphemism for GOD'S SONS interfering and forcibly fornicating w humans, who were just starting out in God's creation. And like i said, we see there were MANY SONS OF GOD guilty of this abomination! **This kinda rains on the parade of Jesus being THE ONLY SON. And mankind is BLAMED.**

------ Sunday, Dec 5, 2021 ------

Me (1:23 AM)

Instead of God PUNISHING HIS 'SONS'... Heck, forget about 'punishing' them for forcing themselves on VIRGIN HUMAN GIRLS out of their lust, how about God simply PREVENTING HIS 'SONS' from doing so IN THE FIRST PLACE!! God is omnipotent and all knowing, so he would have to have ALLOWED his non human 'SONS' to 'TAKE' those human girls for themselves as they chose...<u>So THIS is his 'holy plan' u think is 'the Light'??</u> **THIS is part of Gods 'holy plan' that u accused me of blaspheming for pointing out HIS (& HIS SONS') PITCH BLACK EVIL that is inherent in ALL OF IT?? Get real!** To ALLOW that origin of corruption and 'sin' ADMITTEDLY brought on by GODS OWN 'SONS', and then to respond by BLAMING MANKIND, (oh, and of course blaming the innocent virgin girls who 'tempted' GODS SONS to come 'take them') And to then use this corruption, brought on by GODS SONS, to CONDEMN mankind to GLOBAL GENOCIDE... **There is obviously NOTHING 'holy' about such a 'plan'. It is of course the PINNACLE OF EVIL!**

------ Monday, Dec 6, 2021 ------

Me (2:38 AM)

Let's continue our repetition of some of the blatant lies i have detailed for u from your own Bible, and the EVIL they undeniably reveal about 'GODS PLAN' as u recently referred to it: God speaking to the Jews regarding other NON Jewish people & cultures they go to war with, in Deuteronomy chap 2O, vs 13-15: **"And when the Lord thy God hath delivered it into thine hands, thou shalt SMITE EVERY MALE thereof with the edge of the sword: BUT THE WOMEN AND THE LITTLE ONES...even all the SPOIL thereof, thou shalt TAKE UNTO THYSELF."** Sound FAMILIAR?? Like what God ALLOWED 'his sons' to do in our last lesson, only to then condemn humanity to genocide for the 'fornication' and 'sin' the SONS OF GOD instigated? But in this passage in Deut 20, God doesn't simply ALLOW IT, HE TELLS the Jews to 'take' the women and 'little ones' as THE SPOIL of war! **Its HIGH TIME you stop burying your head in your 'religious sandbox' Mother. I shouldn't have to tell u that this is THE OPPOSITE of 'The Light'...THE OPPOSITE of Love...THE OPPOSITE of spiritual truth!**

------ Tuesday, Dec 7, 2021 ------

Me (3:18 AM)

"BUT THE WOMEN AND THE LITTLE ONES...even all the SPOIL thereof, thou shalt TAKE UNTO THYSELF." Do i 'BLASPHEME' such a false and EVIL depiction of God, who would tell his "CHOSEN PEOPLE" to commit genocide of all the MEN of those non Jewish cultures, but TAKE THE WOMEN & LITTLE ONES FOR THEM SELVES?? **YOU BET YOUR BOTTOM DOLLAR I DO MOTHER!!** And this was no one time pedophile/rapist SPLURGE God ordained for the male Jews to 'ENJOY'...**Far from it, this was a repeated practice in the Bible as 'GODS HOLY PLAN'**! Not only did we just see it practiced by GOD'S SONS to the 'fair' virgin daughters of men in two lessons back, but doesn't this ring a bell from ANOTHER passage i detailed for u in Numbers 31, vs 17-18?...Lets read of 'GODS HOLY PLAN' as it is clearly described there: **"Now therefore kill every male AMONG THE LITTLE ONES, and kill every woman that hath known man by lying with him. BUT ALL THE WOMEN CHILDREN THAT HAVE NOT KNOWN A MAN (virgin little girls) KEEP ALIVE FOR YOUR SELVES."** Can it get more evil than that Mother??

------ Wednesday, Dec 8, 2021 ------

Me (2:02 AM)

I am forcing u to FACE THE EVIL **at the fundamental ROOT** of what u and i were programmed to believe from a very early age, about the nature of God. <u>My purpose is to preach spiritual truth, and expose these man made lies MASQUERADING as 'Gods Word'</u>. It is not MY MESSAGE that is the evil 'blasphemy' of God Mother! **It is THE BIBLE'S man made lies and HOLY LIBEL that are the blasphemy of 'The Light' and UNCONDITIONAL LOVE, which is the TRUE nature of what 'God' is**...NEVER advocating mass harm, mass genocide, mass infanticide, mass CHILD VIRGIN RAPE by Jewish men **or 'SONS OF GOD ' taking virgin girls/little ones for themselves as the 'spoil of war', etc.!!** You MUST wake up now, not only for your sake, but for me, your daughter's sake, who you cant be ignorant of the extent that i am a victim of such sick condemning beliefs, simply because i had the courage to make my physical gender correct w my true gender identity. **I need you to wake up now and stop ignoring the sick patriarchal pattern all throughout the Bible's Old and New Testament, of demeaning women as just property & sex objects, <u>shamefully in the NAME OF GOD</u>!**

------ Thursday, Dec 9, 2021 ------

Me (1:47 AM)

Lets cont our review of this PATTERN OF EVIL i have shown u, that u so defensively referred to as 'Gods plan'...1st Samuel 15, vs3 reads:"Now go and smite Amalek and utterly destroy all that they have, and spare them not, <u>but SLAY BOTH MAN AND WOMAN, INFANT AND SUCKLING</u>..." **Also, remember as we already saw in John 1, vs 1 in the New Testament, Jesus and God are defined as SYNONYMOUS by Christianity, ONE AND THE SAME**, and therefore do not think anything CHANGED w the arrival of Jesus. For as i have already shown u in Matt 10:34, he CONTINUES w this pattern, <u>saying he DID NOT come to bring peace, BUT A SWORD!</u> I have also shown previously that Jesus made his 'FINAL SOLUTION' worldwide genocidal plans very clear to his disciples, decreeing he would destroy ALL non believers like Sodom and Gomorrah upon his return, which i showed u he GUARANTEED would occur IN THEIR GENERATION. And of course, it did not. **But such a genocidal decree by 'Jesus', and the subsequent long history and legacy of 'The Crusades' and many other imperialistic genocidal and enslaving campaigns toward 'non believers', native Americans, African Americans and other cultures**

162

by Christianity since then, undeniably shows that the <u>VERY SAME</u> <u>man made, bigoted & weaponized pattern continued w the New</u> <u>Testament & Christianity.</u>

------ Friday, Dec 10, 2021 ------
Me (2:33 AM)
As we cont our review of these consistent patterns throughout the Bible, **it cannot be denied that it is pure unadulterated EVIL written by bigoted men**, as i have explained to u before, who were not only seeking to control the masses teaching their children such fear and propaganda, but in so doing were determined to DEIFY THEIR CULTURE above ALL others! Their intent was to deify their bigotry and GENOCIDAL HATE toward those cultures **who their weaponized, TOTALLY CONCOCTED 'deity' condemned**. But in truth, if one is honest with one's self, at this point in these lessons, we plainly see it was only those lying bigoted men who **fraudulently PORTRAYED 'God' as such**. Turn pls in our review to Hosea chap 13, vs 16 where these lying Jewish writers describe God as not just angry at the Samaritan culture for their rebellious behavior, but it reads**:"...they shall fall by the sword. <u>THEIR INFANTS SHALL BE DASHED IN PIECES, and their</u> <u>WOMEN W CHILD SHALL BE RIPPED UP." Gods 'holy plan'?</u> <u>NO. Pure evil.</u>**

------ Saturday, Dec 11, 2021 ------
Me (1:01 AM)
As we see from those few examples, just a sampling out of SO MANY MORE throughout the Bible, God's 'Holy plan' **constantly displays a specific patriarchal demeaning & denigrating of women, especially young child virgins, defining them not just as 'second class', but on the level of sexual property, and 'spoil of war' like cattle**. I cant stress to u enough Mother, that THIS IS KEY in how we can ABSOLUTELY SEE that all of it is NOT HOLY, but on its face is nothing but man made evil bigotry that has SHAMEFULLY been taught to the masses as 'Gods word'! This has resulted in indescribable harm to humanity, and to WOMEN & CHILDREN ESPECIALLY, over approx four thousand years!! I am one voice of a growing number who are shining The Light of REAL spiritual truth on that PITCH BLACK DARKNESS that has so deceived u about the nature of God, and about the HOLY NATURE OF MAN! That's right, your true nature is NOT SINFUL! **You and ALL of your fellow humanity of ALL diversity are a HOLY PERFECT ASPECT of God**

------ Sunday, Dec 12, 2021 ------
Me (2:18 AM)
It's been part of this sick man made programming to LIE to u <u>not just</u> <u>about who & what "God's" nature is, but about YOUR nature being evil</u> <u>and bad</u>. This was KEY in their mass psychosis programming, to PREVENT u and i and the masses of humanity they seek to control, from realizing our SHARED HOLY NATURE as eternal parts of what God is, here in this physical dimension. If u were here with me now, i would ask u to look at my hands, and i would tell u, **"These are the holy hands of** **God" as i wrapped them around u to hug u and show u my** **unconditional love**. What God is CANNOT and would NEVER 'rig' a situation like the Exodus story of the Egyptian Pharaoh, <u>in order to get to</u> <u>a final curse of infanticide of babies & children</u>, after Pharaoh as I showed you, tried MULTIPLE TIMES before that to let the Jews go, and 'God' INTERFERED W HIS FREE WILL DECISION to do so!! **Such a** **sick, deliberately false depiction of God is nothing but man made** **EVIL and we see it on display, as i have shown u, ALL throughout** **the Bible, <u>including by Jesus' admitted "Final solution" plans for</u>** **<u>non Jews.</u>**

------ Monday, Dec 13, 2021 ------
Me (1:49 AM)
Just to clarify that last line, Jesus' FINAL SOLUTION' genocidal plans that he decreed would take place upon his '2nd coming' as i detailed for u earlier<u>, were of course intended also for all NON BELIEVING JEWS, in</u> <u>addition to ALL NON JEWS</u>. **As i showed u in Matt chap 10, he** **specifically told his disciples NOT to take his 'gospel' to NON JEWS** (i.e. the Gentiles). As i showed u in precise detail in those earlier lessons, Jesus undeniably is quoted in **not one, not two, but THREE** different 'gospels', giving his specific answer to his disciples, after they came to him privately asking WHEN the END TIMES & his '2nd coming' would occur. I showed u Jesus' actual quotes GUARANTEEING his 2nd coming would b IN THEIR GENERATION**, and that THEY, his** **disciples, would SEE the END TIMES, and telling them many of** **them would die in the GREAT TRIBULATION**. And i even showed u where Jesus identifies John the Baptist as the return of Elijah FULFILLED, and his quote that some listening to him would NOT DIE before his 2nd coming!

------ Tuesday, Dec 14, 2021 ------

Me (2:54 AM)

So if Jesus, who the Bible says is synonymous w 'God' as we read in John chap 1, vs 1... If he is quoted making such a 'VERILY I SAY UNTO U' guaranteed prophecy to his disciples, in answer to their private direct query about WHEN his 2nd coming would occur, to the degree that i was able to show those quotes in THREE diff so called 'gospels' saying it would occur in THEIR generation, **and to the degree that in at least one of them, Jesus gets so precise as to say there are some standing here now who will not taste death before his 2nd coming w the kingdom of heaven**... What does that mean Mother? You cannot any longer pretend those passages of Jesus' FALSE PROPHECY are not there for all to see. You know what it means. Just like i showed u John's desperate quotes right at the beginning and at the end of Revelation, that reveal he was still clinging to that false prophecy of Jesus in relation to ALL the end times visions he described in the VERY FIRST VERSE as **"things which MUST SHORTLY come to pass"**

------ Wednesday, Dec 15, 2021 ------

Me (1:20 AM)

Its important to understand what i shared w u in a prior lesson...
Precisely because Jesus made those fraudulent guarantees to John and the other 3 disciples in the passages i previously detailed for u, of his 2nd coming certain to b in THEIR generation, and **precisely because** Jesus told John and the others THEY WOULD LIVE TO SEE THE END TIMES, and some would surely b persecuted and killed as they would SEE the 'great tribulation', and **precisely because**, as i showed u in your own Bible, Jesus told John and the others, in response to their questioning Jesus about WHEN would they see the required FULFILMENT of Malachi's prophecy that Elijah would return as forerunner to herald Jesus' return, **and Jesus answered John & the others, telling them it had ALREADY BEEN FULFILLED, that John the Baptist WAS ELIJAH'S 2nd coming!** And obviously because of that, as John writes 'Revelation', he is desperately still believing that FALSE prophecy...**And precisely because of those facts, undeniably, it is clearly a GIANT LIE by the church to continue to pretend that Jesus' false prophecy to his disciples of his '2nd coming' is yet to come!!**

165

------ Thursday, Dec 16, 2021 ------

Me (2:07 AM)

I asked u what such a fraudulent prophecy means. If u r honest w yourself, after all this undeniable evidence i have shown u in your own Bible, you r finally beginning to realize those were NOT God's (i.e. Jesus') fraudulent words! **Agn, they were man made concocted lies.** WHAT THAT FRAUDULENT PROPHECY MEANS IS that there is not going to be any Jesus coming down from the sky riding a white horse w his army of fiery sword wielding angels committing Jesus' worldwide 'final solution' slaying and condemning of all 'non Christians'. That is nothing but the man made, PITCH BLACK DARKNESS BIGOTRY u and i were programmed to believe from kindergarten age. **It's the EXACT OPPOSITE** of 'The Light of the world'... **It's the EXACT OPPOSITE** of unconditional love & forgiveness that is the all encompassing nature of what God is. As i shared w u before, we are NOT to be saved by a genocidal savior who will CONDEMN all others. **We are meant to awaken to our COLLECTIVE ONENESS w what 'God' is, and save, heal & ACCEPT one another, AS WE NEED THE SAME FROM THEM!**

------ Friday, Dec 17, 2021 ------

Me (2:03 AM)

Sometimes, when people who have been so fraudulently programmed, when they hear the truth for the first time that in all our diversity, WE ARE ALL PART OF what God is, they mistakenly think such a statement is a sinful ego trip. But that again is because of their false programming to see themselves as horrid & sinful, SEPARATE from what is Holy & Divine. **The truth is the OPPOSITE of an ego trip Mother**. When u begin to awaken to the truth that your nature is NOT sinful, but that you are PART OF WHAT GOD IS, **it is powerfully HUMBLING!** Suddenly, spiritually, things snap into proper focus and u realize everyone in the world is ALSO a diverse part of 'God'. Thats what is humbling, because u realize your responsibility to BE THE LOVE, to be the healing and acceptance that others need, REGARDLESS of their varying diversity and path they are on, JUST THE SAME AS U NEED THAT FROM THEM! **You realize it is a man made bigoted COP OUT to think 'salvation' is an imagined GENOCIDAL 'savior' coming to destroy all 'non believers'.**

------ Saturday, Dec 18, 2021 ------

Me (2:59 AM)

Cont with todays lesson, i want to repeat the last portion of yesterday's msg. That last concise portion succinctly encapsulates 'The Light' of spiritual truth where REAL HEALING begins, as it spotlights the overarching **man made lies of the Bible that have fraudulently programmed u to believe you are evil and bad by nature**. Please take a look again from the msg yest regarding the HUMBLING & HEALING RESPONSIBILITY that is felt, in coming to the true spiritual awareness that you and all humanity are NOT sinful 'by nature', but are ALL an eternally HOLY PART of what God is: "u realize your responsibility to BE THE LOVE, to be the healing and acceptance that others need, REGARDLESS of their varying diversity and path they are on, JUST THE SAME AS U NEED THAT FROM THEM! **You realize it is a man made bigoted COP OUT to think 'salvation' is an imagined GENOCIDAL 'savior' coming to destroy all 'non believers'."** Mother, it is a sick perversion of spiritual truth that portrays such a blood lusting genocidal God.

------ Sunday, Dec 19, 2021 ------

Me (1:53 AM)

In yesterday's lesson i reminded u that it is nothing but a sick perversion of spiritual truth that portrays such a blood lusting genocidal God. The LAST thing the fabricators of JudeoChristianity wanted was to recognize the spiritual truth that all of humanity, in all of its diversity, are and forever will be EQUAL with them! **Thats WHY they force the bigoted belief that they are either the 'CHOSEN ONES' or the 'ONLY SAVED ONES', all others worthy of eternal torture & damnation**, teachings which, as i have shown, we find RAMPANT all through the man made lies of the Bible, first in the Old Test, then cont in the New Test as corrupt, warmongering, empirically obsessed Rome and its dutiful sycophant servants the Roman Catholic church, carefully & diabolically crafted their new state religion of Christianity. And talk about **'u shall know them by their FRUITS'! As i have discussed previously, the FRUITS of JudeoChristianity's MASSIVE, long legacy of imperial warmongering & evil genocide are hypocrisy beyond belief.**

167

------ Monday, Dec 20, 2021 ------

Me (1:28 AM)

Speaking of the early Roman Catholic crafters of 'The New Testament', those of course being the Roman bishops who were ordered by the Roman emperor Constantine to officially craft & put together their condemning, oppressive, guilt & fear dominated version of that **new Roman state religion of Christianity (<u>i.e. the version IN YOUR KING JAMES BIBLE that i have been sourcing in these lessons</u>**) We return now to PAUL, the master con artist & liar who was arguably MORE CHIEF among the material the Roman Bishops used to concoct that new state religion than even the MANY DIFFERENT so called 'words of Jesus', that were violently being fought over by MANY DIFFERENT FACTIONS at the time, all claiming diverse versions of Jesus' teachings. **The Catholic church of course wanted to craft it as condemning to ALL WHO DID NOT ACCEPT IT, mandated by Rome as a prime weapon of control of the masses,** and ALSO strategically to help them divide & finally conquer their long protracted conflict w the Jews, who they recognized as being severely divided by those factions at the time.

------ Tuesday, Dec 21, 2021 ------

Me (2:26 AM)

Continuing w Paul, who as i said, is arguably <u>the CHIEF liar and con artist among all of the New Test,</u> ALL of which accept for about 7 of Paul's letters, are authored by ENTIRELY UNKNOWN writers, **who put the apostles' names on the books AS THOUGH THEY actually wrote them!** So the lies begin w the BOOK TITLES, before we even GET to the CONTENT! Most Christians have NO CLUE of this fact, and they blindly trust w 'child like faith' that Matthew, Mark, Luke, John & Peter all actually wrote the 'Gospel of Matthew', the 'Gospel of Mark', etc. Not only did they NOT write them, and no one knows WHO DID, <u>they were written between 100 to 200 years AFTER THEIR DEATHS!</u> Back to Paul...'SAINT PAUL' as hes fondly revered ESPECIALLY by Catholic priests and bishops...No wonder they hold him in such HIGH honor, what with that MONSTER of a lie he inserted into Christianity for them, that we discussed in Romans chap 7: **"...how to perform that which is good i find not..." 'but its NOT ME who cant stop doing it, its SIN!'**

------ Wednesday, Dec 22, 2021 ------

Me (12:24 AM)

Like so many other glaring hypocrisies all throughout the Bible, Paul talks out of MULTIPLE sides of his mouth, pretending in many passages, like in Romans chap 12, that HE IS ALL ABOUT demanding a holy, moral **'transformation by the renewing of the mind'**, etc. YET, as we have already covered in detail, his passage in Romans chap 7 (one of the most popular passages u will hear preached from the pulpit) Paul tells the reader that **its TOTALLY OK if u are like HIM, and though u KNOW what is good, u cant seem to do it, and though u KNOW what is evil, evil IS what u CONTINUE to do, <u>but he says don't worry, its NOT YOU doing the evil that u know u shouldnt do!</u>** He says Christianity is all u need, because God understands u CANT STOP doing evil, and the blood of a human sacrifice satisfies God, therefore its OK that u keep doing evil like him, even though u know better! **<u>Romans 7, vs 19: "For the good that i would I DO NOT, but the EVIL which i would not, THAT I DO. Now if i do that i would not, it is no more i that do it but SIN..."</u>**

Me (11:51 PM)

Obviously, you can't say 'If i do what I KNOW IS WRONG, it's not really me doing it'. OF COURSE IT WOULD BE YOU DOING IT! No one had a knife to Paul's carotid artery forcing him to do evil that HE ADMITS he knows is evil, <u>after he has supposedly become an APOSTLE of this new 'gospel'</u>! Paul admits that he KNOWS its evil hes routinely CONTINUING to engage in, but says it is a sinful, evil nature that he   forever just cannot help but CONTINUE to engage in. **And it is this specific diabolical MONSTER of a lie from Paul, that is exactly what pedophiles like UNTOLD NUMBERS of Catholic priests use as an excuse and fraudulent 'atonement' for their continuous evil predatory behavior toward children**, not to mention untold numbers of Christians in general who LOVE to hear this monumental horse shit whenever it is preached, so they too can feel like they dont really have to CHANGE. <u>They WANT to believe such a blatant lie that says they can't help the things they r doing that they KNOW r wrong. It is a masterful 'con act'</u>.

------ Thursday, Dec 23, 2021 ------

Me (11:31 PM)

As i have assured u all along in these lessons, the TRUTH is the OPPOSITE! The vast majority of humanity ARE NOT LIVING IN SIN! The vast majority are loving and moral, irrespective of their diverse beliefs about God, **because they are living THE GOLDEN RULE, which has been long ago proven to predate the cultures and writings of JudeoChristianity by MANY THOUSANDS of years!** The writers of the Bible did what we call PROJECTING with the giant 'con' they fabricated as they sought to 'deify' their cultures above others. Based largely on their bigotry and intolerance toward the diversity of other people & cultures they didnt understand, **they 'projected' THEIR evil acts & sinful ignorance onto ALL mankind, but then claimed they had the ONLY 'salvation'**. Hopefully u r beginning to see the fraud i am showing u. Imagine if i came to u and said that i found the ONLY true religion…Yes it has a legacy of genocide and pedophilia, but a human blood sacrifice means when u keep sinning IT ISNT U!

------ Saturday, Dec 25, 2021 ------

Me (1:15 AM)

Cont today's Christmas Eve msg where i left off yest, asking u to **"Imagine if i came to u and said i found the ONLY true religion…Yes it has a legacy of genocide & pedophilia, but a human blood sacrifice means when u keep sinning, IT ISNT U!"** How would u react if u weren't programmed from childhood to MAKE EXCEPTIONS for all of that OBVIOUS EVIL in the name of God?? You'd say "CONNIE, THAT IS A SATANIC CULT!" U would IMMEDIATELY KNOW, once i told u that at its core this religion i joined involved animal and ultimately a HUMAN BLOOD SACRIFICE to satisfy a 'blood lust' to this 'God', **and its writings were RAMPANT w genocide and infanticide and ordaining pedophilia and the rape of young 'virgin' girls** (as i have repeatedly shown u God ordaining in the Bible many times) U would KNOW that it was evil, and u would help me to SEE that. U would show me all the massive hypocrisy of such sick cult like beliefs **that contradict what THE GOLDEN RULE, LOVE & FORGIVENESS are FUNDAMENTALLY about**.

Me (10:46 PM)

Cont from the msg yest... That's precisely what u have needed me to do for YOU, show YOU the monstrous evil and mind blowing lies & hypocrisy of what we both were programmed w from such an early age. And i have carefully and patiently done so over this entire year, not only for u, **but out of my own desperate need for a healed, healthy minded mother**. Now here we r on Christmas Day, one year from when those SAME programmed 'beliefs' of yours caused u to want to HANG UP on your daughter when I tried to call u at Christmastime, simply because I asked u to talk to me about what it was u think u have done in your past that makes u think u r so bad...**Beliefs i have proven the dishonesty of in these lessons over the past year**...Beliefs that u KNOW are assoc w such indescribable denigration toward honest, loving & healthy people like myself, or my gay childhood friend June, just for having the courage to b TRUE to who we are.

------ Sunday, Dec 26, 2021 ------

Me (9:55 PM)

There's a reason i am sending u these 2 special pics now, and it is DIRECTLY on the topic of the evil, man made PITCH BLACK DARKNESS of religious bigotry u have been so fraudulently programmed with, and that i have been steadily helping u to see over this past year. The pic of myself i took today, & the perfectly gorgeous blooming roses i took a few weeks ago when i saw them just off stage at a music venue where i perform. **LOOK AT ME MOTHER. See who i truly am. Now look at that perfect blooming rose. That rose is me, your daughter. It's an exact metaphor**. This is undeniable. Now look closely at the rosebud that has <u>NOT yet bloomed</u> in the pic, and i want u to imagine that some sick person put a tight rubber band around it so it would NEVER b able to bloom! THAT is what i am showing u has been done to u, w the man made Bible based bigotry u are so harmfully embracing at your daughters expense**. I had the courage to SEE those lies, & take the band OFF. I am now helping to take it off of u too.**

------ Tuesday, Dec 28, 2021 ------

Me (12:35 AM)

Agn, u r preferring to embrace OBVIOUS bigotry & condemning lies that u KNOW r at your daughter's expense, **INSTEAD of embracing ME w the unconditional love i extend to u**. I have shown u MANY detailed examples proving the massive undeniable evil, hypocrisy & dishonesty of the Bible & JudeoChristianity, that was fraudulently fabricated by men as they sought to 'deify' their respective cultures and elevate them above others as <u>'The Chosen Ones' or the 'Saved Ones'</u>, with all others deserving destruction & damnation... And also to control the masses under them, **ESPECIALLY OPPRESSING WOMEN.** All this i have shown u many examples of from your own Bible. So if i can see these lies as the OBVIOUS evil man made PERVERSION of Love & The 'TRUE LIGHT' of Divine spiritual truth, **and if i can find the courage to heal myself by taking their imprisoning band off of my mind, i KNOW YOU CAN TOO, <u>especially with my help. I didnt have your help, i just had God's help, my 'Higher Self', showing me those lies.</u>**

------ Wednesday, Dec 29, 2021 ------

Me (12:34 AM)

Mother, apart from the huge denigration and hateful rejection your belief system targets me your daughter with, simply because of my gender change - Apart from that, let me assure u that u dont get to believe whatever bigoted & condemning Bible beliefs u want, to the mass detriment of the diversity of billions and billions of OTHER LOVING PEOPLE, without **A.) My forever holding u accountable** for such sick & harmful beliefs, and **B.) Without YOUR paying a heavy price in this life for deliberately ignoring the healing truth & life example i am showing u,** and for your deliberately choosing to look at your fellow diverse brothers and sisters as evil and 'going to hell' **simply because they r following their DIFFERENT path that was meant for them, as an EQUAL PART of what 'God' is**. A LOT of the suffering u have and are experiencing is NOT because God wants u to prove your faith by 'taking up a CROSS and having others persecute u', etc. **That is yet another GIANT LIE by the crafters of such a sick lie about God! No, your suffering is from such UNHEALTHY THOUGHT.**

------ Thursday, Dec 30, 2021 ------

Me (2:45 AM)

Healing and 'The Light', as i have shown u, **ARE NOT found in 'thoughts' rooted in beliefs that teach that YOU are in a 'saved' preferred status, with ALL OTHERS being 'evil' & 'living in sin'! Those are PITCH BLACK DARKNESS thoughts.** The truth is, as i have shown u, such thoughts are the result of utter man made bigotry & they are the **PINNACLE OF HYPOCRISY** to the healing ALL INCLUSIVE, UNCONDITIONAL love & forgiveness of spiritual truth & 'The Light'. I have been so blessed to have been given the answers & the wisdom about how to bring healing to my life & others, which i steadfastly have prayed for all my life since childhood. **Simply put, EVERYTHING IS THOUGHT!** As such, healing is resisted by many for one MAIN COMMON REASON, which is because healing REQUIRES CORRECTING UNHEALTHY ADDICTIVE thoughts. Accordingly, it requires a willingness to jettison unhealthy thought addictions, and CHANGE to adopt the healthy loving NEVER CONDEMNING thoughts that Love & 'The Light' REQUIRE. **My life is meant to show u this by example**.

------ Friday, Dec 31, 2021 ------

Me (12:52 AM)

I will return shortly w more exposing of the fraud and lies of the Bible, but i want to continue a little more here, in showing u the REAL ANSWERS found when we r willing to let go of such sick, man made destructive & condemning lies about the nature of God. **As i told u, we r ALL A PART of what God is, and what we r fundamentally is THOUGHT. We r all, in ALL our beautiful diversity like the colors of the rainbow, an eternal part of the DIVERSE THOUGHT OF GOD!** That eternal divine thought is what science refers to as 'consciousness'. U and i and everyone are holy aspects of The Divine, and we r meant to BE IN HARMONY here in this physical plane, recognizing our SHARED & DIVERSE HOLY NATURE w one another. The reason these lessons i am bringing u are SO important is because the man made lies and massive fraud of the Bible (and Koran) are the BIGGEST 'THOUGHTS' standing in the way of humanity healing and unifying as we were meant to do! **Thoughts/beliefs at the deliberate EXPENSE of others serve only to BLOCK healing.**

Chapter Twelve

------ Saturday, Jan 1, 2022 ------

Me (3:20 AM)

This special New Year's Day msg will be a 'three parter' over 3 texts...The fraudulent, 'libelous' crafters of the Bible DELIBERATELY perpetrated mass psychosis on those they sought to control, and the Romans & the Roman Catholic church agenda was of course <u>to control and conquer THE WORLD (as has been the agenda of Islam also)</u>. And EACH of what i call the Big Three organized religions forced damaging, condemning, fear and guilt based, fraudulent HARMFUL THOUGHT ADDICTIONS on those in their respective spheres of global control. **It is critical for u to understand Mother, that <u>this is the PITCH BLACK DARKNESS u and the rest of the family are in, and that my life example is meant to help free u from</u>**. As i have shown u, Divine Love & The Light by nature CANNOT HARM and CONDEMN! By nature Divine Love & The Light CANNOT COMMIT INFANTICIDE and GENOCIDE, as I've shown you your own Bible over and over decreeing it to be 'ordained by God' because those infants and people were not 'CHOSEN ONES' or CHRISTIANS! And theres a very simple reason WHY Divine Love and The Light CANNOT EVER harm and condemn...Its because **THEY DONT NEED TO!! <u>Divine Love & The Light can only HEAL & FORGIVE. The sick 'thought' that others deserve ETERNAL HARM is pitch black darkness and 'Holy Libel'</u>.**

Me (5:41 PM)

Theres an intention w these lessons to finally bring healing that is desperately overdue NOT just on the 'MICRO' level for u Mother, but just as importantly on the 'MACRO' level, <u>for ALL our diverse holy sisters & brothers on this planet.</u> Your level of deep-seeded bigotry and condemnation toward the diversity of others in the name of 'God' is so intentionally embraced by u, that u would rather believe those lies to the eternal harm & damnation of others...**You would rather continue to align yourself w those who use them to condemn and denigrate the genuine, honest and loving life of your daughter, than to HEAL & stand by me, and help bring healing to their minds**. I realize that u may take such bigoted beliefs to the grave, and only realize these spiritual truths AFTER u r gone to the 'other side'. **Though you are forgiven, the indescribable pain caused to me from your NEEDLESS sustained life of bigotry, will b left for me to contend with & remember u by...**

Me (6:06 PM)

Also related to the important MACRO healing intention of these lessons in spiritual truth, it is VITAL FOR YOU to understand something Mother: WHATEVER it was that u did earlier in life, that led to you thinking you had to embrace such sick condemning man made false teachings about God in order to be 'SAVED'...**Whatever it was that made u embrace such harmful 'addictive thought patterns' that told you that u r only forgiven IF u believe them, to the mass detriment of others**... WHATEVER it was, whether an abortion, or some other equally painful act u feel responsible for that had to do w either another life, or possibly your having been sexually abused and somehow u feel massive guilt as a result, <u>WHATEVER it was, YOU ARE FORGIVEN</u> **and that forgiveness IS NOT based on such sick adherence to animal & human blood sacrifices, and mass genocide & condemnation of the natural diversity of all others!** THEY ARE FORGIVEN TOO, as they learn THEIR lessons here, which is also part of the 'MACRO' level intention of these lessons **for ALL of our universally holy sisters and brothers**, here on our shared universal family home we call earth.

------ Sunday, Jan 2, 2022 ------

Me (5:22 PM)

In the bigger, MACRO importance that these lessons in REAL spiritual truth and Light bring, it is fundamental to understand that those in positions of power in their respective Jewish, Greco-Roman & Islamic cultures, in their respective bigoted world view, sought to ELEVATE THEMSELVES & THEIR CULTURE as ABOVE ALL OTHERS, 'preferred' by the 'God' **THEY CRAFTED, for that very DIVIDING PURPOSE, which has shamefully and inexcusably cont TO THIS DAY.** My purpose here in detailing such 'HOLY LIBEL' is to awaken and heal not just u Mother, but all of humanity, to this fundamental man made EVIL LIE <u>that is the primary thing preventing humanity from healing by understanding our SHARED, DIVERSE HOLY ONENESS with each other,</u> **all of us BEING THE HANDS OF GOD for each other!** The liars who crafted the OPPOSITE, 'libelous' msg of the Bible & Koran, fraudulently claiming it to be the 'Word of God'(as they sought to dishonestly portray God), did so in order to DELIBERATELY PREVENT the masses from learning that **we all individually are sovereign HOLY ASPECTS OF GOD. They wanted the masses divided, paralyzed in fear & guilt, totally ignorant & under their complete control.**

177

------ Tuesday, Jan 4, 2022 ------

Me (2:48 AM)

These monstrous, needlessly DIVISIVE man made lies, primarily by JudeoChristianity & Islam, are not only the biggest ROOT CAUSE of the majority of genocide, slavery and wars throughout history (while all three ostensibly claimed "THOU SHALT NOT KILL" as such a SACRED commandment) but the sick unnecessary TRIBALISTIC DIVISION in the name of 'God' they have caused **is the FUNDAMENTAL reason why we have thermo nuclear warheads aiming at each other ready to blow up the world.** And what is even MORE dangerous about Christianity & Islam specifically, is they hold the sick belief, as we have seen from Jesus' words i detailed in an earlier lesson**, that such a MASS HOLOCAUST destruction of all 'non Christians' (or 'non Muslims' in Islam's case) is believed by them to be DESERVED and EXPECTED!! The result being that we have the INSANE danger of those false, tribalistic & bigoted 'beliefs' in the name of God being potentially 'SELF FULFILLING' of a nuclear holocaust, to the mass harm and detriment of others.**

Me (10:15 PM)

For a little more clarity on this, what i mean is the damage that was done long ago, i.e. the MASS PSYCHOSIS LIE deliberately perpetrated on most of humanity by the elite power brokers, who fraudulently forced their false teachings in the name of God on most of the world, that we are all 'evil' & 'sinful by nature', and only THEIR belief system provides 'salvation' from deserved genocidal destruction & eternal damnation, **this 'salvation' dependent on animal blood sacrifices (and ultimately in Christianity's case, a human blood sacrifice) all to satisfy such a sick 'blood lust' of this 'God'**...The mass psychosis damage of this massive lie, while not the ONLY reason, but being the PRIMARY reason, has led to such an extreme thermo nuclear, mutually assured destruction threat to ALL of humanity, **all because mankind has deliberately NOT been taught the healing truth about our TRUE SPIRITUAL NATURE.** The good news is, a growing number of us are teaching it, so this world healing knowledge of our Divine Oneness is beginning to dawn in the minds of more and more of humanity every day!

178

------ Wednesday, Jan 5, 2022 ------

Me (9:53 PM)

Humanity is LONG OVERDUE to awaken from those needlessly dividing man made religious lies...If we had NOT been so deliberately and falsely programmed for thousands of years **by such 'organized religious bigotry' in the name of God**, we SURELY WOULD have awakened to these uniting healing truths before now, and such hateful divisive tribalism would NOT have grown and led to such an insane, **extreme nuclear threat** to all of our holy sisters & brothers on this our sacred & shared home together. This agn underlines what i showed u in a previous lesson, that being how one of the fundamental lies of JudeoChristianity (& Islam too) is that our only 'hope' or 'salvation' CANNOT come from each other, **but must come from an imagined future 'messiah', or a 'savior'** riding down on a white unicorn in the clouds...I know, its a white horse, not a unicorn. But let me ask u, <u>if the writers of the Bible had said it was a white unicorn, would THAT have been enough for u to see the harmful fairy tales for what they are?</u>

------ Thursday, Jan 6, 2022 ------

Me (9:33 PM)

Like i have stressed to u before, if u just simply held obvious harmless fairy tale ideas about God that WEREN'T CONDEMNING TO EVERYONE ELSE who thought of the Divine in their own harmless ways, i wouldn't have to go to this extent to hold u accountable for such bigotry. **But your fraudulent bigoted monstrous, nightmare fairy tales about God have caused more evil, hypocritical mass genocide and harm, OFTEN as i have shown here from your own Bible**, targeting INNOCENT CHILDREN, INNOCENT VIRGIN LITTLE GIRLS, w God allegedly telling the Jewish men to kill all the boys, but take the virgin girls for themselves! **And u think thats 'The Light'?? ENOUGH with such false teachings about God!!** ENOUGH w teaching such horse shit to children, that they are evil by nature WHEN THE TRUTH IS THEY ARE PRECIOUS & HOLY BY NATURE!! **<u>Enough w holding on to such OBVIOUS harmful addictive thought patterns standing in the way of humanity's healing by awakening to the realization that WE CAN & MUST SAVE EACH OTHER!</u>**

------ Saturday, Jan 8, 2022 ------

Me (3:11 AM)

These carefully crafted lies i am showing u are what have blocked yours, & much of humanity's spiritual growth, with as i said, <u>one of the biggest of those lies being that only those of ONE belief can b 'saved', and</u>

179

ONLY by an external 'messiah' who then must kill & condemn ALL others by committing mass genocide YET AGAIN, **like he already has done w the 'flood' in Genesis**, and w all of the other many examples i have shown u from your own Bible, of God ordering the mass genocide of 'non Jews' or the mass infanticide of Egyptian innocent children, on and on w such PITCH BLACK EVIL DARKNESS, **of course all portrayed as 'HOLY' by the bigoted men who wrote such lies in the name of God.** As i have stressed to u in prior lessons, it is the obvious unnecessary weaponizing of these beliefs that expose their massive fraud, and their being the HYPOCRITICAL OPPOSITE of divine spiritual truth and 'The Light', **which DOESNT NEED TO HARM AND COMMIT MASS GENOCIDE! 'The Light' only heals & forgives, UNCONDITIONALLY**.

------ Sunday, Jan 9, 2022 ------
Me (2:12 AM)
These destructive lies have denied u the proper understanding of the healing, REAL TRANSFORMATIVE power of awakening to realize that not just you, but ALL of humanity are HOLY ASPECTS of the Divine, <u>and as such, are always forgiven, never condemned</u>. **And we r meant to BE THE LOVE & ACCEPTANCE that others need who r different, just like we need it from them, without condemnation!** THAT is what LOVE is! U were meant to understand that we SAVE EACH OTHER w unconditional love, and by recognizing this SHARED HOLY NATURE in everyone, **with no one 'saved' or 'chosen' or 'preferred' over others!** I shared w u the wisdom i was given, that healing comes from correcting unhealthy addictive THOUGHT PATTERNS, especially thought patterns that are rooted in 'beliefs' that are entirely at the EXPENSE & condemnation of your other holy sisters & brothers of DIVERSE ideas about how to conceive of 'God'. **I need u to at last wake up Mother, and help me bring this Light & healing to so many who need it. <u>We save each other, not sick 'BLOOD' from a 'human sacrifice'</u>.**

------ Monday, Jan 10, 2022 ------
Me (2:02 AM)
Now let's resume exposing these evil lies that couldn't b more OPPOSITE of 'the Light' of spiritual truth, by returning to the 'LIAR IN CHIEF'. Remember in prior lessons i detailed the UNDENIABLE fraud of Paul's so called 'conversion', as i compared & contrasted his hypocritical call to transformation, virtue & holy living in Romans 12, vs 1**, contrasted w his hugely popular passage pastors LOVE to preach,**

due to its fantastic recruiting appeal for new converts, where Paul tells everyone the EXACT OPPOSITE is the case! That there is NO 'good' in us, and truth b told, even as Christians we CANT HELP but to keep doing evil! I showed u this shameful monstrous lie in your own Bible, in Romans chap 7, vs 17-20. I showed u how Paul tells the 'believer' that we cant help but continue to do evil, but then the 'Liar in Chief' says GOOD NEWS! Because all you have to do is 'believe' HIS GOSPEL, which decrees that **it really ISNT YOU anymore, doing those evil things u cant stop doing!** Cliff hanger: What if i told u Paul even openly ADMITTED LYING in not one but TWO places in the New Test?

------ Tuesday, Jan 11, 2022 ------
Me (1:46 AM)
Not that we should NEED his open admission of lying in what he calls 'HIS GOSPEL', as we can see the blatant dishonesty on its face as i have shown u. But let's look at a few more examples before i show that to u. Turn pls to Acts 10:34, which is actually a lie from Peter, but it LEADS TO MORE blatant lies from 'Saint Paul'. Practically EVERYTHING i have shown u is rooted in man made bigotry, otherwise defined simply as being a 'RESPECTER OF PERSONS'. Yet in Acts 10:34 Peter tries to decree that God is nothing of the sort, saying "...of a truth i perceive that God is NO respecter of persons." Well, as i have documented for u here over & over, **that's a WHOPPER of a lie, not a 'truth' by any stretch!** Turn pls to Deut chap 7, vs 6 where God is supposedly being quoted speaking to the Jews: "...**the Lord thy God hath CHOSEN thee to be a SPECIAL people unto himself, ABOVE ALL PEOPLE THAT ARE UPON THE FACE OF THE EARTH".** We'll see Paul's lies on this tomorrow.

------ Wednesday, Jan 12, 2022 ------
Me (1:45 AM)
I have diligently 'studied to show myself approved unto God, someone who need not be ashamed, RIGHTLY DIVIDING the word of truth.' That's what i have done here for u w these detailed lessons every day over the past year. **My life is dedicated ONLY to rightly dividing spiritual truth from man made religious lies.** Of course for some readers who may not b familiar, that passage i put in quotes comes from 2nd Timothy chap 2, vs 15. **The 2 books of Timothy r of course among those attrib to our Liar in Chief, 'Saint Paul'.** We r going to look at his lies related to Peter's lie that 'God is NO respecter of persons', but first, since it's close to 2nd Tim 2 vs 15, lets catch another of his lies in

vs 19: "...Let EVERYONE that nameth the name of Christ DEPART FROM INIQUITY". **Hmmm, gee whiz, that doesn't quite sound like what we read from ole 'Saint' Paul in Romans chap 7, now does it Mother?? What was it agn, 'For the good i would i do not, but the evil i would not, that i do. But its no more me, but SIN in me'**

Me (10:12 PM)
Does that sound like Paul had 'departed from iniquity'?? OBVIOUSLY NO. **It undeniably shows the contrary!** And it is the PINNACLE OF LIES & HYPOCRISY regarding spiritual truth! Paul's writings r constantly making LIP SERVICE references to condemning evil and 'departing iniquity', all the while accusing ALL OTHERS who believe in many diverse ways other than 'HIS GOSPEL' as being the 'evil doers', even declaring to young Timothy in 2nd Tim chap 3 that he will recognize the 'last days' **when he sees many engaging willfully in evil behavior while having what?? Vs 5: "Having a form of godliness".** And THAT is exactly what PAUL is doing! He's openly admitting his ONGOING evil behavior he knows is evil, but claiming he CANT HELP BUT KEEP DOING! And if that's not dishonest enough, then he absurdly proclaims **how 'HIS GOSPEL' decrees that 'ITS NOT ME'! I am no longer held responsible due to 'my gospel' or 'form of godliness' that i am claiming makes it ALL OK! Thats what honest holy people in The Light call horse shit.**

------ Thursday, Jan 13, 2022 ------
Me (11:07 PM)
'The Light' of real spiritual truth **NEVER** displays such hypocrisy. But let's use that as an example. Imagine if, in these lessons on spiritual truth i have been bringing u, and after all the lies of the Bible i have been showing u...Imagine if i made the assertion Paul made! Imagine if i suddenly claimed that 'The Light' i am showing u allows us to KEEP DOING EVIL **though we know better, but can't help ourselves**, and 'The Light' says that's OK, because it's NOT YOU, it's 'sin' in u that u can't help but engage in. **You would KNOW such a claim was a FRAUD! But u ignore that very same obvious fraud in the Bible??** Now, regarding Peter's absurd lie that God is no respecter of persons, lets chk out 1st Tim chap 2, vs 11:"Let the woman learn in silence with all subjection. But i suffer not a woman to teach, nor to usurp authority over the man, but to be in SILENCE." This is the epitome of male bigotry **and all about a belief rooted in being a respecter of persons not just of Jewish ethnicity, or Christian belief, but gender.**

------ Saturday, Jan 15, 2022 ------

Me (12:38 AM)

Then in vs 13 & 14 Paul shamefully & dishonestly tries to claim that women are to be subservient to men <u>because the man was made by God FIRST</u>. Mother, by now, this man made bigotry i am showing u HAS to b sinking in! All of this is nothing but male 'patriarchal' bigotry pretending to b 'the word of God', all because **the men who crafted these lies had as one of their FUNDAMENTAL objectives, women from childhood being taught that they are inferior to men**. In vs 14 Paul shamefully lies agn trying pitifully to cast Eve as the 'only transgressor', being the only one 'deceived'. This is a GIANT lie. Like i showed u, that Genesis 'Garden fable' <u>actually says ADAM WAS WITH EVE</u> at the time of their being preyed upon by 'Satan', not elsewhere, w Eve being alone, and then seeking him out as the 'weak evil seductress', as Paul **(ADMITTEDLY a continuing evildoer AFTER his so called road to Damascus 'conversion', claiming he can't help it)** would have the reader to believe! So they were BOTH deceived in their childlike innocence, not because Eve's being female made her inferior.

------ Sunday, Jan 16, 2022 ------

Me (2:25 AM)

As i repeatedly showed u in those early lessons on the fundamental lies the Bible begins w in that Garden of Eden fable, OF COURSE BOTH Adam & Eve would b deceived, in their complete CHILDLIKE INNOCENCE, <u>not having the knowledge of what 'sin' was</u>, until God ALLOWS Satan, a master predator & deceiver, **to prey upon their total innocence!** This on its face shows how that Bible story of their 'choosing to sin' and betray God is completely unfounded. I showed u how the story says that it was EVE who told Satan they had NO intention of eating from the tree as instructed by God. **So left to their own volition, without being deceived in their innocence, it was SHE, not Adam, who told 'Satan' in the story that they were not going to eat from the tree!** It wasnt until God ALLOWS them to b preyed upon in that innocent state, not even knowing what 'sin' was, that OF COURSE both of them would b easily deceived like any childlike minds would! It wasnt because Eve was weak-minded, inferior and by nature a seductress as The Vatican, Judaism, Islam and their respective church/synagogue doctrines have sought to falsely characterize the fable. **These r <u>shameful, patriarchal bigoted lies by JudeoChristianity and Islam at women's expense.</u>**

183

------ Monday, Jan 17, 2022 ------

.Me (2:00 AM)

Lets look at another of Paul's writings in Galatians that completely contradicts his 'decree' that women are inferior to men and must remain silent in the church, etc. Turn pls to Galatians chap 3, vs 28: "There is neither Jew nor Greek, there is neither bond nor free, **there is NEITHER MALE NOR FEMALE,** for ye are all ONE in Christ Jesus." So HERE Paul is stating that in God's eyes there is NO superiority of the male gender, but that BOTH genders are EQUAL AS ONE! Hmmm, yet more talking out of TWO sides of his mouth! But as i have told u before, **the oneness and EQUAL BALANCE of male & female IS what 'God' is.** The teaching that God is a 'MALE ENTITY' who created an inferior 'female' gender as an afterthought to 'serve' his primary male creation, **is on its face OBVIOUSLY MALE BIGOTRY, and sick denigration & oppression of women, who are AN EQUAL HOLY ASPECT of what God is.** Well then, can we also take from "there is neither bond nor free", that Paul is at least condemning the evil of slavery??

------ Tuesday, Jan 18, 2022 ------

Me (2:00 AM)

Cont where i left off, asking if we can take from his phrase "there is neither bond nor free", that Paul is at least condemning the evil of slavery?? What if i told u that not only is the answer a giant 'NO', but that Paul actually PRAISES Christian slave owners, as being WORTHY OF ALL HONOR?? What if i told u not only that, but Paul commands ALL slaves to HONOR their masters **or be guilty of BLASHEMING the name and 'doctrine' of God??** See, the thing is, MOST people who call themselves 'Christians' have ZERO knowledge of the Bible's content...its massive evil, genocide, infanticide, denigration of women, routine endorsement of SLAVERY, condemnation of all other beliefs, etc, that i have steadfastly taken the past year to detail here. WHY? **Because they don't actually READ the Bible!** But, when actually SHOWN such evil in black & white, they recoil in disgust & horror AS THEY SHOULD! They then make it clear that they didnt know that was in the Bible, and it certainly is NOT what they believe.

------ Wednesday, Jan 19, 2022 ------

Me (12:58 AM)

I haven't forgotten to show u where Paul actually ADMITS lying in presenting his 'gospel', and i will show that to u soon. But like i have said, with all these blatant examples of lies in the name of God i am showing u, why would we even need Paul's rare 'honest admission' to his

184

horse shit?? We will need that BIG WHEEL BARROW & SHOVEL for these next lies, as i show u Paul's decree to **HONOR the institution of slavery or be guilty of BLASPHEMING GOD! Turn pls to 1st Timothy chap 6, vs 1.** First, understand that it is a fact that the word 'servants' here means 'slaves'. Bible scholars agree the word comes from the Latin word 'servus', translated as 'servant', and truly meaning 'slave'. **Chap 6, vs 1 reads "Let as many servants as are under the yoke count their own masters worthy of all honor, THAT THE NAME OF GOD and his DOCTRINE be not blasphemed." In Ephesians chap 6, <u>Paul calls for slaves to honor the slave owner as they would honor CHRIST! Mother, this is PITCH BLACK DARKNESS, not The Light.</u>**

------ Thursday, Jan 20, 2022 ------
Me (2:48 AM)
As i have been giving u these lessons in spiritual truth, imagine if i suddenly stated that spiritual truth **requires that those who r slaves must HONOR their slave owners or b guilty of blaspheming God.** You would immediately KNOW that my words were FRAUDULENT and rooted in bigotry. But yet, like many other such examples i have detailed, u accept it as 'HOLY' when u see such sick shameful, evil words in your own Bible. <u>It is time for u to step away from all of these Bible lies by men</u>. There is NOTHING 'holy', **NOTHING about 'The Light'** in ALL of these evil diabolical examples i have shown u from your own Bible! As i am trying to teach u, they have been and cont to b what has been preventing humanity from understanding our SHARED DIVINE ONENESS, <u>and preventing us from HEALING EACH OTHER</u> and our shared home here on earth. **<u>OBVIOUSLY 'The Light' always condemns ANY form of human slavery! The TRUE 'blasphemy' is to read that from Paul, and readily WANT to believe it to be the holy words of God!!</u>**

------ Friday, Jan 21, 2022 ------
Me (2:31 AM)
The man made hypocrisy is beyond belief! Paul wants to b seen writing many passages like Ephesians 4:23-24 (much the same as what i showed u in Romans 12:1) saying "And be renewed in the spirit of your mind, and that ye <u>put on the NEW MAN</u>, which after God is created in <u>RIGHTEOUSNESS and TRUE HOLINESS</u>". Then in at least THREE other of his books incl Ephesians, Colossians and 1st Tim chap 6 he declares that anyone, **especially any slave** who does not HONOR the Christian slave owner **is guilty of BLASPHEMING the holy name and**

doctrine of God! Thats the result of being 'renewed in righteousness and true holiness'?? **NO. Thats PITCH BLACK DARKNESS!** But its no surprise after what i showed u in Romans chap 6, of Paul's own ADMISSION that he has of course NOT been 'renewed' from committing evil after his previous claim of 'life transformation' on the road to Damascus, telling the reader that he (and they too**) just CANT HELP but keep doing what they KNOW is evil...But it ISNT THEM DOING IT anymore!**

------ Saturday, Jan 22, 2022 ------
Me (1:43 AM)
But Paul not only defends the massive wealth generating institutions of slavery growing in practice exponentially at the time by the Greco-Roman empire, he actually goes the EXTRA 'EVIL MILE' and demands HONOR of the slave owners, telling slaves they are to obey & honor their slave masters AS THOUGH THEIR MASTERS WERE JESUS, **and decrees that anyone doing the contrary is guilty of blaspheming the holy name and 'doctrine' of God!** (And 'by their fruits ye shall know them' eh?) How many Southern Baptists do u suppose often quoted these very verses by Paul, the LIAR IN CHIEF of the New Testament, as they waged one of our nations BLOODIEST wars, **primarily for the purpose of PRESERVING their states' right to continue this HOLY, GODLY institution and 'ministry' of slavery??** This is just another in a long list of undeniable 'GAME OVER' examples i have shown u from your own Bible, that clearly reveals massive man made fraud as being the REPEATING FUNDAMENTAL UNDERPINNING of the entire Bible.

------ Sunday, Jan 23, 2022 ------
Me (2:47 AM)
Cont where i left off yest regarding the man made lies and fraud that r undeniably the fundamental underpinning of the entire Bible...As i have said, at this point it should come as no surprise when i show u not one, **but TWO** places where Paul finally confesses to the reader that he has LIED in preaching 'HIS gospel' (as he often likes to refer to it) Turn pls to 2nd Corinthians chap 12. First lets look at vs 11 where Paul wants to berate the Corinthians for not honoring him as he boasts to them that he is not just an apostle, **but the CHIEFEST of apostles!** "I am become a fool in GLORYING. Ye have compelled me (meaning YOU made me do it) for i ought to have been commended of u: for in nothing am i behind the very CHIEFEST of apostles." A few verses later in verse 16, this self proclaimed CHIEF APOSTLE then confesses how he has 'caught them

with GUILE'. **Verse 16 reads "But be it so i did not burden u: NEVERTHELESS, BEING CRAFTY, I CAUGHT YOU WITH GUILE." Obviously, 'guile' is NOT 'gospel'**

------ Monday, Jan 24, 2022 ------
Me (2:03 AM)
We know the word 'guile' generally means fraud, deception, corruption, dishonesty, evil and the like. But just to b extra resourceful for this 'Ultimate Deprogramming Guide to the Lies & Fraud of the Bible', lets cite a couple of trusted dictionary sources. Merriam Webster defines 'guile' as **"deceitful cunning"** and also uses the synonym **"duplicity"**. Isn't that interesting, after i have made note multiple times in the lies i have shown u from Paul's writings, how OBVIOUSLY hypocritically dishonest he was being **by so often talking out of two sides of his mouth?** His agenda each time was to make allowances for blatant, undeniable evil & bigotry, or his own ADMITTED ongoing evil behavior, all in the name of 'his gospel'. So I'd say that's a good call by Merriam Webster to include 'duplicity' as a dishonest element of 'guile'. The Cambridge Advanced Learners Dictionary captures the essence of 'guile' saying its **"the practice of DECEIVING people or using other dishonest methods to achieve your aims."**

------ Tuesday, Jan 25, 2022 ------
Me (11:16 PM)
Let me say that agn...'The Light', the TRUTH of God, that which is Divine spiritual truth, is NEVER taught or 'glorified' by lies and 'guile'. It never hypocritically says "We are transformed" and "born again" at one moment, but then in another moment, **"We all STILL can't help but KEEP doing evil, because we r so full of sin, but WE are not responsible anymore for it, IT ISNT REALLY US continuing to do what we know is bad/sinful/evil". That which is TRULY the Divine Light doesnt ENDORSE the institution of the slave trade!!** That would OBVIOUSLY b man made bigotry seeking to establish such evil with the fraudulent claim that it is not only SANCTIONED by God, but SO ORDAINED by God that it is BLASPHEMING His 'doctrine' for slaves not to 'honor' their slave owners **AS THEY WOULD HONOR JESUS!** Just that example i have shown u right there all by itself is enough to see the overall man made fraud masquerading as the 'holy gospel' of God. The Truth & Love of 'The Light' ALWAYS exposes bigotry in ALL forms.

------ Wednesday, Jan 26, 2022 ------
Me (10:26 PM)
Now that i have shown u the overwhelming number of lies, fraud and undeniable evil all throughout the Bible, fictitiously portrayed by bigoted men as being the 'Holy Word of God', **you have a RESPONSIBILITY to now step away from it Mother**, just as i have, in the name of TRUE DIVINE HOLINESS that these bigoted man made lies have DELIBERATELY HIDDEN from humanity for thousands of years. Its just like a highly addictive drug, and then someone shows u the facts of how it is toxic & harmful, **and u realize u have to enter rehab and separate from that destructive addiction thats been BLOCKING healing in your life**. But those who WANT to b addicted & embrace these horribly bigoted and condemning thought patterns r WORSE than someone who's just addicted to some chemical drug. A chemical drug addiction mostly harms the user (though it often hurts family & friends too). **But these false bigoted 'beliefs' are at the expense of the GENUINE holy diversity of ALL OTHERS, condemning their genuine diversity.**

------ Thursday, Jan 27, 2022 ------
Me (11:44 PM)
Deep down i know that u DO know what i mean when i refer to '<u>genuine</u>' <u>diversity</u>. It's the genuine, NATURALLY diverse personalities, cultures, sexual identities and orientations, concepts of conceiving of things spiritual, of ALL of our naturally diverse & Divine brothers & sisters. **When u are truly walking in The Light, u recognize humanity's genuine 'differences' as PART OF the HOLY diversity of what 'God' is.** U recognize my hands, the hands of my childhood gay friend June, the hands of a Hindu, the hands of a Buddhist, even of an atheist who is yet to grow to their understanding of 'God', on and on, as ALL being the beautifully diverse and blossoming HANDS OF GOD, SAVING & HEALING ONE ANOTHER, here in this physical dimension. **But when one is walking in PITCH BLACK DARKNESS, they have been conditioned & programmed w condemning, superstitious 'delusions' to see ONLY THEMSELVES as 'saved' by their man made false concept of 'God'**. That bigotry is NOT God's Love. The Light cannot 'condemn'.

------ Friday, Jan 28, 2022 ------
Me (11:57 PM)
As i have explained before, **The Light doesn't need to 'eternally harm' others with 'vengeance' and 'condemnation'. Those concepts r from**

the evil men who created a God in THEIR BIGOTED IMAGE, not the other way around! They in their bigotry, they in their desire to denigrate and subjugate women and **treat them as property**, they in their desire to **DEIFY & elevate their race and culture ABOVE all others**, they in their evil designs of enslaving other races, **primarily black/African people**, they in their desire to commit genocide after genocide of other cultures they hated and/or just wanted the real estate those other cultures lived on, they in their claim that God told them to **kill all the boys, but take the virgin girls for themselves as plunders/spoils of war**, THEY in all of that evil WERE NOT created to think that way in God's image! What i have been showing u, that has caused so much needless division and war for humanity, **is that THEY created a fraudulent God in THEIR bigoted image**.

------ Saturday, Jan 29, 2022 ------
Me (11:47 PM)
The brief list i just gave of but a few of many more sick examples from the Bible of hateful bigotry & advocating for slavery, of genocide and CHILD VIRGIN RAPE, etc, are all examples of **MONUMENTAL EVIL** that is at the root of the same behavior that has continued for thousands of years to the present from JudeoChristianity. And the important thing to remember is YOU CANT SAY 'well that was from mans sinful nature', because THE ENTIRE POINT of all of these lessons, and all these 'scriptures' i have repeatedly shown u in careful detail from your own Bible, of hate, bigotry and evil genocide and infanticide, **ARE ALL DESCRIBED AS BEING CALLED FOR & ORDAINED BY GOD!!** SO NO NO NO, you can't have it BOTH ways, and call such undeniably sick & evil behavior 'SINFUL NATURE' when OTHER beliefs or cultures engage in it, but out of the other side of your mouth call it 'GODS HOLY PLAN' when those liars who wrote the Bible try to portray God CALLING FOR IT! **Thats them 'concocting' a bigoted God in THEIR IMAGE.**

------ Monday, Jan 31, 2022 ------
Me (3:21 AM)
The deep harmful psychological effects of these Bible lies about such a condemning vengeful God become SO addicting that as i said, it's equivalent to a powerful drug addiction. The 'drug' is the programmed 'belief' that SO OFTEN, **as with u and me, began being 'dosed' into our highly impressionable brains not long after we learned to talk...as early as preschool age!** The desire to 'BELIEVE' for many reasons: Not wanting to b CONDEMNED for imagining God in the

189

'wrong way', & not wanting to disappoint your family u look up to, & **wanting to 'believe' that a 'savior' is going to come down on a cloud & FIX EVERYTHING,** riding a white horse w millions of angels to destroy all NON 'believers', and u think u MUST 'believe' A.) because u have been paralyzed w fear that otherwise, u could b one of those 'sent to hell' for NOT 'believing' correctly, and B.) u desperately WANT to b given the 'mansion' in heaven on the 'golden paved streets'. **And the 'drug' LIES & says it's your only 'salvation'.**

Me (10:24 PM)
That man made lie, programming u to think such nightmarish beliefs are your only 'salvation', **is what has BLOCKED humanity from healing!** That man made lie about 'God' is what has thus far KEPT humanity from realizing that **WE are our ONLY SALVATION,** when we awaken from such horribly bigoted, dividing and condemning beliefs toward others, and finally learn to see our beautifully diverse brothers & sisters as EQUAL HOLY PARTS of 'God', just as we need them to understand about us! That is where our only 'salvation' comes from Mother, not in looking at those who 'believe' differently, or have a different sexual orientation, as being condemned!! U only BLOCK the healing & salvation u need when u dogmatically hold on to beliefs that eagerly await a 'savior' coming down to kill and damn everyone to eternal torment because they didn't feel right about holding such condemning beliefs toward u & others! **You have a responsibility now to step away from such harmful beliefs, and help me bring healing.**

Chapter Thirteen

------ Tuesday, Feb 1, 2022 ------
Me (7:45 PM)
To further illuminate this point, i am going to share a real world example that just happened today. It will likely take 2 or 3 texts to cover it...I am currently networking and promoting my live music show in Las Vegas this week, making connections w booking agents and live music venues. While starting my day at Starbucks, **a VERY injured, extremely emaciated homeless young woman came hobbling out of the bathroom,** w an apparent broken foot that she was trying to force walking on, but couldnt put weight on it. She hobbled painfully to a table w a glass of complimentary water from the barista. **She was very weak & slumping over in her chair, and i went over to inquire about her health.** She had a black eye, scabs and cuts, and was beyond 'thin as a rail', likely from a major drug addiction. I confirmed later w the police that she is apparently a prostitute. Anyone w any experience at all w such health challenged homeless prostitutes knows they usually are preyed upon quickly and die soon...

Me (8:04 PM)
Her name is Ashley. I asked her if she had been beaten up, and she said yes. She let me get her some oatmeal to eat. I could see from how swollen and both red & purple her ankle and foot was, that it was a **severe injury**. I told her she cant keep trying to walk on it. I told her i thought it was broken, and she immediately replied **'I think it IS broken'**. I explained to her that she had to get emergency treatment right away. I ended up having to call 911 for police and paramedics to respond to hopefully intervene & get her the medical attn she desperately needed, but was unreasonably resisting, not exercising proper judgment for herself. The police & paramedics came, **but refused to intervene** & told me it was because she told them she refused their help. That is of course, patently absurd, and shameful to witness. One of the officers was a young woman of similar age to Ashley. I explained that Ashley was in an obvious exigent emergency health crisis situation, not using proper judgment...

Me (8:25 PM)
But the Las Vegas P.D. officers did not exercise proper judgment on Ashley's behalf, & the paramedics didnt even wrap up her foot w a bandage! They just left her there, not even checking her vitals/blood

pressure etc, for possible internal injuries from being so beaten up. The police stood & watched her, w not one but THREE personal bags on her shoulder, hobbling away down the sidewalk into another cold winter Las Vegas night. I had been trying to reach local homeless advocates for over half an hour, and no services would answer the phone. **QUESTION: Where is Ashley's ONLY SALVATION Mother?** This is precisely what i have been trying to teach u. Ashley is not a 'condemned sinner' who's "going to Hell" for being a drug addicted prostitute. **Shes in desperate need of salvation from US, FROM THOSE PARAMEDICS & COPS who let her down & left her in such dire straits**. It isnt that Ashley must be 'saved' by 'believing' one way about 'God', but she needs to awaken to the healing truth that she is a HOLY part of God, **and OUR HANDS 'save' her!**

------ Thursday, Feb 3, 2022 ------
Me (1:10 AM)
What is imperative to understand about this real world example, is that Ashley is not only a HOLY PART OF GOD, even in her current addictive state, harming herself on the streets of Vegas, <u>but she is an eternal PART OF YOU AND ME!</u> Those who have been programmed w their own JUST AS HARMFUL addiction of believing that THEY r 'saved' and all others living like Ashley r NOT saved, but r condemned by God, **they have been conditioned to look at someone like Ashley as SEPARATE from them, & SEPARATE from what God is. As a result, healing is BLOCKED**. Ashley is engaging in self harm, but to her credit, <u>at least she isnt holding such harmful condemning beliefs toward others</u>! I use Ashley's example to show the synonymous nature of 'harmful addictive thinking' and 'unhealthy thought patterns' that for YOU have become JUST LIKE the heroin or meth addiction that is at the root of why Ashley refused to receive the healing she needed yesterday. **Healing comes when such harmful addictive thoughts finally STOP.**

Me (4:26 PM)
Listen closely, because this is SO important. Ashley & ALL of us r simply on our own timeline, path & schedule <u>to learn the life lessons we need to learn, and LEARN THEM WE WILL in time, the sooner the better for being able to properly effect healing in others lives, not just ours</u>. A FUNDAMENTAL key to this truth, as i keep reminding u, is that those healing, CORRECTIVE lessons will b learned & taught by 'The Light' we r ALL a part of by nature, **WITHOUT THE NEED FOR CONDEMNATION OR 'ETERNAL TORTURE & DAMNATION'**, etc, as the man made lies of Christianity blind u with such dogmatic

superstitious, bigoted fear. And due to such blinding, harmful thought addictions & chemical addictions that many refuse or are slow to let go of, much harm and negative consequences and blocking of healing continues, **UNTIL WE LEARN TO LET THOSE UNHEALTHY ADDICTIVE THOUGHTS GO! Until we wake up to the wisdom that u, me, Ashley and EVERYONE are EQUAL & HOLY ASPECTS OF 'GOD', <u>here to BE the hands of God for each other</u>.**

------ Friday, Feb 4, 2022 ------

Me (5:35 PM)

But, we r NOT the loving hands of God <u>when we eagerly embrace 'weaponized' condemning beliefs in the name of God toward our fellow Divine sisters & brothers</u>, simply because they believe differently, and are DIVERSE from us in all kinds of genuine ways, **just like the natural blending of the diverse colors of the rainbow!** This is fundamentally how u can KNOW u r in utter PITCH BLACK DARKNESS Mother: It's when u hold ANY sort of 'belief' that looks at your fellow genuinely diverse sisters & brothers as deserving of eternal torture and 'damnation' by 'God' because of their diverse but GENUINE identities & beliefs...**Just because they r happily and genuinely thriving from being TRUE TO WHO THEY ARE! You r in PITCH BLACK DARKNESS as long as u refuse to recognize humanity as EQUAL HOLY PARTS of what God is here in this physical dimension.** Humanity is OVERDUE to awaken to that healing wisdom that the Big Three bigoted, divisive, tribal organized religions have intentionally BLOCKED from much of humanity for too long!

------ Saturday, Feb 5, 2022 ------

Me (5:30 PM)

As i have detailed before, those barbaric, superstitious animal and human 'blood sacrifice' tribal, man made beliefs **A.)were NOT ORIGINAL**, but copied, counterfeited & modified FROM the original & much more ancient loving, all inclusive, NON weaponized metaphors and myths that were NEVER INTENDED to b 'literalized' and weaponized as the Jews, Christians & Muslims did, using their respective tribal bigotry to 'bastardize' those myths they learned from the ancient wisdom & ORIGIN OF ALL CIVILIZATION, that being Kemet (later named Egypt by Greek conquerors) and **B.) were intentionally crafted to b a call to divisiveness and race superiority, fraudulently in the name of 'God' ('HOLY LIBEL')** and to control the masses of their respective cultures w intense misplaced GUILT & FEAR, twisting those myths **that were intended to TEACH u of your powerful TRUE HOLY**

193

NATURE as an eternal PART OF GOD, <u>and instead deliberately</u> <u>HIDING that truth from the masses, teaching them the 'Holy Libel'</u> <u>lie that they r evil and condemned by nature.</u>

------ Sunday, Feb 6, 2022 ------
Me (5:48 PM)
And what i have been carefully detailing for u over & over **in your own KJV (King James Version) Bible,** & reminding u of the subsequent mass genocidal, warmongering, bigotry & slavery intensive LEGACY of those 'bastardized' man made lies of JudeoChristianity, that have been the overarching fundamental HALLMARK of the so called <u>'MANIFEST DESTINY' HORSE SH#T used by the JudeoChristian Roman, British &</u> <u>other Western imperial conquerors and 'settlers' of The Americas</u>...In spotlighting these things from your Bible, I am simply **trying to get u to THINK instead of just blindly REFUSING to do so**, and instead of thinking, just 'believing' such horribly harmful, bigoted & condemning false images of God, designed by those whose entire purpose was to program those weaponized lies about God in the minds of their cultures & those they sought to control, by LEVERAGING those bigoted, divisive 'beliefs', **<u>as a RALLYING CRY to wage genocidal, slavery</u> <u>intensive 'Crusades' and world imperialism, fraudulently claiming</u> <u>such horrors in the name of God were 'HOLY DESTINY'! On the</u> <u>contrary, it's all 'HOLY LIBEL!'</u>**

------ Monday, Feb 7, 2022 ------
Me (6:11 PM)
One more note and comparison i meant to mention already about my example of Ashley earlier: The common denominator between Ashley & you Mother, is **BOTH of u have been at least MENTALLY, if not physically/sexually abused** (sexual abuse a virtual certainty in Ashley's case).The ROOT EFFECT of that abuse, whether just mental or both, is the traumatic harm that **BLINDS u to your true HOLY, SINLESS, INNOCENT identity & mind, & that traumatizes u and paralyzes u with UNECESSARY GUILT**, the result of that traumatizing religious and/or just sexual abuse being, u then FALSELY see yourself OPPOSITE from the TRUE, UNCHANGEABLE, PERFECT & HOLY PART OF GOD that u are by nature! <u>U then are programmed to believe</u> <u>that u DESERVE 'condemnation'</u>, as taught to u by those man-made Bible lies. In the coming lessons of this definitive guide to the lies and fraud of the Bible, i am going to detail **the much older ORIGIN of where these myths and fables were copied, counterfeited and weaponized by JudeoChristianity & Islam**.

------ Tuesday, Feb 8, 2022 ------

Me (7:53 PM)

Pope Leo X, one of the most prominent Popes in the history of Catholicism is renowned for his surprisingly revealing, honest & damning quote regarding their fraudulent & oppressive 'concoction' of Christianity. Pope Leo was behind closed doors at a posh Good Friday banquet attended by Cardinals, Bishops & other 'Vatican insiders'. His quote, <u>documented by not one but two Cardinals in their letters & personal diaries,</u> was the following admission: **"How well we know what a PROFITABLE superstition this FABLE OF CHRIST has been for us and our predecessors".** All that i have been carefully detailing for u over this past year about the massive man made lies & fraud of the Bible, doesn't get MORE CONCISE on high authority than that! To further underscore the lies of the 'fable of Christ' and Christianity, we find w just a tiny bit of research (NOT ON CHRISTIAN WEBSITES OR BOOKSTORES) **that this fable itself was NOT EVEN ORIGINAL**! It was counterfeited & weaponized w bigotry & condemnation from MUCH OLDER myths.

------ Wednesday, Feb 9, 2022 ------

Mother (11:50 AM)

Watch "I AM NOT ASHAMED OF THE GOSPEL LYRICS" on YouTube
https://youtu.be/WNS5tGUoBCs

Me (10:24 PM)

I checked the song out. Mother, Listen to me. The never ending barrage of emotional **'human blood sacrifice'** intensive music is a MAJOR tool in how they get u to 'believe', and those emotional songs rarely if ever sing the truth in your Bible i have shown u, <u>of the genocide & infanticide & pedophilia/rape of virgin little girls, etc. And THE SONGS r actually one of the most effective ways the church uses to begin programming the little children at PRESCHOOL age!</u> Two of the simplest, prettiest melodies programmed into all of us as toddlers were 'Jesus Loves Me' & 'Jesus loves the Little Children'. Which children? Well OF COURSE the catchy song says **ALL the children of the world! As comic actor Jim Carey would say: RRREALLLY??** ALL of those Bible verses i showed u of God/Jesus (one in the same) ordering the infanticide & genocide & RAPE of the virgin girls of NON Jewish cultures by the Jewish males **is a God who LOVES ALL THE CHILDREN?? That is PITCH BLACK EVIL MOTHER, and God/Jesus ORDERED IT! So**

195

think again…Contrary to the title of that song you sent, you have MUCH to be ashamed of with such beliefs, and for teaching such beliefs to children!

------ Thursday, Feb 10, 2022 ------
Me (11:28 PM)
Actually they DO COME VERY CLOSE with a few, SHAMEFULLY having children sing about topics entirely related to those constant acts of genocide of NON JEWS, ordered by GOD/JESUS. But they VERY CRAFTILY make it seem to the kids like its just an innocent game as their Sunday School teacher has them holding hands together, walking in a circle, as they sing "Joshua bid the battle of Jericho", with the kids all falling down when they sing the line: "and the walls came tumbling down". **But MY, MY, MY, i wonder why they DIDNT include a verse for the kids to sing about the MASS INFANTICIDE & GENOCIDE that happened NEXT in Joshua chapter 6!!** GOD/JESUS commands Joshua's soldiers to KILL EVERY MAN, WOMAN & CHILD of Jericho! This 'inspirational Christian song' example u used, only further profoundly illustrates ALL the blatant hypocrisy i have been carefully cataloging for u thus far. Songs like that are one of the MOST EFFECTIVE tools of 'mass psychosis' & subtly programming people w the Bible's lies.

------ Friday, Feb 11, 2022 ------
Me (9:14 PM)
To further address the MISLEADING lyrics in the song u shared, where they refer to suffering from being 'mocked', **agn that's dishonest, hypocritical 'SPIN' Mother**. You r being HELD ACCOUNTABLE for the almost indescribable degree of evil, worldwide imperialistic genocide/infanticide, rape of innocent virgin little girls, oppression of women as inferior to men, outright & frequent ENDORSEMENT of the institution of **SLAVERY (Paul decreeing any dissent to contrary as BLASPHEMY of the DOCTRINE of Jesus/God, even ordering slaves to 'HONOR' their masters as though their masters were your 'precious Jesus')** For THOSE reasons you are MORALLY being 'mocked' if u want to call it that! But its really just all of us in THE TRUE LIGHT holding u ACCOUNTABLE for your shameful pretending that believing in Jesus is only about bringing peace and safe harbor for the weak and downtrodden. As i have repeatedly shown u, **that is the fraudulent 'FACADE' on the surface so often perpetuated w such psychologically manipulating 'songs'.**

------ Sunday, Feb 13, 2022 ------

Me (2:15 AM)

For another shameful example of beginning this subtle psychological programming method w little preschool children, using such dishonest but 'fun', game-like songs, u will recall the UBIQUITOUS Christian children's song **'ONWARD CHRISTIAN SOLDIERS'**. Now what is this supposedly fun innocent song NOT EVEN SUBTLY referencing? The infanticide & genocide of the massive wide scale 'CRUSADES'! Just a few lines of the song, as the Sunday School teacher often tells the little children to MARCH TO THE BEAT, are: **"Onward Christian soldiers marching as to WAR...With the cross of Jesus, going on before" A RED CROSS was emblazoned on all the genocidal crusaders swords.** WHY? Because of the passages of JESUS which I have shown u previously, DECREEING all 'NON BELIEVERS' deserved worse genocidal destruction & torment than even what he did to SODOM & GOMORRAH! They believed they were COMMISSIONED by Jesus as a result, to kill EVERY MAN WOMAN & CHILD they encountered. **And they rope the children in w the 'fun' of the marching to that song.**

Me (6:22 PM)

Bottom line Mother, U and your brothers and everyone else in your current circle of **PITCH BLACK DARKNESS** have nothing but MANY reasons to be utterly ashamed for eagerly embracing such bigotry & evil falsely in the name of 'The Light', and then having little children sing about such evil unknowingly, using such methods as 'fun' songs THAT ARE ACTUALLY ABOUT such ordained genocide by God/Jesus! U r shamefully choosing to embrace sick superstitious beliefs that call for the CONDEMNATION of 'non believers' - sick beliefs of animal & human blood sacrifice rituals, Eucharist/communion ADMITTEDLY being a human blood sacrifice ritual in which u practice **not just the sick belief in GODS need for that 'bloodlust' to b satisfied, but u practice the BEYOND SICK ritual of DRINKING THE BLOOD & EATING THE FLESH of Jesus, this being delusional symbolic CANNABALISM!** I've detailed for u Jesus' FALSE PROPHECY of his so called 2nd coming w world-wide genocidal destruction of all 'non-Christians', decreeing it WOULD b in his disciples Gen, **but u shamefully WANT that to happen.**

197

------ Monday, Feb 14, 2022 ------

Me (6:33 PM)

Like I've told u before, IF u held bizarre superstitious fairy tale beliefs that <u>DID NOT</u> cause & continually CALL FOR such massive harm, evil, slavery, oppression of women, genocide & harm for all others...IF your superstitious belief <u>DID NOT</u> have that **PITCH BLACK DARKNESS & EVIL** as its fundamental teachings in its 'scriptures', then it would not b any concern. As much as u know how beautifully healing & genuine my gender change has been for me, and as much as u know how much i love u & need u, **its beyond shameful that u would PREFER to embrace such condemning harmful beliefs at your daughters expense. My life was meant to b an example of The True Light in your life.** The Light ONLY HEALS & FORGIVES Mother. It HAS NO NEED TO CONDEMN, OR DESTROY & DAMN ALL DIVERSE BELIEVING HUMANITY BY GENOCIDAL ANGELS, OR CALL FOR THE RAPING OF VIRGIN CHILDREN OF 'NON BELIEVING' CULTURES, OR ORDAIN THE INSTITUTION OF HUMAN SLAVERY AS THE 'DOCTRINE OF GOD' etc! <u>**U have MUCH to b ashamed of the Gospel of Christ!**</u>

------ Tuesday, Feb 15, 2022 ------

Me (9:53 PM)

Over this past year, I have done a more than thorough & effective job using your own Bible, proving to u and showing u the MASSIVE amount of evil genocidal bigotry, fraud and lies RAMPANT in the Bible. I have painfully detailed for u the SHAMEFUL, almost indescribable degree of MIND BLOWING MALICIOUS HARM <u>deliberately targeting women & often targeting INNOCENT CHILDREN, specifically including calling for rape of 'virgin little ones' of 'non believers'</u>, all an evil & bigoted product of the tribal 'weaponized' beliefs at the root of JudeoChristianity, **w the 'scriptures' i have shown DECREEING those repetitive acts as being CALLED FOR by God/Jesus (one and same as i reminded u from John 1:1.)** Divine Love & The Light OF COURSE DO NOT ENGAGE IN SUCH EVIL & GENOCIDAL HARM Mother!! Where are u burying your head turning such a willful blind eye, deliberately trying NOT to see this truth?? Agn, The Light & Divine Love r the true spiritual nature of all of us. <u>**The Light of 'God' is what WE ALL ARE. The Light & Love ONLY HEALS & FORGIVES, & NEVER HARMS**</u>

198

------ Wednesday, Feb 16, 2022 ------
Me (8:07 PM)
I'm going to stress the last few lines of yesterdays lesson, because they are critically important in exposing the SHAMEFUL, weaponized 'harm-oriented' pattern the writers of the Bible eagerly and fundamentally employ, **that are AT THE ROOT of JudeoChristianity**, but that so many such 'inspirational Christian songs' like the one u sent, deliberately NEVER include lyrics about, instead always pretending Christianity and 'Jesus' are only 'all loving' & 'all peaceful'. But as i have detailed over & over this past year from your own Bible, **the OPPOSITE is its overarching genocidal, condemning message for 'all unbelievers'**, not just commonly calling for such genocide & harm in the Old Test, but Jesus, as i have shown u in previous lessons, DECREEING THE CONTINUATION OF SAME upon his 'Second Coming' in the New Test! Here r those last critically important lines from yest: **"The Light & Divine Love is the true spiritual nature of all of us. The Light of 'God' is what WE ALL ARE. The Light & Love ONLY HEALS & FORGIVES, & NEVER HARMS"**

------ Thursday, Feb 17, 2022 ------
Me (6:57 PM)
Anytime u have a religion or philosophy that CLAIMS to b the 'only salvation' for all, while advocating such diabolical harm, mass genocide and not just physical harm, but SO bigoted that it portrays 'The Light' as calling for all 'non believers' to not only be WIPED OUT from the earth, but ETERNALLY TORTURED... **Anytime u find such evil, weaponized, harm- oriented elements at the core foundation of a religious belief system as we see RAMPANT IN THE BIBLE, u obviously know immediately that it has ABSOLUTELY NOTHING to do w 'The Light', & ENTIRELY to do w just an evil, man made institution of cult-like fear-based lies to program the masses under its influence**, using such fraudulent divisive fear & guilt brainwashing from an early age, as both u and i were victims of Mother. Another subtly programming song shamefully taught to little children is 'AMAZING GRACE'. **It tells the child they are a 'wretch', meaning evil by nature, seeking to hide from them the OPPOSITE TRUTH, their innocent HOLY NATURE!**

------ Friday, Feb 18, 2022 ------
Me (4:22 PM)
So i wrote some NEW lyrics to replace the lies of 'Amazing Grace', and that reflect the Spiritual Truth about the Divine & Holy 'hands of God'

199

WE ALL ARE, temporarily here in the physical dimension, <u>removing the man made EVIL LIE that u are a **'wretch'**</u>. Here are 2 verses of the new healing lyrics mankind has never more desperately needed to understand: **"Amazing grace, how sweet the sound, the VOICE OF ALL mankind, We save each other here on earth, with HOLY HANDS DIVINE. (Vs2) We're all a Holy PART OF GOD, what can there be to fear? Its ONLY EVIL THAT CONDEMNS, BUT OUR LIGHT CAN ONLY HEAL!"** I used this example before, and it bears repeating in this deprogramming guide to the massive lies of the Bible: Imagine how u would react if i came to u and said, "Mother, u and everyone on earth r going to b killed & then eternally tortured if u dont 'believe' in this 'savior' that i do. **AND IF U BELIEVE, <u>u have to do a ritual of symbolically EATING his flesh & drinking his blood." You'd KNOW that was sick.</u>**

------ Saturday, Feb 19, 2022 ------
Me (4:40 PM)
In the upcoming next 2 lessons we are going to expose the lie even more w <u>the shameful lyrics of the 2nd verse of 'Amazing Grace'</u> most people are not familiar with, which underlines the fraud of Christianity in a huge way. First of all, as i have told u many times now, the basic fundamental foundation of 'The Light', i.e. Love & spiritual truth is that it **NEVER CONDEMNS OR DOES HARM, IT ONLY HEALS, CORRECTS & FORGIVES.** It restores your understanding of your SHARED HOLY NATURE as a PART of the universal Divine consciousness we call 'God'. As such, the only thing it destroys is condemnation, 'hate/bigotry' & 'fear', <u>fear & ignorance being where hate, bigotry and belief in the condemnation of others comes from</u>. Simply put, 'The Light' is THE OPPOSITE of 'fear', as its nature is healing, love & FORGIVENESS EQUALLY FOR ALL, WITH NO EXCEPTIONS. **On the contrary, u know u are in PITCH BLACK DARKNESS when selective 'condemnation', 'bigotry' and FEAR have ANY part of your beliefs, let alone are the CORNERSTONE of them!** Tomorrow we look at verse 2 of 'Amazing Grace'.

------ Monday, Feb 21, 2022 ------
Me (10:58 PM)
Grace is just another word for <u>'The Light'</u>. <u>Grace & The Light are what WE ALL ARE, and as such we can NEVER be separated from Grace or The Light, NO MATTER WHAT MISTAKES WE MIGHT MAKE in our personal journey here in the physical, in learning our respective lessons!</u> And why these lessons in spiritual truth that i have

steadfastly been bringing u this past year are SO important, is precisely because of how the crafters of JudeoChristianity **deliberately sought to HIDE this empowering truth from the masses!** And as i said, they discovered long ago that one of the MOST EFFECTIVE ways of programming 'believers' w such lies was not only to use fear & guilt to hide the truth of your HOLY, DIVINE NATURE, <u>but to use repetitive beautiful emotional music & 'MELODIES'</u> from as early an age as possible, to reinforce those man made fear & guilt lies, deliberately programming u to think of yourself as 'evil by nature', WHEN NOTHING COULD BE FURTHER FROM THE TRUTH! **<u>Grace DID NOT teach your heart to FEAR! MAN MADE LIES DID THAT!!</u>**

------ Wednesday, Feb 23, 2022 ------

Me (12:19 AM)

This spiritual truth & wisdom I've been showing u, THAT WE ALL ARE the 'Grace' & 'Light' of God...THAT understanding is what is going to HEAL and UNITE humanity, after thousands of years of the Big Three religious institutions of JudeoChristianity <u>shamefully DOING THE OPPOSITE w their divisive, bigoted message that "WE ARE SAVED OR 'CHOSEN' AND ALL OTHERS ARE CONDEMNED"</u> etc! As I've said before, one of the most ABSURD questions i have ever heard some ignorant people say so they dont have to actually FACE the massive evil and genocide repetitively called for by God/Jesus in both the Old & New Test, **is the stupid question, "What harm is there w someone's religious beliefs?"** Those who ask such a willfully blind, ignorant question have their heads buried somewhere, just as much as the person does who eagerly WANTS to align themselves w such bigoted, condemning, genocidal beliefs in the name of God. **<u>Humanity will finally heal as we realize WE ALL ARE the Grace and the HANDS OF GOD for each other!</u>**

------ Thursday, Feb 24, 2022 ------

Me (12:35 AM)

Grace & The Light of spiritual truth <u>NEVER HAVE ANY element of 'fear' or 'condemnation'</u> in their Divine nature. And as i have been teaching u, that fear-free Holy Divine nature is what YOU ARE, and what I am, and what ALL OF HUMANITY IS in ALL OF ITS BEAUTIFUL DIVINE DIVERSITY, blending seamlessly and artistically together like the diverse colors of the rainbow! **As soon as FEAR is brought in to a belief system claiming to be 'the only way to salvation', YOU IMMEDIATELY KNOW IT IS MAN MADE FRAUD, the opposite of the FEAR-FREE unconditional love &**

forgiveness of Grace & The Divine Light. As i have told u, Grace & The Light HAVE NO NEED TO CREATE FEAR! Only bigoted ignorant men need to peddle in such superstitious bigotry & lies about God, that claim they r 'saved' over all others who r condemned. Lets use the rainbow as another example of this...**U were not meant to see the rainbow as a symbol of worldwide genocide by God! Lying Bible writers polluted the image of the rainbow using FEAR!**

------ Friday, Feb 25, 2022 ------
Me (1:15 AM)
Many who call themselves Christians but haven't really READ the evil, genocidal condemning content rampant in the Bible (same as is also found rampant in the Muslim Koran)... Many such Christians reading this for the first time, probably think it sounds CRAZY that the beauty of the rainbow would be polluted by Bible writers claiming it was created specifically as a symbol of Gods promise never to use a FLOOD again in order to commit worldwide genocide. Many who call themselves Christians haven't read that part of the Flood story, **so they think it sounds NUTS. And guess what... THEY ARE RIGHT to think it sounds NUTS! Because it is!** Grace & The Light OF COURSE would not destroy virtually all of humanity, especially when the story beginning in Gen 6 vs 2 (as we covered in much earlier lessons in depth) states that the 'sin' & so called 'corrupt fornication' was CAUSED BY THE 'SONS OF GOD' forcing themselves on the daughters of men! **Mankind was victimized by THE SONS OF GOD, and then 'Grace' is to blame mankind?? That is obviously nothing but absolute, total HORSE SH#T!!**

------ Saturday, Feb 26, 2022 ------
Me (1:52 AM)
I'm lingering on this topic of the perversion & pollution of the nature of 'Grace & The Light' and the synonymous perversion & pollution of one of the most innocent and beautiful manifestations of the universe, **that being the rainbow.** I'm lingering on this a bit because its the PERFECT example in a nutshell, of the man made fraud and lies of the Bible & JudeoChristianity. Its the perfect example of how men traumatized the masses, shamefully lying and polluting what 'God', 'Grace' & 'The Light' are, fraudulently portraying them to the **masses based primarily on their being condemning, vengeful, genocidal entities SEPARATE from what we are, as such using paralyzing, traumatizing FEAR as their PRIMARY tool in programming the masses w those lies.** As i said in the last lesson, it is utter HORSE SH#T to believe the rainbow is

202

a symbol of God promising that IF he decides to commit worldwide genocide again, it won't be by FLOOD. **U normally would SEE that, if not for the sick FEAR programming**.

------ Sunday, Feb 27, 2022 ------
Me (1:41 AM)
Grace DID NOT teach u such a fear based superstitious belief that the gorgeous rainbow is a symbol that God wont destroy mankind 'by flood' agn...**of course w all OTHER methods to destroy it always remaining 'on the table'**, there agn showing the fundamental fear based nature of such sick teachings **the church seeks to begin programming KINDERGARTEN AGE CHILDREN WITH!** Grace did not teach u the sick child abuse story that Abraham was told by God to SACRIFICE HIS LITTLE BOY ON THE ALTAR! SHAMEFUL!! **Do u ever stop to think of the trauma and degree of child abuse that is, just to teach that false TERROR BASED concept of God to a little child?** Usually its at the age when the child is only just then being introduced to the idea of 'God' for the first time! Grace didn't pervert & pollute your concept of God w such lies. Sick men did who sought to HIDE the truth & the power that comes to everyone who awakens to the understanding that **WE ARE HOLY PARTS OF GOD! It is NOT GRACE that taught u that u r evil by nature! And u are OVERDUE to awaken now!**

------ Monday, Feb 28, 2022 ------
Me (1:36 AM)
It's NOT GRACE that taught u that YOU are 'saved' and all others who don't share your condemning beliefs are NOT SAVED, but are condemned. GRACE DID NOT TEACH YOU THAT LIE MOTHER...Man made bigotry taught u that. As i have repeatedly told u, Grace & Divine Light have NO ELEMENT of 'fear' or 'condemnation'. They only bring healing correction and forgiveness! **Its NOT GRACE that taught your heart to 'fear' as that 2nd verse of 'Amazing Grace' begins.** It was the sick lies of the crafters of the Bible that sought to control the masses with fear & guilt, and to HIDE from u the spiritual truth that u are a DIVINE HOLY PART of what 'God' is. As we discussed in many early lessons, Grace DID NOT condemn childlike Adam & Eve after SETTING THEM UP to be preyed upon by an evil master deceiver, when the story admits they DID NOT HAVE ANY KNOWLEDGE OF WHAT SIN WAS, **or what 'good & evil' was, before they were deceived in their innocence to eat of the tree of the knowledge of 'good & evil'! Grace OF COURSE would FORGIVE such a childlike mistake.**

Chapter Fourteen

------ Tuesday, Mar 1, 2022 ------

Me (12:54 AM)

One of the obsessions i have encountered in those who have been so programmed w the fraudulent fear and condemnation-based Bible image of God, **is their obsession w the need for 'punishment'**. And as i have shown, the man made bigoted lies that r RAMPANT throughout the Bible, both Old & New Testament, all program u to think that such punishment **should not even be just temporary to bring correction, but must be ETERNAL DAMNATION for all those who would dare take a pass on such condemning, OBVIOUSLY FALSE teachings about God**. So when i share w such programmed people the spiritual truth i have been sharing w u, that Grace HAS NO NEED TO CONDEMN, because of its all powerful HEALING CORRECTION and forgiveness it brings…As they hear this and struggle w their inner self that deep down KNOWS THIS IS TRUTH, their fear and condemnation programming kicks in and they often say, **"Well then where is the punishment?" And i have to remind them that i said The Light brings HEALING CORRECTION for all!**

Me (11:32 PM)

Dont misunderstand. Grace & The Light DO NOT allow unhealthy evil acts & behavior to go unaccounted for! That's NOT what i am teaching u. All of us, as eternal PARTS of God here in the physical, have our own personal paths & LESSONS to learn. And the overarching primary lesson is for us to learn to live THE GOLDEN RULE. It is as simple as that in a nutshell. **We r to learn to recognize ourselves and the Divinity of God IN EVERYONE ELSE, IRRESPECTIVE OF THEIR DIVERSE 'BELIEFS' or whether they are heterosexual or gay or transgender, etc.** Those who, in their current ignorance & PITCH BLACK DARKNESS, prefer to wallow in 'beliefs' that DO NOT recognize the shared holiness of God in the diversity of humanity ARE OBVIOUSLY NOT LIVING THE GOLDEN RULE, but are choosing to engage in elitist, bigoted behavior toward others, in DIRECT OPPOSITION to the purpose of all of our being here in the first place! **Grace & The Light dont need to 'CONDEMN' you for that. But, they WILL bring healing correction.**

------ Thursday, Mar 3, 2022 ------

Me (1:48 AM)

And that healing correction is ALREADY coming to u strongly through me, not from any 'punishment' angle, **but only w my unconditionally loving, forgiving, healing life example that destroys and evaporates your 'condemnation' superstition**. Healing correction is already beginning to awaken your shared Holy mind w ALL humanity, with these Holy lessons from the wisdom of spiritual truth that i have been SO BLESSED to learn, & from the long list of undeniable lies, evil & fraud i have detailed for u from your own Bible. Even if u choose to willfully remain in such a fraudulent bigoted belief system that condemns those who, out of love and acceptance of others, DONT share your condemning beliefs…even if u ignore all opportunities i am affording u to heal & awaken, and finally be a healthy minded mother to your daughter... **When u sadly take that false religious bigotry to the grave, u WILL be corrected on the other side, & while forgiven for a lifetime of bigotry, it will b too late to help me as I so need you to do in this lifetime**.

------ Friday, Mar 4, 2022 ------

Me (12:24 AM)

Now in the final chapter of this **'definitive guide to the lies & fraud of the Bible'**, i am going to teach u the TRUTH of how these fraudulent, deliberately concocted, twisted & perverted, condemning concepts of 'God' in the Bible ARE NOT EVEN ORIGINAL to the crafters of JudeoChristianity! As i have briefly touched on before, they were totally counterfeited & weaponized after being copied from MUCH OLDER ancient cultures from whom they originated as NON weaponized, NON literal myths and anthropomorphized metaphors largely derived from their reverent study of astronomy, constellations & the seasons, **but FIRST & FOREMOST from their fundamental recognition of 'THE SUN' of God as the source that sustains all life.** For example, as they anthropomorphized the SUN, that is where the concept originated of 'The SON of God' and the phrase 'The Light of the world.' These METAPHORS were meant to help their cultures understand THEIR ONENESS w all people and all things in nature & the universe.

------ Saturday, Mar 5, 2022 ------
Me (2:25 AM)
As i have briefly explained before, science, archeology & Egyptology have all confirmed that the most ancient defined culture of humans were Africans in the Nile Valley, who predated the Sumerians, and long predated the Jews' origin defined by the Old Test by ten thousand years or more! After thousands of years developing, they eventually became known as KEMET (**renamed EGYPT by Greek conquerors thousands of years later.**) The wise people of this amazing early culture of Kemet we now know were the pioneers of civilization and spirituality. It is established fact that ALL other developing cultures, over thousands of years after Kemet invented civilization, spirituality, astronomy & the study of the stars, agriculture incl irrigation, science & medicine (incl forms of surgery), art & music, etc...ALL other developing cultures would routinely send emissaries and often 'spies' to learn from and copy the world renown wisdom, knowledge & spirituality of Kemet, **where the world's FIRST UNIVERSITY was established!**

------ Sunday, Mar 6, 2022 ------
Me (12:06 AM)
Another of the huge GAME OVER examples exposing the man made lies of the Bible is this long known, undeniable & scientifically proven fact that **there existed other MUCH older civilizations of people at least SEVERAL THOUSANDS of years BEFORE the Bibles' defined timeline claims that the Jews & their 'CHOSEN RACE' seeded mankind**. That fact alone exposes JudeoChristianity for the clear bigoted man made fable that it is. The people & culture who would later call themselves the Jewish nation were known to have not only visited Kemet/Egypt, but were welcomed into Kemet and allowed to sojourn there as refugees during a severe time of famine, during which long period they learned from all the Kemet spirituality, knowledge & culture. Then later they took a lot of the spiritual tenets Kemet had pioneered and taught them, **and sought to portray themselves as the origin of it all...of civilization, and even mankind! Then later as i will soon address, the founders of Christianity did the same.**

------ Monday, Mar 7, 2022 ------
Me (1:39 AM)
One of the biggest lies programmed into the minds of most European & Western people to this day, even beyond the massive fraud & lies of the Bible, is the Greco-Roman & 'Euro-centric' deliberate lie that tries to rewrite history to say the Greeks & Romans were the 'architects of

civilization', as they sought to forever hide the fact that they LEARNED & COPIED the vast majority of their knowledge of 'civilization', incl architecture, agriculture, science, medicine, astronomy, art **and spirituality** from KEMET/EGYPT! And of course in tandem w that fictional 'revisionist history' came the fictional, weaponized, genocidal & imperialistic fabrication by the Roman Catholic Church, that being the man made lies of Christianity, much of which I've detailed here, and not the LEAST of which incl Paul's ENDORSING the institution of human slavery in multiple places, **decreeing ANY word to the contrary as BLASPHEMING the gospel, & telling slaves to honor their masters as though they were JESUS.**

------ Tuesday, Mar 8, 2022 ------
Me (1:24 AM)
As i touched on earlier, we now know from undeniable archeological evidence originally reported in the '80s by National Geographic Magazine & Newsweek, **that mankind DID NOT originate from the Jews, but in fact originated (hold on to your seat) IN AFRICA, OVER 190,000 YEARS EARLIER** than the Jewish fable writers of Genesis document in their 'Adam to Abraham' genealogy timeline of early humanity, supposedly being seeded by their race, which virtually all theologians & Bible scholars agree clearly dates humanity's age as only 6 or 7000 years. **Let me also cite here The Houston Baptist University as confirming this fact on their web page entitled "Bible Timeline: Chronological Index of the Years and Times From Adam"**, in which they confirm the number of years from Abraham back to Adam and the BEGINNING of humanity totaled 2078 years. Counting forward from that to present day is approximated at only 6 to 7000 years! **The Jews being God's 'CHOSEN RACE' and the ORIGIN OF HUMANITY is another absurd, GAME OVER lie by JudeoChristianity.**

------ Wednesday, Mar 9, 2022 ------
Me (12:39 AM)
Biologists using mitochondrial DNA from the bones of these African (Ethiopian area) humans dated them to be **AT LEAST 200,000 YEARS OLD!** So with this scientific factual knowledge (**rather than Jewish fairytales to brand themselves 'The Chosen People of God'**)...With this factual evidence of mankind originating at least 200,000 years ago in Africa, it should b no surprise that AFRICANS would have the earliest civilization & culture. As i have said, history that Greco-Roman Europeans unsuccessfully sought to HIDE reveals this truth, that not only

did Africa have the earliest culture & civilization of mankind, THEY INVENTED AND DEFINED IT! As i touched on earlier, not only did they define 'civilization' and 'culture', but in that process we now know they invented & pioneered scientific research, medicine and early forms of surgery, agriculture and irrigation of crops, astronomy & the study of the stars w relation to the seasons, art & music, **and most importantly, they pioneered SPIRITUALITY!**

------ Thursday, Mar 10, 2022 ------
Me (1:19 AM)
And as i will detail shortly, all of the fundamental precepts of JudeoChristianity were NOT ORIGINAL, but <u>were copied & counterfeited FROM the original NON condemning, NON weaponized & NON literal spiritual metaphors & myths of the world renown model of civilization & culture of Kemet</u>, that much of the rest of the world was learning from and modeling themselves after. 'MODELING' is one thing, but stealing, counterfeiting & WEAPONIZING those innocent, loving, 'Golden Rule' teaching metaphors, & **then using those weaponized counterfeited teachings to LIE to the masses** in order to decree that YOUR race or YOUR belief are the 'CHOSEN ONES' or the 'ONLY SAVED ONES', while decreeing all others as 'condemned infidels' is obviously another EVIL, diabolical thing altogether! **The late preeminent scholar, professor, author & historian Asa Hilliard often taught about how Kemet established a world renown educational & spiritual system in the area of Luxor founded by this amazing African culture...the world's FIRST 'university system'.**

------ Friday, Mar 11, 2022 ------
Me (1:44 AM)
Speaking of Kemet(Egypt) having been the vanguard & civilization model around the world for newer nations seeking to learn from, emulate & model themselves after, Hilliard further describes how when the fledgling, albeit imperialistic & warmongering **Greek culture** heard about & initially encountered Kemet (The Egyptians), they were also greatly impressed with its incredible educational & spiritual system. **Just as so many other budding nations had done before them, they quickly and jealously sought to learn & 'adopt' the wisdom & knowledge of Kemet**. Kemet was a very open, trusting culture toward all who came their way seeking to learn from them. They were NOT a warmongering culture seeking to conquer the world as were, unbeknownst to them at the time, the Greeks. After many thousands of years of pioneering & freely sharing their civilization, & their

208

unparalleled knowledge, wisdom & defining of spirituality with the rest of the world, **their kindness & trust was their ultimate downfall**.

Me (11:24 PM)
By the way Mother, on a side note, my phone service provider lets me know when a text i send is 'received', and then a separate notification when it is 'read', which is why occasionally i have told u i was resending the previous day's message, since it didnt indicate 'delivered', just to make sure. But lately it is no longer indicating u r opening any of the most recent messages, **esp this last chapter as i am detailing the ORIGIN of the spiritual motifs & myths that were later counterfeited, weaponized and called Judaism & Christianity.** If u r thinking u can just ignore these lessons & facts i am informing u of, so that u dont have to face them, that is just burying your head in the sand, **like a child who refuses to hear the truth that Santa Claus doesnt exist.** So please at least muster the courage not to hide from or ignore this knowledge & true history i continue to diligently take the daily time to share w u, that has been deliberately hidden from u all these years by the church.

------ **Saturday, Mar 12, 2022** ------
Mother (3:13 AM)
I have asked you not to keep sending me these heartwrending, and heartbreaking "lessons" as you call them...again, I ask you, please stop sending me these texts!!! My heart cannot bear the position you have taken regarding GODS INERRANT HOLY WORD, AND HIS MERCY TOWARDS US IN THE HOLY, HOLY, HOLY SACRIFICE OF HIS SON, JESUS CHRIST, FOR OUR SIN!!!...It is "your choice" to believe as you do, though it continues to be "my sorrow" that you have chosen as you have!!!/...until THE LORD RETURNS OR TAKES ME HOME, I will pray FOR HIS MIRACLE of "opening your eyes and heart" to see how wrong you are!!!/and for you to be set free, at last, BY YOUR OWN PERSONAL BELIEF AND FAITH IN HIS WORD, AND HIS SON JESUS CHRIST'S HOLY SHED BLOOD FOR YOUR SINS!!!

Me (3:43 AM)
Mother, after what I have already detailed for you here, for you to STILL WANT to write such a response to me only shows how very sick and bigoted of a woman you are. But I know you, and I KNOW that you are NOT so sick that you can't clearly see the massive amount of lies and hypocrisy that i am showing you...YES, in these 'LESSONS'. As i have

shown u from your own Bible, **OBVIOUSLY there is NOTHING HOLY about decreeing 'THOU SHALT NOT KILL!' and then all through the rest of the Bible, portraying God/Jesus calling for JUST THAT**, the genocidal killing of non Jewish cultures! And if that ISNT OBVIOUS ENOUGH for your programmed mind Mother, portraying God/Jesus calling for the RAPING by the Jews of VIRGIN LITTLE GIRLS & cutting up the pregnant wombs of non Jewish mothers! And Pauls ordaining the institution of slavery under penalty of 'blaspheming God', demanding slaves look at their masters as JESUS! **There is NOTHING HOLY about your defining God in such a sick way, & thinking your 'salvation' is Jesus returning w genocidal angels to destroy all who DONT share your bigoted beliefs! The LESSONS continue**.

Me (7:22 PM)
Before i cont w the history u have not been taught of the REAL spiritual origin of the counterfeited & weaponized lies of the Bible, and in response to your last bigoted, condemning outburst, (again on helpful display here for other readers to see as an example of the 'harm' & danger of Christianity) its time for me to make something crystal clear to u Mother. **You are not the woman you were MEANT to be, hence the healing i have been so steadfastly bringing u w these lessons in REAL Grace, and the Divine Light of REAL spiritual truth.** Over this past year, i have detailed & exposed for u the massive amount of MAN MADE evil & bigoted lies ALL THROUGHOUT the Bible, **fraudulently MASQUERADING as "God's word",** a deliberate divisive, man made weaponized INVERSION of the truth of what you & ALL humanity are - NOT evil & sinful by nature, but all of us HOLY PARTS of The Divine Light, **here to BE THE HEALING HANDS OF GOD for one another in ALL of our unique & varying diversity, WITHOUT CONDEMNATION...**

Me (7:37 PM)
You & your brothers (my uncles who i love more than i can describe, but who have so horribly denigrated & rejected me) **were NOT MEANT to hold such condemning bigoted beliefs about God!** Thats a primary reason why my life circumstances came into all of our lives. Thats a primary reason why my close childhood friend June's being gay came into our lives, & her finding the love of her life and getting married. It was for YOU to see how RIGHT it was for June, just like it can be right for you if it is who u r NATURALLY, **& just as u can see IF u r honest, how right my gender reassignment was for me**, & how early

210

on in childhood i even told u how right such a change felt. Again, as i have said before, i WATCHED you all my life growing up, being gay, and being physically intimate w women! You were NOT meant to condemn and denigrate such diversity w your sick bigoted Bible beliefs! **A huge part of my life's purpose has been to have the courage to stand up against your horribly wrong beliefs about God.**

------ Monday, Mar 14, 2022 ------
Me (12:33 AM)
As I've said before, MOST who call themselves 'Christians' have not READ much of the Bible, & unless they read a comprehensive guide like this one, they often remain surprisingly unaware of the Bible's overarching, <u>fundamental foundation of condemnation of ALL 'non believers', & its sick, hypocritical & frequent call for the genocide (& infanticide) of non Jews & non Christians,</u> all through the Old Test, then cont w Jesus' repetitive decree of the same (making Hitler's 'Final Solution' genocide of the Jews look tiny in comparison) **that being Jesus' own 'END TIMES' version, vowing upon his 'RETURN' to rain genocidal destruction on ALL HUMANITY who are not 'believers. (detailed extensively in earlier lessons here)** And in those earlier lessons, i SHOWED u in your own Bible, in not one but THREE of the 'gospels', that Jesus GUARANTEED his 2nd coming would be IN HIS DISCIPLES GENERATION!! Read those lessons Mother! **There is NOTHING HOLY about such HARM BASED bigoted beliefs toward others!**

------ Tuesday, Mar 15, 2022 ------
Me (1:36 AM)
So what am i REALLY showing u in those many lessons in which i detailed for u all the proof from the books of Matthew, Mark & Luke QUOTING JESUS, repeatedly guaranteeing his '2nd coming' & his destruction of ALL 'non believers' would absolutely occur IN HIS DISCIPLES GENERATION? **What am i REALLY PROVING to u?**... When u see these unequivocal quotes of Jesus in your own Bible, repeatedly telling his disciples (IN ANSWER to their specifically asking to know WHEN his 2nd coming would be) that they themselves **would actually EXPERIENCE & be persecuted & killed DURING 'the Tribulation'** (so it's very clearly NOT yet to come) & that THERE ARE THOSE STANDING THERE AMONG THEM WHO WOULD NOT TASTE DEATH BEFORE HIS 2nd COMING…When I show you this, what am I REALLY showing u from your own Bible Mother?? **Obviously at a minimum, i forced u to see Jesus is repeatedly making**

211

a fraudulent prophecy of his 2nd coming, and I'm showing u that NONE of that prophecy in your Bible was true, quoted by the person u were told was 'GOD'!

------ Wednesday, Mar 16, 2022 ------
Me (2:01 AM)
The answer for healing humanity IS NOT holding superstitious beliefs of needing a HUMAN BLOOD SACRIFICE (**after 2 millennium of ANIMAL SACRIFICES**, all to satisfy a God who not only needed such a 'BLOOD LUST' satisfied, but also tells u that u must regularly engage in the ritual of **EATING HIS BODY & DRINKING HIS BLOOD** (Eucharist/communion) to be 'saved'...And the answer for healing humanity IS NOT believing that everything will only 'heal' when this imagined 'savior' returns w his army of genocidal angels to kill & condemn everyone who does NOT believe such weaponized, condemning beliefs toward others, **& who DOES NOT 'eat of the flesh & drink of the blood' of such a sick imagined 'savior'!** I've been showing u the TRUE ANSWER for the healing of humanity, as we r finally exposing these bigoted Bible & Koran lies of JudeoChristianity & Islam, & as we finally awaken to the truth that **WE create heaven on earth! WE ALL ARE the healing hands of God! WE HEAL ONE ANOTHER, not condemn one another.**

------ Thursday, Mar 17, 2022 ------
Me (12:03 AM)
And THAT is what the ORIGINAL spiritual myths & metaphors were entirely about, created by the culture of Kemet TEN THOUSAND years or more BEFORE the Bibles' timeline of the beginning of the Jewish 'Chosen Race'. They included ALL the main tenets u have been falsely led to believe were original to Christianity. They were NOT. The Nile Valley African culture pioneered the metaphor of a **'Resurrected Savior' being the 'Son of God'** (often referred to as the 'savior God/man' myth). They originated the **'VIRGIN BIRTH/immaculate conception' myth**. They originated the **'Holy Trinity' metaphor, meant to be 'father, mother & son/daughter'(the family unit)**. SO OF COURSE, as this was counterfeited by the patriarchal crafters of Christianity who sought to define women as inferior, they TOOK OUT the sacred equality of the 'mother', and made up the replacement of a 'holy spirit' instead. But these original spiritual metaphors were all about SYMBOLIZING humanity's shared DIVINE ONENESS w what God is.

------ Friday, Mar 18, 2022 ------

Me (12:24 AM)

Before i cont w the details of the ancient origin, ten thousand years or more BEFORE Christianity, of the 'resurrected Son of God' myth that Christianity counterfeited & weaponized, lets return to my earlier question. <u>What am i REALLY showing u Mother</u>, when i carefully detailed for u, using your own King James version Bible, (**from not one but THREE of the four so called 'Gospels'**) Jesus' BLATANT FALSE PROPHECY, guaranteeing to his disciples in answer to their question, that his 2nd coming to destroy all 'non believers' & establish his so called 'kingdom of heaven on earth' **WOULD OCCUR IN THEIR CURRENT GENERATION?** There is NO grey area about those MULTIPLE SPECIFIC QUOTES & passages of Jesus, declaring this guarantee to his inquisitive disciples in those THREE GOSPELS, as i detailed for u over many lessons here. **What I am REALLY showing u is how you have been LIED TO by the church w a fraudulent fable, one that Jesus is quoted promising his own disciples would LONG AGO HAPPEN! Read those lessons.**

------ Sunday, Mar 20, 2022 ------

Me (4:53 AM)

Just for clarity on that last point in the lesson from yest thats SO important, and this agn is something i showed u and proved to u in those earlier lessons. That verse that pastors and church leaders love to quote about Jesus saying "No man knows the day or the hour" is always used WITHOUT including the critical context of ALL that he is quoted saying <u>IMMEDIATELY BEFORE that verse</u>, where he tells his disciples they may not know the day or hour, but he detailed for them how THEY would experience the 'Tribulation', **and that the 2nd coming of Elijah as prophesied by Malachi had ALREADY come, that being 'John the Baptist'**, & while he ends up telling them at the end of his false prophecy how they must 'watch diligently' because 'no man knoweth the day or hour', he said that only in the context of telling them **they WOULD know the GENERATION, and as i showed u in multiple passages in Matt, Mark & Luke, Jesus makes it absolutely clear that his 2nd coming WOULD happen in THEIR generation.**

Me (10:17 PM)

Again, i am deliberately using very focused repetition of key important evidence I've covered earlier **because this is a DEPROGRAMMING guide** as well as a guide of evidence exposing the massive amount of man made fraud & lies all throughout the Bible and 'church doctrine'.

213

Those like my Mother who have been so deeply brainwashed & programmed w such superstitious, genocidal & condemning lies, fraudulently in the name of God, **need to be reminded frequently of things covered earlier**, because the tendency of someone so deeply programmed is to combine 'selective memory' with a subconscious or even conscious effort to try to forget truths they have been shown that start to resonate w their true spiritual self deep down, as these truths i have repeatedly detailed here will do for all who read them. DEEP DOWN, under all of my Mother's man made bigoted programming from the Bible, **her true innocent Divine nature KNOWS what i am teaching here is REAL SPIRITUAL TRUTH. Any hope of healing her traumatized mind requires repetition.**

------ Monday, Mar 21, 2022 ------
Me (11:03 PM)
Now to return to the primary topic of the TRUE ANCIENT ORIGIN of the spiritual metaphors & myths that were counterfeited by Christianity MANY THOUSANDS OF YEARS AFTER they were created by the Nile Valley African creators of civilization & spirituality, **that being the amazingly wise African culture that came to b known as Kemet, later renamed Egypt by Greek conquerors.** It should b noted that the Greeks ALSO copied Kemet's popular spiritual motifs & myths even before the Romans copied, literalized & weaponized them, as they crafted Christianity with Roman Catholicism. As i mentioned earlier, the Kemetic reputation of their DEFINING example of civilization, including spirituality, culture, science, medicine, astronomy, agriculture, art, music & more, became world renown, & most newer cultures & nations that followed sought to learn all they could from the Kemetic (early Egyptian) people, **& until the 'weaponizing' of those myths by Christianity, they were understood to b metaphors, NOT LITERAL**.

------ Wednesday, Mar 23, 2022 ------
Me (12:39 AM)
As i mentioned several lessons back, this ancient African culture of Kemet originally created the myth/metaphor of 'the Son of God' AND the myth/metaphor of 'The resurrection of the Son of God'. They did so with one of, if not THE OLDEST spiritual myth models in history, that being their myth of Osiris the 'Sun' of God/'Son' of God. As i mentioned earlier, the ORIGIN of the creation of a 'Son of God' metaphor derives from this Kemetic culture's **prime reverence toward the SUN**, which contrary to what Christians often want to believe, was not worship of an inanimate object as 'God', but a wise spiritual recognition on their part of

214

the sun being the primary most powerful ASPECT & REPRESENTATON of God in the physical universe, precisely because they knew the sun was the PRIME SOURCE that maintains all life. The expression 'THE LIGHT OF THE WORLD' originated from them as they worshipped the Divine THROUGH the sun, **& their 'Osiris' myth was an anthropomorphizing of the sun into a 'savior'.**

------ Thursday, Mar 24, 2022 ------
Me (1:39 AM)
It is very important to understand that the original correct spiritual wisdom of the Nile Valley Africans (who later became the Kemetic culture)was NOT LIMITED to their reverence for the sun! Their correct, ancient spiritual wisdom was their understanding that ALL the DIVERSITY of the universe, ALL the diversity of nature, and ALL the diversity of mankind **are ALL aspects of 'God', manifesting the 'Divine' here in the physical realm**. Their original defining of the myth model of the 'Son of God', with Osiris being an anthropomorphized (humanized) 'Son of the Holy Sun' was, as i have said before, NOT meant to be taken literally!! It was a SYMBOLIC metaphor. LISTEN to me Mother, as i explain what the 'Son of God' myth was MEANT to 'symbolize'. It was meant to symbolize YOU! It was meant to help humanity understand that **WE ALSO not only came from the SOURCE of life (symbolized to them by the sun) but WE ALL will be 'resurrected' & transformed BACK to our Divine, Holy spiritual state at death.**

------ Friday, Mar 25, 2022 ------
Me (2:52 AM)
Again, the Nile Valley African culture who would later become Kemet(Egypt) were not only the original creators of the 'Son of God' myth/metaphor, but were also the original creators of the myth/metaphor of 'the resurrection of the Son of God' many THOUSANDS of years BEFORE the Roman empire & their fabrication of Christianity counterfeited it. Author & religious historian E.A. Wallis Budge makes this fundamental fact front & center in the TITLE of his book **'Osiris & The Egyptian Resurrection'**, and writes in his opening preface that the central figure of the ancient Egyptian religion was Osiris, and the chief fundamentals were the **belief in his DIVINITY, DEATH & RESURRECTION**. There is today a voluminous amount of source material by many Bible scholars, theologians, anthropologists, Egyptologists & religious historians (among many others) who have documented how JudeoChristianity came along LATE in the history of

215

humanity and **APPROPRIATED the popular myths of long pre-existing cultures**.

------ Saturday, Mar 26, 2022 ------
Me (1:44 AM)
Before i continue, let me list just a fraction of the VOLUMINOUS documentation on this topic: **"Pagan Origins of the Christ Myth"**, **"Christianity Before Christ"** & **"Man, God & Civilization"** by John G. Jackson, **"16 Crucified Saviors"** by Kersey Graves, **"Nile Valley Contributions to Civilization" by Anthony Browder**, **"Stolen Legacy of African History" by George James**, **"The Jesus Mysteries"** by Timothy Freke & Peter Gandy, **"The Christ Conspiracy - Greatest Story Ever SOLD" by Acharya S, "The Power of Myth"** & **"Creative Mythology - The Masks of God" by Joseph Campbell**, **"Forgery in Christianity" by Joseph Wheless** and **"The Egyptian Book of the Dead"** by Gerald Massey and **"Astrology of the Old Testament"** by Karl Anderson, this list again only barely scratching the surface of the authoritative source material on this subject.

------ Sunday, Mar 27, 2022 ------
Me (4:20 AM)
John G. Jackson describes the Greek/Roman/European fictional **'revisionist history'** they deliberately fabricated in their desire to hide the truth of the much more ancient African & Asian source of their civilization and spirituality they merely learned from, copied & dishonestly tried to take the credit for originating...He writes in chapter 18 of **'Man, God & Civilization'**: "Nearly all the so-called world histories and histories of civilization, so popular in contemporary academic circles, are based mainly on what is known as European civilization. **This species of parochialism gives a false picture of human history**; and few students become aware of the fact that European civilization, speaking historically, is a product of the RECENT PAST(my emphasis) and that European culture was not indigenous, but was derived from the older civilizations of Africa and Asia." He adds that **"The first civilized Europeans were the Greeks, who were largely civilized by the Egyptians, who were Africans."**

Me (10:52 PM)
First & foremost, this wise ancient African culture was the origin of what we now call 'THE GOLDEN RULE', that many other cultures & religions learned from their example & adopted. Their term for it was **the Divine principles of Ma'at**, which they originally detailed as truth,

216

equality, harmony, morality, justice & law, to name but a few. This 'UNIVERSAL EQUALITY' ensuring moral tenet they taught, of seeing the Divine Oneness in ALL others & treating others as YOU want to b treated, **was counterfeited by Jews & Christians MANY THOUSANDS of years later**, pretending THEY created it, but was NOT original to JudeoChristianity. NOR, as I've thoroughly detailed & proven here in these lessons, have the FRUITS of JudeoChristianity displayed it, with their weaponized, imperialistic, often genocidal legacy & condemning Bible 'beliefs' **toward 'non believers' & vulnerable indigenous cultures they routinely sought to kill, conquer & ENSLAVE, ironically like the Africans & Native Americans for example**!

------ Monday, Mar 28, 2022 ------
Me (10:34 PM)
I'm going to repeat the last part of yesterdays lesson, since its SO important in answering the BEYOND ignorant question of **"What's the HARM of religion?"** BOTH the so called 'holy scriptures' of the Bible & the overall HISTORY of JudeoChristianity have MADE A MOCKERY of their claim that they stand for The Golden Rule! They have BOTH INTRINSICALLY displayed **the OPPOSITE of the Golden Rule** since their counterfeited & weaponized crafting of The Old & New Testaments, as I've thoroughly detailed & proven here in these lessons. The FRUITS of JudeoChristianity have regularly displayed a weaponized, imperialistic, OFTEN GENOCIDAL legacy decreeing over & over as i have shown u, bigoted man made teachings **MASQUERADING as being 'ordained by God' because they r the CHOSEN RACE or the ONLY SAVED ONES** w their condemning Bible 'beliefs' toward 'NON believers' & vulnerable indigenous cultures they routinely sought to kill, conquer & ENSLAVE, ironically like the Africans & Native Americans for example!

------ Wednesday, Mar 30, 2022 ------
Me (2:08 AM)
As i stated earlier, there's a PLETHORA of historical, scientific & anthropological evidence documented by trusted scholars, showing humanity's TRUE HISTORY, **as opposed to the 'Greco-Roman revisionist history'**, & that documents the undeniable evidence that Africans (particularly in the Nile Valley region) r the ORIGIN of world civilization, culture, science, astronomy & spirituality. Subsequently, this same undeniable evidence has revealed the truth that **they were also the ORIGIN of the counterfeited main tenets of JudeoChristianity &**

217

Islam. This evidence confirms they were the universally recognized center of world culture in Kemet. Kemet is known to have been established in approx 3100 BC (which means **'Before the Common Era'**, not 'Before Christ') Kemet was ruled by 30 Dynasties, & the anthropological & indisputable scientific evidence shows that the Nile Valley culture that would ultimately FOUND Kemet & world civilization predated Kemet by at least 10,000 years or more!

Me (11:06 PM)
It's not about what you **want to 'BELIEVE'**, or what you deeply feel you **need to 'BELIEVE'** Mother, ESPECIALLY when all the scientific historical FACTS show those 'beliefs' to b deliberate man made fraud. And IF your 'beliefs' did not have the bigoted, genocidal legacy that i have exposed & detailed here, and **IF your 'beliefs' didn't eagerly await that SAME SICK genocidal 'Final Solution' style return of a 'savior' w an army of angels to come soon & destroy and condemn all who DONT hold your 'beliefs'**, then it wouldnt b of such paramount importance to hold u accountable for that SHAMEFUL PERVERSION of the TRUTH about God! I could just accept the fact that u were like an adult who refuses to believe Santa Clause doesn't really exist. But your sick 'beliefs' r the ROOT of the lack of humanity's proper understanding of our SHARED HOLY ONENESS, **not just w one another, but our SHARED HOLY ONENESS w God, the spiritual truth & awakening that was meant to bring healing to ALL of us long before now!**

------ Thursday, Mar 31, 2022 ------
Me (11:51 PM)
The sick VIOLENTIZATION image of 'God' in the Bible, fraudulently programming the masses to 'believe' God is SEPARATE and OUTSIDE of what you are by nature unless u 'believe' ONE WAY, etc...And accordingly this violentized God's elevation of a 'Chosen Race' ABOVE ALL OTHERS in the Old Test, w its accompanying constant bigotry in numerous forms, and its condemnation of all NON believers, & its **frequent 'ordaining' by this man made CONCOCTED 'God' of genocidal imperialism,** to ESPECIALLY include worldwide genocide of all non believers upon Jesus'(falsely prophesied) so called 2nd coming as i have detailed here earlier from your own Bible... THAT, as i have said before, (& this is SO IMPORTANT to understand)**... THAT is the ORIGINAL crafting of 'mass psychosis propaganda' to control the masses w a weaponized religion, in LOCKSTEP PARTNERSHIP w the ruling class, first of the Jews, & of course much later w Rome &**

218

the Roman Catholic Church. Put another way, <u>it was the original MASS MEDIA to control the masses using guilt & fear.</u>

Chapter Fifteen

------ Saturday, Apr 2, 2022 ------

Me (12:27 AM)

But as I've stressed before, those orig spiritual metaphors & myth models, STOLEN, POLLUTED & WEAPONIZED by JudeoChristianity & Islam, were **intended for the EXACT OPPOSITE spiritual practice & understanding!** Their OSIRIS 'savior god man' & orig 'Son of God' myth model that this ancient, very wise African culture created, was meant NOT to symbolize 'God' and his 'Son' as being SEPARATE from u!! Again, **it was MEANT to symbolize WHAT YOU AND I ARE TOO!** This wise culture of Kemet came up w the FIRST 'Son/Sun of God' myth model, AND the FIRST 'RESURRECTION' myth model many thousands of years before EUROPE or the clans that later would call themselves Jews ever existed! And they came up w these myths to use to help people, especially THEIR people, to see that we ALL are ONE with a Divine universe, only temporarily here in the physical. They created those myth METAPHORS, **not to use to condemn others who 'believed' differently, but to teach the UNIVERSAL spiritual truth that we r ALL SONS & DAUGHTERS of God!**

------ Sunday, Apr 3, 2022 ------

Me (12:13 AM)

And as they understood that we r ALL 'Sons & Daughters of God', **this metaphor also included the creation of the ORIGINAL 'TRINITY' myth model!** The Kemetic culture and its ancestors understood that where there was a 'God', there must also be what?? A GODDESS! This is critical for u to understand Mother. That original 'Son of God' myth INCLUDED the **'Daughter of God'** who was Osiris' mate, that of course being 'ISIS', and the myth included their child, who was called 'Horus'. **This was understood as the orig Trinity/Godhead of three.** But agn, it was NOT to symbolize those three as SEPARATE & above what humanity is! On the contrary, it was intended to symbolize the **HOLY FAMILY UNIT, father, mother & child as being the IDEAL EXAMPLE of what 'God' is,** as they understood we r ALL diverse PARTS of God here in the 'physical'. They were a matriarchal society, **and held the absolute EQUALITY of male & female as SACRED, precisely because they knew that God was NOT a 'male', but both male & female!**

------ Monday, Apr 4, 2022 ------

Me (2:01 AM)

The original 'Father, Mother & Son' Trinity metaphor, represented by Egypt's 'Osiris, Isis & Horus' as the FIRST Godhead of three, **is OF COURSE the perfect myth model to symbolize what 'God' is here in the physical realm.** But the bigoted, male-centric oppressive culture that sought to craft a new weaponized religion of maximum control, especially crafted to emphasize the subjugation of its female population, relegating them to 'servant status', **would sooner ADD AIR CONDITIONING TO HELL than to accept a 'Godhead' myth model that included the Mother/female as EQUAL w the FATHER/male.** This ancient Kemetic 'Godhead' myth, like all the OTHER myths they copied, was a very popular & easy spiritual concept for people to grasp & understand. These myths, as i said, had been around for many millennium already, so cultures knew better than to forsake them altogether in crafting their efforts to CONTROL their cultures w NEW 'beliefs'. **So they copied it PARTLY, deleting the Mother, <u>and replacing her instead with a 'GHOST'!</u>**

------ Tuesday, Apr 5, 2022 ------

Me (1:08 AM)

But hold on to your seat, because the extent to which the crafters of Christianity counterfeited the orig Nile Valley African myths gets much deeper! The VIRGIN BIRTH itself was counterfeited as i have already said, but it gets deeper than THAT! **Even the date of Dec 25th for the birth of Jesus was fraudulently counterfeited, as was the NATIVITY MYTH of his being born in a stable & laid in a manger w wise men coming from afar guided by a bright star.** That story was entirely STOLEN from the orig ancient, very popular myth for guess who? <u>HORUS, the VIRGIN BORN son of ISIS & OSIRIS on Dec 25th, born in a stable, placed in a manger, etc.</u> And w the ORIGINAL myth, **that date of Dec 25th had DEEP scientific ASTRONOMICAL significance,** which was yet another powerful piece of wisdom that Kemet pioneered & most of the rest of the world's cultures followed ever since, **that being the celebration of the WINTER SOLSTICE which Kemet (having ALSO given us the first CALENDAR) <u>recorded as December 25th</u>!**

Me (11:45 PM)

This important lesson involves a bit more detail, & will take two texts to cover...Now remember, each of these three: Osiris, Isis & Horus, **(the orig 'godhead' & mythical 'saviors')** were just anthropomorphized myths created by the Egyptians to represent the holiness of THE SUN in human form. And there's an astronomical phenomenon that happens in their northern hemisphere that is the SCIENTIFIC REASON for the 'death on the cross' & 'resurrection in 3 days' myths that **this ancient African culture created, NOT CHRISTIANITY!** Every year leading up to the winter solstice, the days get shorter, the cold dark nights get longer, & the sun from their perspective appears to be getting smaller, signifying the end of crops & the coming DEATH OF THE SUN to them. For 6 months the sun has been moving southward and getting lower & lower in its position in the sky, until by Dec 22nd it reaches its lowest point in the sky at or near the horizon, **where this phenomenon occurs of the sun appearing to STOP for 3 days!**

------ Wednesday, Apr 6, 2022 ------

Me (12:42 AM)

This process was very scary for them back then, as much as the sun was SO critical to their survival off the land, & for warmth, & for the ability to SEE any predator threats around them, etc. And the impetus behind WHY they created such a powerful, long lasting spiritual myth and HUGE, UNIVERSAL celebration around this phenomenon from Dec 22nd to Dec 25th, **is when on Dec 25th the 'death of the sun' SUDDENLY REVERSES, and is 'REBORN'** & begins to 'RESURRECT' from the dead, & finally begins to move one degree northward agn, portending the coveted RETURN OF SPRING with its longer days & shorter nights! But thats not all!! Theres also an important scientific astronomical reason for WHY they created the sun's 'death on the cross' myth. As I've touched on before, this ancient first civilization developed a strong understanding of astronomy, **diligently following & mapping the constellations, one of which is the 'CRUX' or 'SOUTHERN CROSS', which is always in the vicinity of the Sun's 'death'.**

------ Thursday, Apr 7, 2022 ------

Me (12:54 AM)

So, w the sun being the MOST HOLY sacred symbol representing God to this ancient African culture due to its being the prime source of all life, and w Horus being anthropomorphized as 'The Son of The Sun of God', **as the sun went through this process appearing to 'die for three days'**

222

always w the Southern Cross constellation visually present in the sky along with it, and it appeared to die on the horizon from Dec 22nd to Dec 25th... As a result of their keen observation of that regular astronomical event, this first civilization then created a detailed sacred myth around that yearly event! The story of Jesus' crucifixion on a cross, dying for 3 days, then resurrecting as 'the Son of God' was NOT genuine or original at all! It was entirely counterfeited from THIS ancient Egyptian ORIGINAL myth, which was based on that scientific phenomenon as i described. They PERSONIFIED the whole process making it a 'play' in effect. **Horus was said to have been 'crucified on the cross' on Dec 22nd, and then resurrecting from that death after 3 days, with Horus' birthday being Dec 25th!**

------ Friday, Apr 8, 2022 ------
Me (12:45 AM)
I should back up & clarify that the 'crucifixion' assoc w Horus is very broadly symbolized in that original process of this culture's seeing the sun (represented by Horus at the time) depicted as 'DEAD' for 3 days w the 'Crux' constellation present. However, the varying writings that developed of the myth of Horus do not describe his 'crucifixion' as his means of death prior to his resurrection. Instead they often depict his death by multiple scorpion stings sent by 'Set'(the original mythical character origin later turned into 'Satan') who was his brother & **the 'Lord of Darkness' & source of 'evil'** that Horus regularly did battle with! **Here agn we see another TRUE ORIGIN of the good vs evil myth, long before JudeoChristianity!** Also, this original, virgin born, resurrected savior god man, 'Son/Sun of God' myth model eventually became copied by multiple other cultures before Christianity literalized & weaponized it. In the next lesson i will list a few of them, **all of them understanding that this myth model was NOT literal**, only a loving 'metaphor of YOU'

------ Saturday, Apr 9, 2022 ------
Me (12:18 AM)
As we approach Easter, about a week away, understand that like Dec 25th & the ancient sacred winter solstice, **Easter was NOT original in ANY way whatsoever to Christianity!** It was yet ANOTHER flagrant example of Christianity's counterfeiting a VERY popular ancient sacred practice & celebration of the RESURRECTION of those ancient cultures' 'Sons/Suns of God' original myths, **& their 'resurrection' seen as represented by the SPRING SOLSTICE, bringing the 'salvation' of the universe w all the renewed life assoc w Spring.** It was turned into

223

the sick, human blood sacrifice ritual that is SHAMEFUL in its fraudulent intent to bastardize such a universally beautiful, innocent celebration of our ONENESS w the annual rebirth of nature & life! As Heather McDougall writes for 'The Guardian' in her article entitled **'The Pagan Roots of Easter'**, "From Ishtar to Eostre, the roots of the resurrection story go deep". She too describes the ancient symbolic story of the 'death of the Sun on the cross'...

------ Sunday, Apr 10, 2022 ------
Me (12:50 AM)
McDougall writes, **"early Christianity made a pragmatic acceptance of ancient pagan practices"** (My note: 'Pagan' DOES NOT mean 'evil' as JudeoChristianity has fraudulently sought to define the label. **'Pagan' simply means NON CHRISTIAN**.) Cont now w Heather McDougall's article in 'The Guardian', she too writes on the topic of the many cultures who followed the custom of the ancient original myth of the Son of the Sun of God dying for 3 days & resurrecting, with their own parallel 'Sons/Suns of God' savior myths...She writes, "The general symbolic story of the death of the son (sun) on the cross (the constellation of the Southern Cross) and his rebirth, overcoming the powers of darkness **was a well worn story in the ancient world**. There were plenty of parallel, rival resurrected saviors too. The Sumerian goddess Inanna, or Ishtar, was hung naked on a stake, and was subsequently resurrected and ASCENDED FROM THE UNDERWORLD." More of such examples to b cont in tomorrow's lesson.

------ Monday, Apr 11, 2022 ------
Me (12:33 AM)
McDougall continues, **"One of the oldest resurrection myths is Egyptian Horus. Born on 25 December, Horus and his damaged eye became symbols of life and rebirth. Mithras was born on what we now call Christmas day, and his followers celebrated the spring equinox."** McDougall also briefly mentions the Greek Dionysus as another Divine Son of God myth model, saying he was also resurrected by his grandmother. She is only including very limited examples & detail in her brief article, but the main point she is making is the same point i have been making in our lessons here, which is that ALL of the main tenets of the Christian 'faith'...The Son of God myth, the virgin birth myth, the resurrection myth, etc., are **NOT ORIGINAL**. And the two main Christian 'holy dates' assoc w them, Dec 25th and Easter Sunday are also long ago proven entirely fraudulent, due to **all of them being**

counterfeited from MUCH OLDER, ancient original popular myths predating Christianity by many thousands of years.

Me (11:16 PM)
As i am showing u WHERE these myths originated **many millennium before Christianity**, its VERY important to also understand the actual astronomical science behind HOW & WHY these 'savior God man', 'resurrected Son/Sun of God' metaphorical myths (including the origin of the sacred symbol of the CROSS, and the sacred nature and significance of the number 12) were all conceived by this ancient culture that would ultimately become Kemet/Egypt. I've shown u some of it already with **how they PERSONIFIED the highly sacred winter solstice astronomical process they observed every year w what they perceived was the death of the Sun of God on Dec 22nd, resurrecting and being REBORN on Dec 25th.** This very wise earliest of civilizations based these & other copied spiritual myths on what is often called 'astrotheology'. As i have shared w u before, their spiritual wisdom was their recognition that the sun, moon, stars & universe... **ALL of us, ALL of nature, are HOLY ASPECTS of what 'God' is...**

------ Tuesday, Apr 12, 2022 ------
Me (11:23 PM)
Before i show u more illuminating detail of various MUCH OLDER 'resurrected savior/Son of God' myth model versions that followed Kemet's original version, & that Christianity also copied & fraudulently LITERALIZED & weaponized much later, let me cont first w some more detail on the astronomical SOURCE often called **'astrotheology'**, since they all derive from sacred observations related to how much this Nile Valley first civilization valued the SUN as the primary source of all life. Author & historian John Jackson quotes writer Arthur Findlay on pg 39 in Jackson's powerfully illuminating book **'Christianity Before Christ'**, **"This return of the savior was assoc by the Babylonians & Egyptians in relation to the sun."** He goes on to explain how in their diligent observation of the moving of the sun, moon & stars, they observed that the sun seemed to them to have a yearly pattern with the same repeating star formations assoc w the yearly seasons, **& from this they made TWELVE 'constellations'**

------ Thursday, Apr 14, 2022 ------

Me (2:23 AM)

This ancient first civilization having also originated humanity's FIRST CALENDAR, the 'STELLAR CALENDAR', observed these 12 star pattern constellations consistently & continually marking the beginning of EACH MONTH of the year in a circular, cyclical pattern. **These 12 constellations were artistically anthropomorphized into 12 'signs' which they called 'The Zodiac'.** The Zodiac was NOT a 'satanic' or 'evil' construct of the Devil' as the Christian church has intentionally mischaracterized it. On the contrary, it was humanity's first effective model of a dependable scientific calendar to measure & mark the seasons of the year. As they understood that ALL of us, & ALL of the universe are HOLY aspects of The Divine, this stellar pattern of the movement of the sun & stars was naturally SACRED! **The SUN was at the center, and called the 'LIGHT OF THE WORLD'. Yes, that expression was ALSO originated by this ancient Nile Valley first civilization! The sun was seen as the prime SYMBOL of 'God'.**

------ Friday, Apr 15, 2022 ------

Me (1:15 AM)

Arthur Findlay is further quoted on this subject in Jackson's book, stating: **"The ancients regarded the various heavenly bodies as visible expressions of divine intelligence, & the twelve constellations were considered to be the sun's bodyguard, this number being given to the Savior-God-man as the number of his disciples."** Before i move on to the consistent repeating details of the popular copying of the Kemetic culture's Osiris & Horus Savior God-man myth model, i want to show u a real world example of the common fraudulent history often put forth by 'mainstream' sources to this day, **that either delib or ignorantly deletes the reality of this ancient Egyptian culture being the REAL origin of civilization spirituality & culture.** In researching for this chapter, i typed 'FIRST CALENDAR' in a Google search. The result falsely said it orig w the Sumerians. However, Britannica got it CORRECT, when i specified 'STELLAR CALENDAR'. They credited ancient Egypt, long before the Sumerians.

------ Saturday, Apr 16, 2022 ------

Me (2:31 AM)

The Sumerians & the Mesopotamians, and EVERY OTHER subsequent culture, learned & adopted that first 'stellar calendar' from Kemet (ancient Egypt). **Kemet invented that calendar a few thousand years BEFORE the Bible's timeline claims to have begun the creation of**

226

man w their fable of Adam & Eve. Kemet's history, <u>meaning that of the MUCH more ancient African cultures who would eventually found Kemet,</u> and who brought much of that orig wise spirituality & culture down the Nile from areas such as Nubia, Kush & Ethiopia, **we now know predated the Jews & the origin of the Old Test of the Bible by at least many TENS OF THOUSANDS of years!** By the way, Kemet was so advanced in science & astronomy that not only did they invent that first stellar calendar based on a 365 day year, but as Britannica explains, **"the ancient Egyptians simultaneously maintained a second calendar based upon the phases of the moon."**

------ Sunday, Apr 17, 2022 ------Me (12:11 AM)
Now, as u learn this for the first time, u r naturally tempted to ASSUME that our 'Western European civilization' certainly must have had to make changes to that 'primitive' calendar into the modern one we use to this day...And you'd be wrong. **As Britannica explains, that ancient Egyptian calendar is the 'basis of the Western calendar still used in modern times', w a minor addition of a 'leap-year' day added by Julius Caesar around 46 BCE.** Now let's look at the truth, that Western European history has delib tried to hide about what civilization pioneered MEDICINE, SURGERY & PHARMACOLOGY, **& who the REAL 'father of medicine' was.** 'Hippocrates' is effusively lauded by our Euro-centric revisionist history books as being the 'Father of Medicine', & from whom the sacred 'Hippocratic oath' is derived from. **But thats exposed as a lie by none other than honest Hippocrates HIMSELF, <u>who credits Kemet's 'Imhotep' as being his teacher & the one to whom he owed all of his knowledge of medicine</u>!**

------ Monday, Apr 18, 2022 ------
Me (1:15 AM)
I'm taking the time to show u these facts because its VERY important for u to finally begin to learn the REAL history of humanity, not the counterfeited one fabricated by the Greco-Roman Catholic 'Christianized' Western world <u>that has fraudulently sought to present itself as the origin of civilization, spirituality & science, when the massive evidence cant b hidden & shows the OPPOSITE!</u> I'm showing u only the tip of the iceberg here, but enough to open your mind to this undeniable truth in general. To finish my last example, there's a fantastic article in the UK 'Telegraph' by Roger Highfield entitled **"How Imhotep Gave Us Medicine"**, Imhotep being Kemet's amazing physician, surgeon, scientist, architect & designer of the Saqqara pyramids around 2650 BCE. <u>Highfield writes, "The Egyptians, not the Greeks, were the true</u>

fathers of medicine". As he explains it was Imhotep, he says **a research team from Univ of Manchester discovered the detailed medical evidence in papyri written in 1500 BCE.**

------ Tuesday, Apr 19, 2022 ------
Me (12:56 AM)
Just to clarify, Highfield makes it clear Imhotep was not the only one, **but was far & away the leader among MANY Egyptian physicians & scientists who taught medicine & pharmacology to the world,** many of their methods & treatments remaining the basis of medical treatments still practiced to this day! As i said, these tip of the iceberg examples are hugely relevant to our overall purpose here of exposing the lies & fraud of the Bible, because these facts BEGIN to help u see that not just JudeoChristianity, but the VAST MAJORITY of what Greco-Roman & Western culture has tried to claim THEY created, is entirely a fraudulent attempt on their part to hide the fact of where it TRUTHFULLY originated, & from whom they learned and counterfeited it from! These few examples of SO MANY more i could list are intended to show u what imperialistic Christianized Western culture has tried to hide, **that being Kemet's MASSIVE WORLD INFLUENCE in ALL disciplines, ESPECIALLY its spiritual mythology models.**

------ Wednesday, Apr 20, 2022 ------
Me (1:19 AM)
Just a couple more stunning examples of this...Just like the fraud & false credit written in our history books that Hippocrates was the 'father of medicine' when he himself declared he learned all he knew from KEMET'S IMHOTEP, the Greeks also tried to claim credit for developing mathematics, when **in fact they learned that discipline also from ancient Egypt!** They fraudulently decreed the Greek philosopher Pythagoras as the first pure mathematician in history. We now know from voluminous evidence that the world's FIRST civilization & culture of ancient Kemet was, as i mentioned earlier, where new budding cultures (**esp the Greeks & Romans**) from all over the world were sending their people to LEARN from them in EVERY major discipline & science incl mathematics, astronomy, medicine, agriculture, art, music, spirituality, etc.! **Well known Greek biographer Plutarch told the truth about Pythagoras in his book 'Parallel Lives', how Pythagoras studied math & astronomy under AFRICANS IN EGYPT.**

Me (11:26 PM)

Before we continue, i need to correct an error i noticed that i made from the lesson of April 10th. In that lesson i was showing u how the 'resurrection' of the 'Son/Sun of God' myth & the related sacred holiday around 'Easter' are NOT original to Christianity, but were LONG before created & celebrated by the Kemetic Nile Valley culture in order to anthropomorphize & SYMBOLIZE what they observed the SUN doing at that time every year. **I was showing u how that sacred annual event was seen as both the 'REBIRTH' & 'RESURRECTION' of the 'Son/Sun of God'. As such it was one of their biggest celebrations of the year**. But i mistakenly referred to it as the Spring Solstice, when it is correctly called the 'Spring Equinox.' Continuing now, theres one more example i want to show u...**At this point it should not b surprising to also learn that ancient Kemet(Egypt) was who ORIGINALLY determined the earth was round, NOT the Greeks as they have fraudulently tried to claim**, like everything else they learned from ancient Egypt! (More on this fact tomorrow)

------ Friday, Apr 22, 2022 ------

Me (1:29 AM)

As u will discover if u do a little searching on the topic of 'ancient Egyptians first to discover the earth was round', u quickly find the typical fraudulent claims by Western history writers who, just like w Hippocrates & Pythagoras, **falsely attribute all the credit to Greek astronomer Eratosthenes**, in yet ANOTHER of seemingly endless efforts to hide the truth that they did NOT pioneer any such scientific knowledge, but instead learned it all from the ancient first civilization of Kemet. We know that Eratosthenes was a director of the world renown Library of Alexandria in 200 BCE, and gained his astronomical knowledge from the ancient Egyptian texts he studied while there! **ALL early Western astronomers incl Galileo learned most of their knowledge from the many THOUSANDS of years of Kemet's prior knowledge**, studying the stars & planets, CREATING the science of astronomy, & subsequently teaching it to the rest of the world in their benevolent SHARING of their knowledge.

------ Saturday, Apr 23, 2022 ------

Me (1:32 AM)

Now, i mentioned something very important at the end of the lesson from yesterday, that being how benevolent & giving the Kemetic culture was in freely sharing & teaching their wealth of knowledge to the rest of the world, that was eagerly seeking to learn that knowledge from them, in such powerful areas like spirituality, science, astronomy, medicine, agriculture, music, art and so much more as i have detailed here. QUESTION: Does such openness, teaching & sharing w outsiders sound like something a warmongering, predatory & imperialistic civilization would do?? Of course not. As i told u, this was the MOST ancient culture of humanity, **who created & DEFINED what 'civilization' & 'spirituality' was many thousands of years BEFORE the Jews, Persians, Greeks & Romans existed, & whose wisdom resulted in their becoming humanity's TEACHER of their wisdom.**

------ Sunday, Apr 24, 2022 ------
Me (1:53 AM)
As i shared earlier, the spirituality Kemet pioneered & created was first & foremost founded upon recognizing the Divine in ALL the diversity of our universe, especially EVERYONE, EVERYWHERE. As i covered in a previous lesson, the Golden Rule of treating all others w the same righteousness, respect, love & harmony as u would want from them **was NOT original to JudeoChristianity, but was created & taught to much of the world by Kemet (ancient Egypt)** It was fundamental to what they called the spiritual laws of Ma'at. With that fundamental Golden Rule dedication to those spiritual laws in how they treated all others, they also created what are called **the 42 negative confessions of Ma'at**, from which the Jews who came along thousands of years later, & sojourned under Kemet's care for quite a long period, would extract & 'appropriate' a portion of those 42 negative confessions, **calling them the TEN COMMANDMENTS & then try to claim they were orig to the Jews as 'The Chosen Race', when they were counterfeited.**

------ Monday, Apr 25, 2022 ------
Me (1:09 AM)
Unlike the warmongering, imperialistic cultures that would betray Kemet's openness to new cultures around the world coming to them to learn, & consequently would ultimately seek to copy, counterfeit & take credit for Kemet's freely shared knowledge w them, **Kemet LIVED The Golden Rule & their spiritual laws of Ma'at w those outsiders by example. Sadly, in doing so they would eventually b taken advantage of, attacked & conquered, first by the Persians, then the Greeks, followed by the Romans**. But for a long time before that happened to them, Kemet DEFINED & TAUGHT the rest of the world not only what 'civilization' & 'culture' was, but they taught the world ALL of the major disciplines THEY had long before developed, incl science, medicine, astronomy, agriculture, mathematics & amazing feats of architecture w

230

their mind-blowing designs of the pyramids! **But possibly the BIGGEST area of powerful influence Kemet had on the rest of the world was their SPIRITUAL influence & Son/Sun of God SYMBOLIC metaphor.**

------ Tuesday, Apr 26, 2022 ------
Me (1:41 AM)
As i have stressed before, & this point cannot b stressed enough: Before much later becoming known as 'Egypt', **the ancient Nile Valley Kemetic culture ORIGINATED & PIONEERED the spiritual mythological practice of 'anthropomorphizing' the sun, stars, constellations & planets, meaning to project human or animal qualities onto them, as a <u>NON LITERAL SYMBOLIC MYTH</u>.** What was their 'personifying' the Sun as 'The Son of the Sun of God' & their creating of the first concept of that Son/Sun of God 'resurrecting' on Dec 25th, 3 days after dying on the winter solstice of Dec 22nd, all meant to symbolize? Like i explained in previous lessons, <u>this practice was meant to symbolize what we ALL are...HOLY SONS & DAUGHTERS OF GOD!</u> The 'resurrection' of the Son/Sun of God mythology they originated was meant to remind us that we ALL can look forward to being resurrected & REBORN upon our physical death, **because we r all ONE w what God is! This beautiful spiritual symbolism of our universal Divine ONENESS was NEVER intended to b 'weaponized' into a condemning dogma!**

------ Wednesday, Apr 27, 2022 ------
Me (1:59 AM)
Generally, w the exception of Christianity and its eventual copying, counterfeiting & weaponizing those popular myths...Other than their man made deliberate misuse in the fraudulent 'literalizing' of those popular, longstanding myth motifs thousands of years later... generally those orig Kemetic myth models of the Sun/Son of God (always the result of a virgin birth or 'Divine conception' not involving human sexual penetration, & the associated 'resurrection' myths) **were otherwise commonly UNDERSTOOD by the rest of the world NOT to b literal or condemning, but were OBVIOUSLY understood as merely SYMBOLIC MYTHS about humanity's shared Divine nature.** I'm going to show u several examples of the influence Kemet's Osiris/Horus 'Sun/Son of God' &' resurrected savior God-man' myth models had on other cultures who learned it from them, and followed the EXACT SAME details w their cultures' versions, **LONG BEFORE Christianity**

sought to literalize & weaponize those popular myths to control the masses w fear.

------ Thursday, Apr 28, 2022 ------
Me (1:46 AM)
As i list some of these examples from other ancient cultures who learned those spiritual MYTH METAPHORS from Kemet LONG BEFORE Christianity, **& followed the exact same details in creating THEIR 'personified' resurrected Sun/Son of God,** keep in mind this brief excerpt by author, historian & archeologist Dorothy Murdock (pen name of Acharya S) from the cover of her eye opening & meticulously sourced book **'The Christ Conspiracy'**...Dorothy writes: "These redeemer tales are similar not because they reflect the actual exploits of a variety of men who did & said identical things, but because they represent the same extremely ancient core of knowledge that revolved around the celestial bodies & natural forces." Again, she too is reminding the reader that these were 'personified' **NON LITERAL MYTHS symbolizing the Sun (& other celestial bodies)** that the Kemetic people recognized as powerful manifestations of the Divine nature of ALL things in the universe, **the 'SUN of God' being seen by them as the source of all life.**

------ Friday, Apr 29, 2022 ------
Me (1:19 AM)
As previously discussed, Kemet originated the 'virgin born' resurrected Sun/Son of God myth model story, w their original 'God head of three'/Trinity myth model of 'Osiris'(Son of the Sun of God) 'Isis' (the Sun Goddess Daughter of The Sun of God) & their immaculately conceived Son of the Sun of God 'Horus'. **I showed u how Horus in particular was the anthropomorphizing of the Sun**, seen as 'DYING' on the 'CROSS' (the Southern Cross constellation) as the sun STOPPED MOVING low on the horizon for THREE DAYS at the WINTER SOLSTICE of Dec 22nd, and was seen to 'RESURRECT' or b 'REBORN' on Dec 25th. But this original symbolic story & 'passion play' of their myth of Horus gets MUCH more 'familiar' in detail! In addition to being the FIRST virgin born savior God-man myth model, **Isis his mother was specifically known as 'Isis-Meri'. The fable has Horus born in a cave & laid in a manger on Dec 25th, with a bright star in the east heralding his birth, and yes, he is attended by THREE WISE MEN.**

------ Saturday, Apr 30, 2022 ------
Me (2:14 AM)

But the familiar details get even MORE familiar! THOUSANDS of years before Christianity, Kemet's mythical passion play of Osiris, Isis & Horus detailed that **Horus was a child prodigy spiritual teacher at age 12, was 'BAPTIZED' in the Jordan River by 'Anup the Baptizer'**, baptism also having orig from KEMET as a spiritual METAPHORICAL 'rebirth' practice/ritual and later counterfeited by Christianity. Also, 'Anup' translates to 'John' in the Greek. To continue, Kemet originated the story of the Son of the Sun of God **having TWELVE DISCIPLES or followers**, and as i explained in a previous lesson, these 12 followers were the 12 signs of the Zodiac calendar SYMBOLIZING the 12 MONTHS of the year that steadfastly 'follow' the 'Sun of God'. The orig mythical story of Horus detailed how he performed many miracles, **WALKED ON WATER, exorcised demons and raised the dead, specifically a character in the orig story named 'El-Azarus' (El-Osiris)! ALL of this copied, & NOT ORIGINAL to Christianity!**

Chapter Sixteen

------ Monday, May 2, 2022 ------

Me (12:48 AM)

As i detailed in a previous lesson, the full knowledge by the Vatican of these undeniable historical truths of the genuine origin of the MYTH & FABLE of the story of 'Jesus' is precisely illustrated by one of the most well respected Popes of the church, **Pope Leo X**. He was quoted as i told u by not one but TWO separate Cardinals who were present w him at a lavish Good Friday banquet, & who documented his quote in their letters & personal diaries. Pope Leo, keenly aware of these widely known historical facts I'm showing u here, openly admitted at this banquet, **"How well we know what a PROFITABLE superstition this FABLE OF CHRIST has been for us & our predecessors."** In addition to the specific details i covered in the last lesson, the terms 'Messiah', 'The Anointed Son of God' & 'The Good Shepherd' were all original to Kemet's myths of Osiris & Horus. **Also as a reminder, so was the sacred term 'THE LIGHT OF THE WORLD', precisely because Osiris & Horus were SYMBOLIC METAPHORS of the sun!**

------ Tuesday, May 3, 2022 ------

Me (12:21 AM)

I'm going to highlight for u a few specific 'spin off' Savior-God-man versions that Kemet's orig myth model story inspired with other cultures who learned the 'Osiris/Isis/Horus' fable from them, LONG predating Christianity. **Unlike Christianity, these cultures UNDERSTOOD it was a symbolic, anthropomorphized sacred myth, not a LITERAL STORY!** It became a popular MYTH model that many cultures were influenced by, to the extent that John Jackson opens chapter 3 on this precise point in his powerfully revealing book i mentioned earlier, **"Christianity Before Christ".** Jackson writes: "Comparative hierologists have discovered records of about THIRTY Savior-God religions." He explains how they existed in very remote times, w clear evidence of a common origin, and he proceeds to list their shared traits w the orig Osiris/Horus story: **Born on or near Dec 25th, their mothers having to b 'virgins', born in a cave or stable, called 'Saviors' who worked for the 'salvation of humanity'...**

Me (8:45 PM)

Jackson further describes how they all shared the Osiris/Horus fable traits **of being 'resurrected from the dead' after descending into 'hell'**

to overcome 'evil powers'...   Remember this is NOT LITERAL, it's all a metaphorical myth from their ancient imaginations & to some degree, their superstitions & fears, that were <u>intended to b SYMBOLIC of their SHARED DIVINE NATURE</u>, and of how they and all humanity too would also resurrect into the spiritual realm and overcome 'evil'. It had ZERO element of condemnation toward other 'beliefs' or diversity, **as JudeoChristianity would later fraudulently weaponize it w its condemning literal version.** Lets now begin looking at a few examples, beginning w 'Mithra' and 'Mithraism', coming from the Persian culture, after learning the myth story from the much more ancient Kemetic (Egyptian) culture, thousands of years before Christianity. **Mithra was also born of a virgin on Dec 25th in a cave, and in his case was attended by SHEPHERDS bearing gifts...**

------ Thursday, May 5, 2022 ------
Me (1:05 AM)
Continuing w the detailed, similar 'Osiris/Horus' pattern of the ancient myth of the Persians' 'Mithra'...**He too, being a Sun/Son of God metaphor personifying the Sun, of course had in his mythical story the 12 'companions' or 'disciples', which were symbolic of the 12 constellations popularized by Kemet w their creation of the Zodiac**, universally adopted as the world's first calendar based on a 365 day year, and as i shared in a previous lesson, upon which our calendar today is still based upon. Mithra too was a great miracle worker and as 'The Great Bull of the Sun', <u>he was said to have sacrificed his life for UNIVERSAL PEACE</u>. Do u see any condemnation or tribal weaponizing of these myths Mother? No! On the contrary, the purpose of these spiritual metaphors was to help all humanity unite in love and peace by understanding we r ALL DIVINE ASPECTS OF GOD, w no one culture or 'belief' being 'saved' w all others 'condemned'. **Mithra also was buried and the he 'resurrected' after 3 days**.

------ Friday, May 6, 2022 ------
Me (12:55 AM)
Lets look at a few more specific examples of this resurrected 'Son/Sun of God' myth motif, influenced by the Osiris/Horus original fable. Lets look at the myth story of the Savior-God-man 'Krishna' of India (dating to approx 900 BCE), <u>approx 1000 years BEFORE Christianity</u>. **Krishna was also born of a virgin on Dec 25th! His birth was heralded by a bright star in the east, & it was attended by singing angels & 'heavenly hosts', as well as shepherds, & he was gifted w spices.** His mythical fable described him as a miracle worker who not only raised the

235

dead, but healed lepers, the deaf & the blind. <u>Krishna used parables LONG before Christianity counterfeited this model in crafting their 'literalized' version</u>. Krishna's story described his using those parables to teach universal love, **with no 'conditional condemnation component'**! His story described the sun darkening at his death, after which he <u>resurrected from the dead & ascended to heaven</u>. Some of his titles incl 'Shepherd God' & 'Universal Word' and of course 'The Sun/Son of God'.

------ Saturday, May 7, 2022 ------
Me (1:17 AM)
Now lets take a peek at the very similar details of the fable of the well known Greek mythical god HERCULES (AKA Heracles). He too was an Osiris/Horus influenced resurrected 'Savior-God-man' myth. **Hercules' myth story describes how he was born of a virgin named 'Alcmene'. There are many parallels between Alcmene and the counterfeited version Christianity would craft several hundred years later w 'Mary'.** <u>Hercules' fable tells how Alcmene's husband refrained from having sexual relations w her until her Divinely conceived child was born</u>! In Hercules' case, instead of 12 followers or disciples, his fable is famous for his '12 labors' which of course also were **simply metaphors for the 12 constellation signs of the Zodiac that the sun passes through each month of the year**. Then, there's the much more ancient, very well known Osiris/Horus influenced 'Sun/Son of God' myth story of the Greek Savior-God-man 'Dionysus'! He is also known as 'Bacchus', or 'the sun personified'...

------ Sunday, May 8, 2022 ------
Me (1:29 AM)
Dionysus' myth story also describes his <u>being born of a virgin at the Winter solstice</u>. His mythical fable describes his being a traveling teacher & miracle worker who was killed, **and then resurrected at the Spring equinox ('Easter' time).** Author Dorothy Murdock explains on page 111 in her book "The Christ Conspiracy" how Dionysus (AKA Bacchus) is often thought of as only being a Greek Savior-God-man myth, **but that in fact "he is a remake of the Egyptian god Osiris."** She explains that his version of the Osiris/Horus myth motif spread popularly over much of the ancient world for thousands of years. And i would add as a reminder, how this popular METAPHOR & myth model **LONG predated ALL of the Bible and JudeoChristianity's counterfeiting of it, and their pretending it was original to 'Jesus'**. It is undeniable that it was NOT, but was copied for its proven, well known psychological

appeal over many thousands of years, **& then deliberately literalized into a weaponized, condemning dogma**.

Me (11:36 PM)
FUNDAMENTALLY Mother, as i have steadfastly reminded u through the course of these lessons over the last year & a half, spiritual truth has ABSOLUTELY NOTHING to do with condemning dogma & 'beliefs' that target others w that condemnation 'in the name of God' just because they rightly SHUN such bigoted, man made 'beliefs'!...'Beliefs' and 'faith' used in such a bastardized & weaponized 'tribal' fashion, primarily by the elite ruling classes of the cultures that crafted the Big Three Abrahamic religions of Judaism, Christianity & Islam. **As those elites began to realize the immense power of MASS PSYCHOLOGICAL CONTROL that 'literalizing' those intended metaphors & myths into fear & guilt based 'BELIEFS' could provide them**, they counterfeited those longstanding non condemning INNOCENT POPULAR FABLES into literalized versions in order to DEIFY their culture ABOVE ALL other cultures, OFTEN TO JUSTIFY GENOCIDE as i have repeatedly shown u using your own Bible, and used those programmed 'beliefs' and 'faith' as a mass psychological weapon of control.

Me (11:53 PM)
Here we r on Mother's Day, which seems like a fitting day for me to conclude this comprehensive guide to the massive degree of man made lies & fraud of the Bible, shamefully masquerading as 'Gods Word'. These lessons have not only detailed & undeniably proven those rampant hypocritical lies, but they have also steadfastly shown u EXACTLY what Spiritual Truth, Love & 'The Light' truly are! **Mother, u NEVER have been 'evil' or 'sinful' by nature! You have NEVER been SEPARATE from what God is!** That was a sick, shameful man made LIE taught to u and to me as little children. It is time now...it is LONG OVERDUE actually, for u to stop clinging to such **'HOLY LIBEL' & PITCH BLACK DARKNESS** as a 'security blanket', knowing how its condemning beliefs eagerly await a 2nd Coming of a 'Savior' that will commit mass genocide of ALL who dont share such sick beliefs! I love you more than words can describe, and I need you to WAKE UP now...**ENOUGH w such religious bigotry in the name of God, and at your own daughter's expense no less! U have no excuse, now that i have taught u the full extent of these man made lies of the Bible, and their deliberately EVIL, FALSE & LIBELOUS depiction of 'God'.** That false, weaponized depiction of God is what has caused more harm

and NEEDLESS DIVISION to humanity throughout our history than from ANY other source. As I've pointed out before, one of the most ignorant questions ever asked is **"What's the harm of religion?"** As I've shown you, <u>the harm is massive, unconscionable & shocking, right there in black & white in your own Bible.</u> That 'Holy Libel' and deliberate man made false depiction of God is what has been the root cause of more wars and genocide throughout our history than ANY other reason…It is what has, up to this point, kept humanity from learning REAL SPIRITUAL TRUTH…It is what has kept humanity from understanding our TRUE HOLY NATURE <u>that is not 'sinful' by nature</u>…It is what has kept humanity from awakening to our SHARED ONENESS with 'God' and each other…**And with this book exposing those lies, it is going to stop now!** There is no 'savior' coming in the clouds to fix everything for you, with all others destroyed who don't share your 'beliefs'…No, the TRUTH such bigoted lies have sought to deliberately hide from you is this: WE are who 'God' is…WE in all of our beautiful, universal collective diversity, like the colors of the rainbow blending together…WE are the shared mind and collective hands of God in this physical dimension! **And when we wake up to this spiritual truth and leave those divisive lies about a condemning God behind, <u>we realize our 'savior' is EACH OTHER</u>.**

Connie Bryan

<u>REVIEW REQUEST</u>: I would love to hear from my readers!

If you would like to help others to discover HOLY LIBEL, please consider taking a moment to review the book on my book listing page at Amazon.com…And you can always find MUCH MORE of my 'truth to power' content on my website & blog at www.ConnieBryan.com.

NOTES

NOTES